CAMBRIDGE STUDIES IN LINGUISTICS

General Editors: B. COMRIE, C.J. FILLMORE, R. LASS, R.B. LE PAGE,
J. LYONS, P.H. MATTHEWS, F.R. PALMER, R. POSNER, S. ROMAINE,
N.V. SMITH, A. ZWICKY

Natural syntax

In this series

* *Issued in hard covers and as a paperback. Other series titles not listed are also available.*

NATURAL SYNTAX

Iconicity and erosion

JOHN HAIMAN

Linguistics Programme,
University of Manitoba, Winnipeg

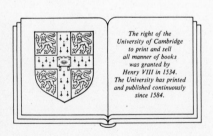

The right of the
University of Cambridge
to print and sell
all manner of books
was granted by
Henry VIII in 1534.
The University has printed
and published continuously
since 1584.

CAMBRIDGE UNIVERSITY PRESS

CAMBRIDGE

LONDON   NEW YORK   NEW ROCHELLE

MELBOURNE   SYDNEY

Published by the Press Syndicate of the University of Cambridge
The Pitt Building, Trumpington Street, Cambridge CB2 1RP
32 East 57th Street, New York, NY 10022, USA
10 Stamford Road, Oakleigh, Melbourne 3166, Australia

© Cambridge University Press 1985

First published 1985

Printed in Great Britain at the Alden Press, Oxford

Library of Congress catalogue card number: 85-5906

British Library cataloguing in publication data
Haiman, John
National syntax: iconicity and erosion–
(Cambridge studies in linguistics; v. 44)
1. Grammar, Comparative and general–Syntax
I. Title
415   P291

ISBN 0 521 26641 6

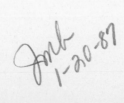

Contents

6 Limitations of the medium: competing motivations 237

Acknowledgements

Research for this monograph was partially supported by a grant from the Social Sciences and Humanities Research Council of Canada, for the study of Papuan languages. For reading portions of the manuscript and offering insightful comments, I am grateful to three anonymous referees from Cambridge University Press, Anna Meigs, Sandra A. Thompson, and, above all, John Lyons.

The book is dedicated, with love and gratitude, to my mother, Emily Czitrom: *millió csókkal.*

Abbreviations

abs.	absolutive	ind.	indicative
acc.	accusative	inf.	infinitive
alter.it.	alternating iterative	int.	interrogative
ant.	anticipatory desinence	irreal.	irrealis
art.	article	loc.	locative
attr.adj.	attributive adjective	med.	medial
caus.	causative	neg.	negative
class.	classifier	obj.	object
comp.	complementizer	obj.foc.	object focus
conc.	concurrent	obl.	oblique
cond.	conditional	part.	particle
cont.	continuative	perf.	perfective
coord.	coordinating desinence	pl.	plural
count.	counterfactual	plpf.subj.	pluperfect subjunctive
dat.	dative	poss.	possessive
decl.	declarative	pred.adj.	predicate adjective
dem.	demonstrative	pres.	present
dl.	dual	prog.	progressive
DS	different subject	p.t.	potential topic
dur.	durative	refl.	reflexive
erg.	ergative	rel.	relative
exc.	exclusive	seq.	sequential
fam.	familiar	sg.	singular
fem.	feminine	SR	switch-reference
fut.	future	SS	same subject
gen.	genitive	sub.	subject
imp.	imperative	sub.des.	subordinating desinence
imperf.	imperfective	subj.	subjunctive
inc.	inclusive	trans.	transitive

Introduction

"... such prisoners would recognize as reality nothing but shadows ..."

Plato: *The republic*

"In the first place it was necessary to give up our consciousness of a non-existent immobility in space and recognize a motion not perceived by our senses; in the present case it is no less obligatory to give up a non-existent freedom and recognize a dependence which we do not perceive."

Tolstoy: *War and peace*

Two approaches to universals

Two pervasive myths underlie the philosophy of all the human sciences. The first, Plato's myth, asserts that things are not what they seem. The second, Tolstoy's, that social phenomena, like natural phenomena, have a life of their own, and are completely beyond our conscious perceptions.

Like all good myths, these simple concepts are not simply compatible with the facts of life: rather, they determine our understanding of what the facts of life may be.

While the essentially romantic appeal of such myths is undeniable, their empirical motivation is another matter. What I should like to do in the next several pages is to review some of the dogmas of linguistics which seem to me to reflect, in their pallid way, the myths of Plato and Tolstoy; and then to present a rather different set of ideas which are opposed to them.

Needless to say, neither Plato nor Tolstoy is ever invoked as an authority in linguistics. Yet the compatibility of some of our most fundamental assumptions with their myths should be readily apparent: and, to some extent, I think these assumptions are correct.

The sound spectrograph has demonstrated that things are truly not what they seem. We hear as "identical" certain utterances which from an objective acoustic standpoint are very different. On the other hand, no spectrograph, however fine, can identify such categories as the phonological segment or the syntactic phrase.

1

Moreover, the laws of language which we refer to as "rules of grammar" have not been legislated by human beings. In fact, we are still unable to identify these laws, let alone control them. Language has a life of its own. But our assumptions go far beyond these observations.

Consider first the notion of the arbitrariness of the linguistic sign. In its crudest formulation, this principle asserts that there is nothing "X-like" about a word "X" in any given language. The word is not what it sounds like; and insofar as the word and its meaning are independent of each other, the word has a life of its own.

The linguistic relativity hypothesis may be viewed as an extension of the notion of arbitrariness. It asserts, first, that the categories of grammar do not correspond in their number or their extent with the categories of reality or experience; second, that the categories of the grammar of one language do not correspond to the categories of the grammar of any other language. Between the real world and our representations thereof lies an "intermediary world" of language: and, as human languages differ in their categories from one another, so too they must differ from the common world they describe, and from our common mental and sensory apparatus which perceives and imagines it. Once again, language, this intermediary world, is seen as having a life of its own.

While most linguists today do not accept the relativity hypothesis, most subscribe without question to a watered-down version of this hypothesis: the emic principle. In phonology, at least, the evidence in favor of this principle seems to be overwhelming: the class of sounds which speakers of a language perceive as identical is determined not (entirely) by the acoustic properties of the sound itself but (at least in part) by the essentially arbitrary way that a language will group different sounds together. The sound classifications which a language imposes on its speakers (as any foreign-language teacher can abundantly testify) is to a certain extent independent of reality. In phonology, then, the intermediary world of language has a life of its own.

Generative grammar has added two very significant ideas to this conceptual inventory of autonomous linguistics. The first is the distinction between deep and surface structures, and the second is the innateness hypothesis.

The distinction between deep and surface structure formalizes Plato's myth: things are not really what they seem. The innateness hypothesis amounts to the contention that the structure of language does not mirror the structure of the external world, but rather, independent properties of the unconscious mind. Clearly, there is considerable evidence, some of a very detailed and specific nature, for both of these ideas.

Nevertheless, my purpose in what follows here is to indicate that these ideas are overstated. There are respects in which linguistic representations are exactly what they seem to be, and there are respects in which human languages are like diagrams of our perceptions of the world, corresponding with them as well (or as poorly) as other diagrams do in general.

The difference between the assumptions of post Saussurean linguistics and the viewpoint of the present book is primarily one of emphasis. That is, I will be presenting a range of uncontroversial facts whose validity may not be in question, but whose significance is presently discounted, simply because they do not support the myths of Plato or Tolstoy.

The general validity of the doctrine of arbitrariness is so obviously correct that it scarcely requires the authority of a Whitney (1875) or of a Saussure (1916) to establish it. We could even go further and inquire what similarity could possibly exist between a *sound* on the one hand, and any non-auditory phenomenon on the other.

Since the stated goal of this book is to challenge the monopoly of arbitrariness, I should emphasize from the outset that there are certain aspects of this doctrine which, for one reason or another, I will not challenge.

I shall not be looking for examples, however vivid, of onomatopoeia. As Saussure correctly pointed out, words like "moo" constitute only a negligible proportion of the words of any language.

Nor shall I try to demonstrate the pervasiveness of "sound symbolism", a constant correlation between submorphemic sounds and meanings: in spite of some suggestive evidence (Sapir 1929, Jespersen 1933, Swadesh 1971, Gregerson ms) to which I will briefly refer in chapter 2, I accept double articulation as an unchallengeable universal. In other words, words of similar sound will not necessarily be words of similar meaning: we should not expect, and do not find, semantic homogeneity among words like *pod*, *pot*, and *pox*.

A language consists, however, not only of an inventory of (admittedly) arbitrary roots, but of a system of grammatical rules for combining these roots to express complex concepts. This system of grammatical rules is our concern, as it is the concern of theoretical linguistics in general.

To what extent is the structure of this grammatical system an arbitrary one? Does it reflect the properties of the world or relatively independent properties of the human mind? When we talk about language universals today, we almost invariably answer these questions in agreement with either Jakobson (particularly 1965) or Chomsky (for example 1972, 1980).

For Jakobson, as for Benveniste, Bolinger, Greenberg, and other writers who are somewhat out of fashion at the moment, many linguistic universals reflect, in a rather obvious way, our common perceptions about our world.

For example: other things being equal, the order of clauses in a narrative will correspond to the order of events that they describe. There is no language known in which stories are regularly told "backwards", with the narrative order being the reverse of the chronological order. Jakobson drew attention to the iconicity of Caesar's famous, and typical, *vēnī, vīdī, vīcī*, "I came, I saw, I conquered"; Eric Kellerman (ms) points out that the latter sequence is emphatically not synonymous with "I saw, I conquered, I came", which "receives a different, but no less iconic, interpretation".

Jakobson pointed out that the relationship in the cooccurring elements of a syntagm (Sentence 1 + Sentence 2) corresponds, in this well-known kind of structure, to the relationship of the events described in S1 and S2: sentences, like events, occur in time, and the medium of language is structurally adapted to the iconic display of temporal succession. This is Saussure's famous "linearity of the linguistic sign": we shall see later how languages may also iconically display simultaneity and temporal or conceptual symmetry.

Another famous example of iconicity, but this time involving paradigmatic rather than syntagmatic relationships between signs, is pointed out by Benveniste (1946). In a very large number of languages–but English is a conspicuous exception–there is a curious asymmetry in the expression of the third person singular, in both verbal and pronominal paradigms. While the first and second persons are typically represented by some personal affix, the third person singular very frequently is represented by zero. Consider the representative paradigms from Hungarian and Hua (the latter a Papuan language) shown in Table 1.

Table 1

	Verbal suffixes in Hungarian		Pronoun objects in Hua	
1sg.	lát-*ok*	"*I* see"	*d*-ge	"He sees *me*"
2sg.	lát-*sz*	"*You* see"	*k*-ge	"He sees *you*"
3sg.	lát-∅	"*He* } sees" "*She* }	∅-ge	"He sees { *him*" { *her*

Benveniste argued that in such cases, the formal contrast between non-null and null forms reflected a conceptual contrast between non-third persons and the third person, a conceptual contrast which the traditional terminology of the Western linguistic tradition had obscured. For the Arab grammarians, the first person was *al-mutakallimu* "the speaker", the second person *al-muhaṭābu*, "the hearer", but the third person, who did not participate in the speech act, was characterized as *al-ya'ibu* "the absent one". The non-person was iconically represented by a non-desinence.

A comparable example is Greenberg's famous universal: "there is no language in which the plural does not have some non-zero allomorphs, whereas there are languages where the singular is expressed only by zero" (1966:94). English conforms with this principle, illustrated in the contrast *dog* + $\emptyset$ (singular): *dog* + *s* (plural). Here again, a formal contrast between some X and zero is an icon of a conceptual contrast between less and more.

In Benveniste's and Greenberg's examples (and, to a lesser extent, in Jakobson's) we are dealing with statistical tendencies rather than ironclad immutable laws: a number of fortuitous tendencies, notably sound change, may obscure these patterns and result in paradigms in which the formal contrasts do not reflect the semantic or conceptual contrasts.

Nevertheless, there is good evidence, even in languages where the correlation between structure and meaning has been obscured, that this correlation has more than a fortuitous character. For there is a well-documented tendency to *restore* this correlation by a variety of different processes.

Watkins (1962) has demonstrated that in languages where the third person singular verbal affix is not null, it will be reinterpreted as null, with a consequent restructuring of the entire paradigm. In Swiss Vallader Romantsch, for example, the third person singular past definite ending was -*et*, added directly to the verb stem: thus, *chant-et* "he sang", *chant-aun* "they sang", and so forth. In the modern language, the erstwhile third person singular ending has been reinterpreted as a characteristic marker of the past tense, so that the same form *chantet* is analyzed as *chant* "sing" + *et* "past" + $\emptyset$ "3sg.". The reinterpretation leaves the third person singular form unchanged but has visible results in the rest of the paradigm, for example, in the new third person plural *chant* "sing" + *et* "past" + *and* "3pl.". The end result of such reinterpretations, of which Watkins gives many persuasive examples, is that the conceptual contrast between the third person singular and other persons is once more iconically reflected in the formal contrast between the third person singular form and other forms.

Anttila (1972:194) draws attention to the restoration of iconicity through extensive *borrowing* when sound changes destroy Greenberg's universal. There was a time in the history of the Slavic languages when the most common ending of the (genitive) plural of masculine nouns (and that which distinguished them from the nominative singular) was the suffix -*ŭ*. When this vowel was lost by a general sound change, the genitive plural became identical with the nominative singular.

As Anttila reminds us, there is not a single Slavic language in which this situation has been permitted to endure. Rather, the denuded genitives of the major declension have been fleshed out with the non-null suffixes that were originally characteristic of the marginal declensions. Following Jakobson, Andersen (1980) points out that there has been a documented tendency in Russian to make *every* plural nominal desinence longer than the corresponding singular.

Jakobson's "Quest" article (1965) discovered an uncharted continent beneath our noses: a realm of the familiar, and yet profound, which current theory consistently ignores. At least part of the reason for this consistent disdain, it seems to me, is the immense, almost charismatic stature of one man: Noam Chomsky.

Over the last twenty-five years, there has been significant change in many of Chomsky's views on the organization of grammars; but on the nature of the interesting universals of human languages, it seems to me that Chomsky has been remarkably consistent. Scattered throughout his writings one can find the credo that

Our interpretation of the world is based in part on representational systems that derive from the structure of the mind itself and do not mirror in any direct way the form of things in the external world (1981:3).

No one could object to this viewpoint, enunciated here with charming diffidence. For a more uncompromising statement, however, compare his remarks in *Language and mind*:

Animal language . . . makes use of a fixed number of linguistic dimensions, each of which is associated with a particular non-linguistic dimension in such a way that selection of a point along the linguistic dimension determines and signals a certain point along the non-linguistic dimension . . . The mechanism and principle, however, are entirely different from those employed by human language . . . (1972:69).

Whether or not this is an accurate characterization of animal communication, I do not know. But I do not think it is quite as alien to human language as Chomsky maintains. And I do not think that Chomsky or his students are driven to his conclusion by the data they consider. Much more likely is the possibility that they are driven to their data by the assumption that the only interesting universals are those which seem to be arbitrary or pointless from a formal or functional point of view. Only these arbitrary universals can provide unambiguous evidence for a specifically human linguistic faculty which Chomsky has come to describe as an organ (cf. 1976:57, 1980 passim).

I should like to emphasize here that there is no way in which the doctrine of innateness is either supported or contradicted by anything in this book. That there is a human propensity for language is sufficiently confirmed by the observation that humans talk and other animals do not. The inventory of characteristics which distinguish human speech from birdsong or the bee dance is sufficiently extensive (cf. Benveniste 1952) without deep structure, the cycle, the empty category principle, or any other structural feature, to establish innateness.

Unlike some of his dismayed supporters, who chided him for his "abandonment" of deep structures (and thus, by tenuous implication, of the innateness hypothesis), Chomsky himself is perfectly aware of the independence of this hypothesis:

If, for example, empiricist or behaviorist theories of learning are unable to account for the acquisition of grammars constructed in accordance with the standard theory . . . then they fail for exactly the same reasons to account for the acquisition of grammars that submit both D[eep] and S[urface] structures to semantic interpretation (1980:158).

This, it seems to me, is absolutely correct. But it is an admission that there is no connection whatever between the putative structure of grammars and the innateness hypothesis. As Chomsky pointed out in his withering review of Skinner's *Verbal behavior* (Chomsky 1959), empiricist and behaviorist theories can account for the acquisition of no grammars at all. For this reason, it seems to me, invocations of innateness are totally irrelevant in arguments about the nature of a grammar. As Bernard Comrie has observed, innateness "is just a name given to the set of language universals and using this name should not blind us to the fact that a name is not an explanation" (Comrie 1980:24).

What *does* have a bearing on the discussion of arbitrariness and motivation, to a large extent, is simply the data that we choose to consider interesting or significant. There is absolutely no way of predicting or legislating which properties of human language are the most significant. That our perceptions of significance are subject, in a large degree, to the influence of personalities and the whims of fashion, no one could possibly deny. For this reason, it is impossible to criticize generative grammarians, or people like myself, for their apparently tedious devotion to theories that derive their support from vanishingly diminutive amounts of data: the only question that matters, in the final analysis, is whether the theory is an "interesting" one. And this is a personal, and social, as well as a scientific matter.

I shall be arguing throughout this book that linguistic structures are often similar to non-linguistic diagrams of our thoughts, such that "selection of a point along the linguistic dimension determines and signals a certain point along the non-linguistic dimension". Arbitrariness creeps into languages as it does into diagrams in general. Wherever possible, I shall try to show that such arbitrariness arises not from totally novel and mysterious human genetic predispositions, but from relatively familiar principles such as economy, generalization, and association. These are principles that are responsible for the impairment of iconicity in diagrams generally, and are therefore relevant in semiotic domains other than that of spoken language.

Inevitably, to the extent that I am successful in my demonstrations and explanations, it will seem that I am reducing the conceptual gap between human language and other semiotic systems. I do not intend to deny that such a gap exists, however. Human language clearly differs from all other systems of (both human and animal) communication, if only in its richness and flexibility.

I do believe, however, that the motivation for a great deal of research in linguistics has caused (or been caused by) the equally mistaken impression that the conceptual gap between human languages and other symbolic systems is totally unbridgeable. Guided by the myths of Plato and Tolstoy, linguists have focussed on marginal and trivial facts which lend support to these myths, while ignoring or dismissing as insignificant vast areas of human language which do not argue so directly for the autonomy of our linguistic abilities.

Some of these areas I hope to explore in the present book. If I can persuade you that they are important and worthy of attention–linguistically significant, in fact–this will be more important, in the end, than the correctness of the explanations that I offer.

Some properties of diagrams

The basic thesis of this book is that languages are like diagrams. In this chapter I will begin by outlining some of the ways in which non-linguistic diagrams are iconic; some of the reasons and the means whereby their iconicity is impaired; and indicate what the linguistic analogs to both sets of properties might be.

The notion of diagrammatic iconicity, which will be crucial to the rest of our discussion, originates with the philosopher C.S. Peirce (1932), who maintained that a diagram is a complex sign, representing a complex concept. There is therefore some correspondence between the *parts* of a diagram and the parts of the concept which it represents. The parts of a diagram do not necessarily resemble the parts of the corresponding concept. In Peirce's terminology, each of these parts may therefore be a symbol rather than an icon of its referent. But the essence of a diagram is that the relationship among the parts of the diagram does resemble the relationship among the parts of the concept which it represents. This (attenuated) resemblance justifies our calling a diagram a kind of icon: a diagrammatic icon.

To appreciate the distinction between an *image* and a *diagram*, consider various systems of numerical notation. Most iconic is a tally system: the number of lines corresponds to the number of objects enumerated. Much less iconic is the roman numeral system: the roman numeral III, for example is similar to a tally notation, and thus perfectly iconic, but the roman numeral L is a symbol of the number "50". The arabic numbers, of course, are almost entirely symbolic. As representations of individual numbers, the tally representation is an icon and the arabic notation, a symbol. However, this is to consider the forms entirely as images.

Consider, now, the arrangement of arabic numerals along a street of numbered houses. Although the numbers taken individually are symbols, their arrangement relative to each other is diagrammatically iconic insofar as the position of a house will correspond to the position of its numerical label along a "number line" (assuming for the moment that the street has houses only along one of its sides).

For example, the house numbered "45" lies between the houses numbered "43" and "47", just as the cardinal number 45 represents a quantity between 43 and 47; moreover, the house 45 and the house 47 will be closer to each other than either is to the house 113, just as the cardinal numbers 45 and 47 represent quantities that are closer to each other than either is to 113; and so on.

The analogy between this simple example and a human language is intended to be understood in the following way: the "words" of the language (the arabic numerals) are themselves symbolic: but their "grammar" (the rule for assigning numbers to houses) is diagrammatically iconic.

Now Peirce acknowledged that the distinction between icons and symbols was not a sharp one, but rather a matter of degree. No sign of any object (except a clone, perhaps) resembles that object completely, and therefore all icons are imperfect: Peirce called them hypoicons. Presumably a sign which resembles its object with respect to a thousand details is more iconic than one which resembles it in only a hundred. And very possibly an attenuated resemblance may come to be perceived as no resemblance at all. When this happens, an (erstwhile) icon becomes perceived as a symbol. In the historical development of any sign system we encounter countless examples of this phenomenon of de-iconization, or *conventionalization*. (The roman numeral *V* originated as a palm with thumb opposed; the letter *A* for "ox" as the head of an ox, still visible if the symbol is inverted; and the Chinese character for "man"人 , as a stick figure more like 大 .)

In the same way, although Peirce did not emphasize this point, it should be clear that the distinction between an icon which is an *image* (like a photograph) and one which is a *diagram* (like a stick figure) is also mainly a matter of degree.

In principle, there is a distinction between the two: an image is an icon of a simple object, while a diagram is an icon of a complex one. But there are no simple objects, and no icon reproduces every detail. Consideration of a typical "image", a photograph, will show how impractical the distinction really is. Unlike a painting, the photograph does not conventionalize: it only shows "what is there". But it certainly doesn't show everything that is there. Like a diagram, it reduces and simplifies the reality it depicts. Three visual dimensions are reduced to two; color reproduction is not exact; auditory, olfactory and tactile sense impressions are not recorded at all; the list could easily be continued. The photograph preserves certain relationships among the colors, lines, and shapes of the object, while suppressing others. A stick figure caricature does exactly the same. It simply suppresses more.

A convenient rule of thumb for distinguishing images from diagrams might be that anyone can recognize the first, while certain conventions have to be understood before we can recognize the second. Surprising as this may seem, this rule of thumb will not distinguish between a photograph and a stick figure in all contexts. Familiar as we are with photographic representation, we assume that photographs are self-explanatory, but in fact we have learned conventions of interpretation that other people may have not. (When living in a Highlands village in New Guinea, I was startled to find that older people did not recognize themselves or members of their families in photographic portraits.)

The neat taxonomy of signs in which image is opposed to diagram and both are opposed to symbol is an idealization. All signs have to simplify and abbreviate what they stand for. Images do so less than diagrams, diagrams less than symbols.

Ideally an iconic diagram is *homologous* with what it represents: not only will every point in the diagram correspond to some point in the reality depicted, but the relationships among these points will correspond to the relationships among the points in reality. I would like to adopt a slightly idiosyncratic terminology and usage here, and break down the concept of homology. into the two independent properties of isomorphism and motivation.

By isomorphism, a one-to-one correspondence alone is intended, without regard for the relative position, importance, mutual relevance, or any other property of points in a diagram. Violations of isomorphism are: many-to-one, one-to-many, one-to-zero, and zero-to-one relations between points in the diagram and points in "reality." All of these violations occur in language, and are familiar as homonymy, synonymy, polysemy, empty morphs, and "signe zéro". They are the subject of chapter 1.

By motivation, I have in mind the property whereby diagrams exhibit the same relationship among their parts as their referents do among their parts. Violations of motivation I shall term distortions. Various kinds of motivation will be the main subject of chapter 2.

While ideally diagrams exhibit both of these properties in abundance, their raison d'être, which is to simplify, makes both of these ideal properties impossible to attain. Simplification is necessary because life is short and human memory finite. It is possible because diagrams need only *represent*, and not necessarily *reproduce*, reality; and it is possible because in order to do this, they need to reproduce only the essential attributes of the objects they denote.

The various kinds of destruction that economy entails may be subsumed under the headings of simplification or reduction, distortion, and the need for auxiliary signs or diacritics: signs which are labels on the diagram, rather than part of the diagram itself.

It may be shown, by reference to three familiar kinds of diagrammatic representations, how each of these inroads on iconicity is imposed by considerations of economy and limitations of the medium. The three representative diagrams are a terrestrial map, a musical score, and a phonetic transcription: two-dimensional diagrams on a sheet of paper. The map represents spatial relationships in a spatial medium, while the score and the transcription are forced to use this medium for the representation of sounds. Nevertheless, the similarities among all three are overwhelming.

In each diagram, there is considerable simplification. The map does not show all the territory. The score does not ensure that every performance of the work is identical. The script does not indicate subphonemic variation or personal indices such as the speaker's age or sex.

In each diagram there is distortion. The shortest distance between two points on a two-dimensional map of the world is not a straight line; Greenland is much too big; the left edge and the right edge of the map represent the same meridian. A low note on the treble clef is higher than a high note on the bass clef; a sharpened note may be higher than a flattened note that is one space higher up on the same clef. One sound is not always represented by the same symbol, even in the IPA.

Each diagram depends heavily on auxiliary signs or diacritics that rectify or override the misleading implications of the structure of the diagram itself. The identity between the left edge and the right edge of the map is indicated by the diacritic label on the meridian; non-spatial information, such as political boundaries, is indicated by lines and reenforced by the use of different colors. Intervals and ranges are accurately indicated in music by means of clefs, sharps and flats. Subtle differences of timbre, and variations of intonation and stress, are all indicated by diacritics festooned over the letters of the alphabet.

Nevertheless, each diagram manifests isomorphism. Except around the edges, each point on the familiar Mercator map corresponds to one and only one point in the world. Each representation of a musical note corresponds to only one pitch most of the time. And again, most of the time, different representations represent different sounds in the IPA.

Each diagram manifests motivation. Broadly speaking, the distance between two points on the map is greater when the distance between the actual places they represent is greater, with the typical result that the coastline as seen by an astronaut really does resemble the coastline indicated on the map. Within the same clef, higher notes are higher than lower notes; the sequence of notes on the page corresponds to the order in which they are played. The order of IPA symbols also corresponds to the order in which the corresponding sounds are uttered.

There is a direct logical connection between economy on the one hand, and the presence of simplification, distortion, and diacritics on the other, in each of the diagrams we are considering. For a gradated example of the trade-off between economy of effort and iconicity, consider the differences between syllabary, alphabetic, and distinctive-feature notation of phonetic data. In terms of "ease of production", the syllabary script, which allows us to represent a whole syllable by a single sign, is clearly the most economical, while the distinctive-feature notation is the most cumbersome. In terms of motivation, however, the syllabary script is a disaster: not only is it totally incapable of representing consonant clusters, but it cannot indicate whether syllables alliterate or rhyme. The difference between *tip* and *top* is no less than that between *tip* and *bug*. The alphabetic script, our happy medium between syllabary and distinctive-feature notations, allows us to represent alliteration and rhyme, but not assonance, or the difference between consonants and vowels, or the fact that /t/ and /d/ are similar to each other in the same way as /k/ and /g/ are. The distinctive-feature notation, foreshadowed by Pitman's shorthand (cf. Abercrombie 1967), is the most totally motivated, and the most wearisome, diagrammatic representation of the sounds of language.

In consequence of the fact that they simplify, all diagrams leave things out, but what it is that gets left out depends on relatively ad hoc definitions of what is essential and what is accidental, relative to the intended purpose of the diagram. In a language without phonemic tone, like English, an acceptable transcription can leave out indications of tone; in the transcription of a melody, on the other hand, it is permissible to disregard indications of timbre.

All diagrams leave things out if they are predictable, even if these things are not irrelevant. A great deal of music for piano includes diacritic indications of fingering, but for difficult passages only. Where the fingering is obvious, it isn't shown.

Nevertheless, all diagrams are capable of avoiding ambiguity where it is important to do so: if necessary, by diacritics which are, strictly speaking, redundant. The exact pitch of a note is fully determined by its position on the staff, the key signature, and the clef, but may be redundantly specified, if the same note in an earlier bar occurred with an accidental, by a natural. A map may indicate a capital city by special lettering, a special symbol, and so on, when any single one of these devices would be sufficient.

Turning now to human languages, we will find all of the same properties. In some cases, recognition of these properties will mean nothing more than relabeling a traditional universal whose validity is not in question. In other cases, it will mean examining some familiar phenomena from an unfamiliar perspective.

Isomorphism, or "the higher, more general principle of 'one meaning, one form', is as old as European linguistics. It has been referred to, among other things, as the principle of optimality (Humboldt), or univocability (Vendryes), and as the canon of singularity (Ogden and Richards) ... the 'one meaning, one form' principle was also connected early with psychological factors, which 'aim to eliminate purposeless variety' (Wheeler)" (Anttila 1972:107).

In human languages, as in other diagrams, the familiar terms synonymy, homonymy, and polysemy denote violations of the isomorphism condition. The next chapter will be devoted to a discussion of these violations and to a demonstration that in general, they either do not exist, or can be attributed to the more general diagrammatic property of economy.

Motivation as a linguistic term was introduced by Saussure (1969 (1916):181) to describe compound or complex signs like the French word *dix-neuf* "nineteen". Although the components of this word are themselves arbitrary, the compound is *in contrast* "relatively motivated". (It is necessary to emphasize Saussure's recognition of the contrast between arbitrariness and motivation, since he gives no definition of "motivation" in the *Cours*.) It is clear from the exemplification that Saussure provided, that his notation of motivation is identical with Peirce's notion of diagrammatic iconicity.

Although Saussure's thoughts on motivation occupy no more than four pages of his famous textbook (1969:180-4), it is amazing how rich and suggestive they are. He recognized that motivation was a relationship among signs, and that the relationship could be either syntagmatic or paradigmatic: *dix-neuf* is a syntagm consisting of two signs, *dix* "ten" and *neuf* "nine", and the meaning of the compound sign is related in some way to the sum of the meanings of its parts; on the other hand, the transparency or motivation of the syntagm depends crucially on the fact that each of its components is a separately intuited sign which can be replaced by others, and diminishes if either or both of the elements of the compound becomes isolated from the paradigm of other forms that can fill its syntactic slot.

Sound change, Saussure pointed out, diminishes motivation because it erodes the structure of the syntagm to the point that it no longer is perceived as having components at all. For example, Latin *in + imicus* (literally "not" + "friend") is a motivated compound meaning "enemy": its semantic contrast with *amicus* "friend" is still apparent, though not as much as in earlier stages of Latin where the word was * *in + amicus*. In later Romance dialects, such as French, sound change has reduced the compound to *ennemi*, a totally opaque and unmotivated word whose semantic relationship with *ami* "friend" is formally no longer expressed. Genetically related languages like French and Latin may therefore differ with respect to their degree of motivation. In fact, the history of any given language could be viewed as a repeated alternation between motivation and arbitrariness: sound change erodes motivation but analogy rebuilds it.

Saussure's most congenial suggestion is that the contrast between arbitrariness and motivation is nothing other than the contrast between lexicon and grammar: "non que 'lexique' et 'arbitraire' d'une part 'grammaire' et 'motivation relative' de l'autre soient toujours synonymes; mais il y a quelque chose de commun dans le principe" (1969:183).

If Saussure's observation were no more than the claim that grammar is regularity, it would be no more than a restatement of a truism that has been around since the Stoic philosophers. It is the nature of the regularity which is in question: does it reflect conceptual structures or is it "based . . . on representational systems that derive from the structure of the mind itself and do not mirror in any direct way the form of things in the external world" (Chomsky 1981:3)?

In view of Saussure's reticence in defining motivation, and his very restricted conception of grammar beyond the level of the word, it would be inaccurate to read too deeply into his intention. My own construction of Saussure, based on his examples, is that in spirit he is opposed to Chomsky's view. Elsewhere he is explicit in claiming that his approach to language treats it as only one of a number of sign systems governed by a common logic (1969:35): "si l'on veut découvrir la veritable nature de la langue, il faut la prendre d'abord dans ce qu'elle a de commun avec les autres systèmes du même ordre". And the common logic of sign systems is the logic of the diagram.

In this book I shall be discussing primarily those kinds of motivation for which the structure of language is particularly adapted: the expression of distance and the expression of asymmetry. Whatever Saussure's intended sense of "motivation" may have been, it will be clear from our discussion that motivation in our sense will mean a correspondence between our perception of the world and our representation of this perception.

We come now to the greatest countervailing tendency of language, which is the tendency to generalize and provide, for the infinite number of objects, events, and relationships that we observe in the sensible world, a small number of category labels. No single property of language is more important. And no linguist has ever done it justice so well as J.L. Borges in his brilliant short story "Funes the Memorious" (1962). This is surely the most haunting meditation on the "emic principle" ever penned. The gist of the emic principle in both phonology and semantics is that for purposes of classification, certain sounds, or certain objects, are treated as though they were identical. In fact, of course, they are not identical, so the emic principle *generalizes*. Rather than recognize an infinity of sounds and of concepts, human languages recognize a limited inventory of phonemes and sememes.

Not the language of Funes. After a mysterious accident which left him paralyzed, the hero of Borges' tale acquires a perfect memory: as the rest of us can recall the array of three bottles on a shelf, so Funes can recall "all the leaves and tendrils and fruit that make up a grape vine," or "the outlines of the foam raised by an oar in the Rio Negro the night before the Quebracho uprising" (Borges, 63).

Unencumbered by a defective memory, Funes devises for his own use an artificial language in which every sensation of his impoverished experience is given a separate name: "It bothered him that (a) dog at three-fourteen (seen from the side) should have the same name as the dog at three-fifteen (seen from the front)" (ibid. 65).

The rest of us not only overlook or fail to notice the difference between the same dog at 3:14 and 3:15, we even overlook differences between one dog and any other every time we use the word *dog*. Undoubtedly we sweep a lot of observations under the rug with the words we use. In doing this, we violate the requirements of a rigorous isomorphism. But there is a curious paradox involved here, which Borges also pointed out.

Endowed as he was, Funes scorned the use of mnemonic classificatory devices that the rest of us depend on, such as a number system: "In place of seven thousand thirteen, he would say (for example) *Maximo Pérez*; in place of seven thousand fourteen, *The Railroad* . . . in place of five hundred, he would say *nine*" (ibid. 64).

Our number system has a "grammar". More accurately, our number system, like any other system, *is* a grammar. One of the functions of such a system, Borges suggests, is to catalog our data according to certain principles. These principles may be either natural or arbitrary, but to a mnemonist like Funes that makes no difference: having no need for either, he rejects them both.

But in rejecting both, he throws motivation out the window as well. His outlandish and impossible language observes a rigorous isomorphism inasmuch as every datum corresponds to a distinct symbol, but this language takes no account of similarities. Every difference is a *total* difference. Motivation, however, depends on generalization, on the perception and recording of *similarities*.

One could argue, of course, that in real life the perception of differences need not obscure the recognition of similarities. It is an open question what the generalizing capacities of mnemonic freaks like Funes might be, although there is some anecdotal evidence (cf. Luria 1968) that mnemonists actually do pay for their phenomenal gift by a corresponding lack of abstract reasoning power. Perhaps the ability to reason abstractly depends on the ability to simplify, and to forget. Certainly human languages bear witness to this generalizing ability. Paradoxically, it is only by virtue of this generalizing function that language is capable of motivation at all.

Diagrams in general use zero representation in two different ways. So far, in my discussion of language, I have been discussing only one, the non-representation, through generalization, of what is treated as incidental. Diagrams also use zero to represent what is predictable. Languages do the same. In the following pair of sentences, the non-representation of the predictable is what distinguishes the second sentence from the first:

(1)   I could kick *myself*
(2)   I should shave ＿＿＿

Both *kick* and *shave* are transitive verbs. In the sentences above, both are used reflexively, that is, the object of the verb is understood to be identical with the subject. In (1), the object is expressed by a reflexive pronoun *myself*, while in (2), it is not expressed at all. What accounts for this difference between the two sentences?

With transitive verbs like *kick* whose objects are typically distinct from their subjects, the information that the subject and the object are in fact *the same* is "newsworthy", an unpredictable fact that must be explicitly recorded. And, in sentence (1), it is recorded by the reflexive pronoun.

Transitive verbs like *shave* are very different. Barbers excepted, people generally shave only themselves. We generally *expect* the object of a verb like *shave* to be the same as the subject. Therefore, when they are in fact the same, as in (2), this fact is not newsworthy, and the object, like the predictable fingering of a piano score, is simply not indicated.

In this, and in many other examples to be discussed in chapter 3, we are dealing with another familiar property of human languages. It was richly illustrated by G. K. Zipf in his classic *The psychobiology of language* (1935). In diagrams, what is predictable is left out. Zipf demonstrated that in languages, what is *familiar* is given reduced expression.

The most obvious limitation of the medium of spoken language is that it exists only in the temporal dimension and is therefore prima facie incapable of directly representing symmetrical and hierarchical relationships. Saussure in his *Cours* alludes to this "linear property of language, which excludes the possibility of saying two things at once" (1969:170), a fundamental principle of language which he ranks in importance with the arbitrariness of the linguistic sign (ibid, 103). In fact, human languages share this limitation with such temporally bound forms as music: and in language, as in music, repetition may be an ambiguous icon of both symmetry and asymmetry. But languages may also circumvent the built-in limitations of form with diacritics like subordinating conjunctions, which indicate that the semantic relationship between two clauses is something other than that suggested by their relative order.

I shall argue that in languages, as in diagrams, there is an inverse correlation between iconicity and economy; and (as a special case of this) that iconicity decreases as the number of diacritics increases. Following a number of distinguished predecessors in the functionalist tradition, among them Henri Frei (1929) and Wilhelm Havers (1931), I believe that the tendencies to maximize iconicity and to maximize economy are two of the most important competing motivations for linguistic forms in general: and the structure of the present treatise reflects this view. In part I, I will attempt to isolate some properties of linguistic diagrams that seem to me to be iconic, while part II will deal with factors which diminish iconicity for a variety of considerations, all essentially economic.

In the final conclusion, as in this introduction, I will return to a defence of this apparently crude and outmoded world view against the various structuralist conceptions of grammar which are much more in vogue today.

PART I
ICONICITY IN LANGUAGE

Like other diagrams, languages are *homologous* with the concepts that they represent insofar as they exhibit both isomorphism and motivation.

In chapter 1, I will discuss isomorphism, and defend, by lengthy discussion of one category (the conditional protasis), a language-learning strategy which I will call the "isomorphism hypothesis":

> Different forms will always entail a difference in communicative function. Conversely, recurrent identity of form between different grammatical categories will always reflect some perceived similarity in communicative function.

The first part of the hypothesis denies the existence of total substitutability between any two expressions: what, following Lyons (1981:50), may be called *total* or *full* synonymy. It says nothing about homonymy, empty morphemes, or meaningful zero morphemes, all of which are also violations of isomorphism, as it might be plausibly understood. I will deal with each of these violations briefly, before turning to the phenomenon of *polysemy* (operationally definable as "recurrent homonymy"), which provides evidence in favor of the second part of the isomorphism hypothesis.

By far the most serious failing of the isomorphism hypothesis, it seems to me, is the fact that it cannot encompass *association*: the process whereby grammatical categories, like words, may regularly acquire logically unrelated meanings as a result of fortuitous or accidental associations between their essential (or core) meanings, and these other peripheral meanings. One such example of grammatical association is the process whereby in a paratactic structure *S1 S2* the first clause typically functions as a protasis. Yet, there may be limits to what associations can do: specifically, paratactic *if* clauses cannot have *all* the meanings of ordinary conditional protases. The limitations on their meaning suggest that association, in at least this case, is constrained by another kind of iconicity, namely *motivation*: a structure without diacritics can only acquire those meanings of which it is itself an icon.

This leads to the discussion of motivation in chapter 2. There I will discuss and defend by example another language-learning strategy which I call the "motivation hypothesis":

> Given two minimally contrasting forms with closely related meaings, the difference in their meaning will correspond to the difference in their form.

The most evident and often-noted iconicity of language structure is the linearity of the linguistic sign, which iconically reflects the linearity of time and causation. But language is also admirably suited to the iconic expression of a variety of symmetrical relationships, and to the iconic expression of conceptual distance, and it is with these that my discussion will chiefly deal.

1 *Isomorphism*

The isomorphism hypothesis is stated in uncompromising fashion by Dwight Bolinger: "the natural condition of language is to preserve one form for one meaning, and one meaning for one form" (Bolinger 1977:x). According to this view, it is clear that such apparent commonplaces as synonymy (several forms, only one meaning), homonymy (several meanings, only one form), empty morphemes (form, but no meaning), and zero morphemes (meaning without form), are simply "pathological" deviations from the norm.

I have nothing useful to say about empty morphemes; I will discuss zero morphemes and markedness briefly in sections 2.3.1 and 5.2 (where I shall argue essentially that formal zero and reduction are both economically motivated); but I think that there is an important asymmetry between synonymy and homonymy which refutes the extreme position taken by Bolinger, and which we are in a position to explain.

1.1 Synonymy and homonymy

In a diagram of any complexity, the same sign, depending on its context, may have a number of different meanings. Linguistic analogs are homonyms and puns, and no language seems to lack them.

The converse, however, is vanishingly rare: of the four kinds of diagrammatic representation discussed in the introduction, only musical notation seems to provide for the "synonymous" representations of the same pitch. In language, of course, synonymy is taken for granted, and regularly exploited in the construction of definitions. Nevertheless, total synonymy in language is as rare as in any other kind of diagram: most probably for the same reasons. A moment's reflection should make it clear why this is so. Consider, for example, a political map, in which different colors are used to represent different polities. It is very difficult, and quite unnecessary, to use a separate color for every single country. A famous

21

theorem of topology asserts that we can get away with using only four, and still avoid the confusion that would arise when neighboring countries share a color. And in fact, all maps are guilty of some homonymy in using colors with different "meanings": blue for lakes and oceans, orange for Afghanistan and Indonesia, and so forth.

Now consider a hypothetical map in which two colors are used totally interchangeably, such that any point on the map which is either blue or orange represents the *same* entity: the color contrast does not denote different countries, different provinces, a different climate, elevation, or religion. On such a map, blue and orange would be totally synonymous. I believe that no such map exists.

It is simply uneconomical to introduce different signs with exactly the same meanings. On the other hand, it is very economical to introduce different meanings for a relatively small inventory of signs.

Economy of the *inventory of signs* (what Frei has called "economy of memory", Frei 1929:33) will therefore sufficiently account for the familiar asymmetry between (very common) homonymy and (very rare) synonymy in non-linguistic diagrams. The situation in human languages seems to be very different inasmuch as both homonymy and synonymy are very common. In fact, however, they are not. Homonymy is incontestable, but total interchangeability between any two linguistic expressions is almost non-existent. Numerous lexicographers and theoretical linguists have asserted that no "total synonymys" exist, none more eloquently than Dwight Bolinger in a series of subtle and sensitive studies (1977).

Traditional lexicography, and, more recently, the tradition of generative semantics, have challenged the validity of this assertion: not only is *kill* synonymous with *cause to die*, it is derived from the latter structure by a prelexical transformation of "predicate raising" (McCawley 1968), the relationship between the two being parallel in every way with that between an active sentence and the corresponding passive.

As Bolinger has pointed out, however, while "synonymys" may be logically equivalent, linguistic meaning includes much more than "logical meaning". "It expresses . . . such things as what is the central part of the message as against the peripheral part, what our attitudes are to the person we are speaking to, how we feel about the reliability of our message, how we situate ourselves in the events we report" (1977:4), and so on.

This recognition of different kinds of equivalence allows us to reconcile the fact that definitions and paraphrases *do* exist with the assertion that total synonymy does not. Think of any utterance you have ever spoken, heard, or written, and you will be able to say it otherwise. All of these paraphrases are perhaps "synonymous" but the chances are that they are not totally interchangeable.

One example for many. The *OED* defines *unless* as equivalent to *if . . . not*, and there are, of course, many cases where the two are interchangeable. But there are many more where they are not. The reader is invited to extend the following rather fragmentary list of differences:

> A. *Unless* cannot occur in counterfactual conditionals. (*If* you had*n't* stolen my wallet, we'd still be friends.)
> B. *Unless* cannot occur in independent protasis clauses which occur as exclamations. (*If* that is*n't* the dumbest idea I ever heard of!)
> C. *Unless* cannot occur in conditionals which assert the contrary of the protasis by an absurd apodosis. (*If* Hitler was*n't* insane, I'll eat my hat.)
> D. *Unless* cannot occur in focussed protasis clauses. (It's only *if* Tommy does *not* wish to stand that I accept the nomination.)
> E. *Unless* cannot occur if the apodosis begins with the resumptive topicalizer *then*. (*If* you're *not* interested, then I'll stop.)
> F. *Unless S* is odd if *S* is very likely to happen. (*If* the sun does *not* rise tomorrow, I'll pay you $100.)
> G. *Unless* cannot be used where the subject of the apodosis is defined relative to the subject of the protasis. (*If* the Syrians are*n't* attacking Arafat, someone else is.)

These differences are systematic: they define whether an expression in some foreign language should be translated as *unless* (thus, for example, Latin *nisi*, French *à moins que*) or as *if . . . not* (thus Latin *si . . . non*, French *si . . . ne . . . pas*). And similar observations may be made concerning almost any pair of expressions.

The observation that "every word which a language permits to survive must make its semantic contribution" (Bolinger 1977:x) is and has been common coin. Frei (1929:84) cites an extensive literature on the topic, deriving from Michel Bréal's famous *Essai de sémantique*, wherein two mechanisms of "linguistic therapy" were actually proposed to get rid of "dangerous and useless synonymy" (Bréal 1897:26). These were the laws of repartition and specialization. By repartition, two or more (perhaps originally?) synonymous forms come to be associated with two different meanings. By specialization, only one form survives. Either way, isomorphism between form and meaning is (re)established.

Unfortunately, there are hardly any case studies on the actual *development* of meaning of words, which alone would demonstrate the validity of Bréal's laws as dynamic principles. We may assume that doublets like *brothers/brethren, worked/wrought* in English, or *culturel/cultural* ("cultural/"agricultural"), *lisable/lisible* ("readable"/"legible") in French (Frei ibid. 85), now manifestly not synonymous, were once semantically equivalent. But how do we know this? Our attestations of these words are often sparse and unsystematic, and important differences between words that may have been used interchangeably in some contexts may thus never come to light.

In the absence of rich attestation – or, better still, of dictionaries written by scholars as subtle and pedantic as ourselves – the only totally reliable data for the validation of Bréal's laws must come from the here and now. Given that there are *now* no perfect synonyms in English, the problem is to prove that doublets like *brothers/brethren* were ever interchangeable at all. On the basis of the hypothesis that the essential characteristics of human languages have remained pretty well unchanged at least since they have been recorded, there is reason to doubt it.

In phonology, total interchangeability is familiar as "free variation": two pronunciations are considered to be in free variation when they correspond to no communicative difference. Recently, of course, this idea of free variation has been called into question by William Labov and his students, who have shown, in a number of fine-grained studies, that most cases of "free variation" are actually socially conditioned alternation conceptually on a par with the different "politeness levels" of languages like French, German, or Hungarian (Brown & Gilman 1960), Japanese (Martin 1964), or Nahuatl (Hill & Hill 1978). In effect, what these studies have done is to confirm with sophisticated quantitative analyses, the kinds of observations made by Fischer (1958) and formalize the wisdom of the man on the street: not only do we know that the forms /m/ and /ŋ/ are not in free variation, we also know which is the more "formal", which is the more likely to be used by "model" boys, and by girls, by schoolma'ams, as the present participle suffix in English.

Presented with contrasting forms, the language learner (whether a fieldworker learning a second language or a child learning his or her first) will either anticipate or possibly even provide two contrasting meanings, in the confident belief that no semiotic system would squander its resources in saying the same thing in two different ways. In other words, the language learner uses as a heuristic the first part of the isomorphism hypothesis, that difference in form must entail some difference in communicative purpose.

Homonymy is a very different matter. The tendency to minimize the inventory of forms, while militating against synonymy, will tolerate homonymy, but not beyond the point where confusion may result. Beyond this point, another kind of "linguistic therapy" may come into play, whereby homonyms are eliminated by a variety of ad hoc means, typically including borrowing and compounding.

Attestation of this particular kind of therapy is sparse, but suggestive. The most famous demonstrations of its existence are those due to the dialect geographer Gilliéron, some of which have found their way into the introductory textbooks (e.g. Bloomfield 1933:396–9). In some French dialects, phonetic changes caused the words for cat (from *cattus*) and rooster (from *gallus*) to fall together. Unlike pears and pairs, cats and chickens belong to the same universe of discourse and may easily be confused. They are conceptually analogous to two countries on a map which share a common border. What happened in these dialects – and only these – is that speakers borrowed a non-homophonous word for chickens from a neighboring dialect. Frei (1929:63–76) gives a variety of further examples from French. Typically, the possibility of confusion increases in direct proportion to the shortness of the word: "the shorter the sign, the smaller the number of phonemes of which it consists, the greater the danger of confusing this sign with others that are subject to the same conditions" (ibid. 65).

Frei alludes to the special processes whereby monosyllabic languages like Chinese remedy this state of affairs. One of these processes, that of disambiguating compounding, is discussed by Li and Thompson in their reference grammar of Mandarin (1981). Of all the Chinese dialects, Mandarin is the one that has undergone the most extensive sound changes and consequently developed the greatest number of homonyms: "where Cantonese, for example, still has a distinction between *yiu* 'want' and *yeuhk* 'medicine', Mandarin has only the single form *yào*" (ibid. 14). On the other hand, Mandarin has by far the highest proportion of polysyllabic words of all the Chinese dialects, possibly over one half of the lexicon, and Li & Thompson suggest that these two facts are causally connected: "the threat of too many homophonous syllables has forced the language to increase the proportion of polysyllabic words, principally by means of . . . compounding processes" (ibid. 14).

In English, the homophony of the word *funny* leads speakers to distinguish between *funny-haha* and *funny-queer*. In very much the same way, Mandarin Chinese has developed a large number of parallel-verb compounds consisting of two verbs which are either almost synonymous or related in meaning: for example, *xìng* "fortunate" has given way to the compound *xìng-fú* "fortunate-blessed" (ibid. 68–70) and so on.

That compounding was originally motivated by the need to avoid confusing ambiguity is strongly suggested by the fact that certain words which require the addition of the now-meaningless compounding suffixes *-zi* (originally "-child") and *-tou* (originally "-worthy"), when they occur as independent suffixes, may drop these suffixes when they combine with another morpheme in a compound (ibid. 44). For example, the root *mù* "wood" as an independent word must be followed by the compounding suffix *-tou*. But in the compounds *mù-bǎn* "wooden board" and *mùtàn* "charcoal", the suffix may be dropped, presumably because the meaning of the potentially ambiguous root is sufficiently clarified by the restrictive nature of the second element of the compound. So, too, the root *hái* "child" must be followed by the suffix *-zi* except when compounded with clarifying prefixes, as in *xiǎo-hái* "small child" or *nǚ-hái* "female child" (= girl) (ibid. 45).

Homonymy, however limited by functional considerations, is both blind and sporadic. There is no reason why pear and pair should happen to sound alike in English, nor do we expect a repetition of this homonymy in any other language. The fact that the two words are homophones in English is as much a peculiarity of the language as the fact that cats are called "cats".

1.2 Polysemy

Matters are different when we consider polysemy: related meanings mapped onto the same form. Operationally, polysemy may be defined as recurrent homonymy, on the strength of the hypothesis that *recurrent similarity of form must reflect similarity in meaning*. (This is the second part of the isomorphism hypothesis.)

The assumption that this is true is the tacit basis for a number of notable semantic analyses in modern linguistics. Thus the formal similarity between indirect questions and relative clauses motivated Keenan & Hull (1973) to find a semantic similarity between them; the formal similarity between relative clauses and clefts suggested to Schachter (1973) that they too must have a common meaning; and the formal similarity between reflexive constructions and passives impelled Langacker & Munro (1975) to propose a common semantic and syntactic origin for these two categories as well.

As one example of such recurrent homonymy, we may consider the striking similarity of conditional protases and polar questions, in English and other languages. The standard mark of the protasis in English is the subordinating conjunction *if*. But this word has other uses: that is, it exhibits some homonymy. As is well known, it may replace the indirect polar question complementizer *whether* in sentences like

(1)   Mary doesn't know whether/if it will rain today

To say that *if* may express either the protasis or the polar question is, at this stage, precisely analogous to the observation that the phonetic sequence /per/ may express either "a couple" or "a species of fruit". However, the homonymy of protases and questions occurs elsewhere, even in English. In certain, not yet entirely archaic forms of the language, but most particularly in counterfactual conditionals, the protasis may be marked, not by the subordinating conjunction, but rather by subject–verb inversion:

(2)   Had it been otherwise, I would have told you

Subject–verb inversion has a number of functions in English, of course, but the most typical is to mark direct questions like (3).

(3)   Had you known of this before Marvin came?

At this point, our analogy with the homophony of /per/ begins to break down. It is as though, in addition to this homonymy, we were to discover that in English, the phonetic sequence /tu/ were also to denote both "a couple" and "a kind of fruit". Provisionally, we may diagram the relationship between forms and meanings as:

FORM: if   subject–verb inversion

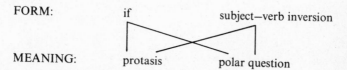

MEANING: protasis   polar question

Without turning from English, we have found that a confusion of polar questions and conditionals is a recurrent homonymy. And it is known to recur outside English. Curme (1931:327) pointed out that the construction was once less marginal in English than it may now appear to be; Jespersen (1940:374) that it is common to all the Germanic languages; Havers (1931:21) that it recurs in French and Greek as well. In all of these languages, *if*-clauses may be signaled by subject–verb inversion or some other mark that is characteristic of direct questions.

We may be inclined to dismiss this shared behavior as a peculiarity of a nest of genetically related languages. We may even wish to account for the etymology of the Russian word *jesli* "if" in the same way. As Vasmer (1953) has pointed out, the form is still an almost transparent compound of *jest'* "be 3sg." and *li* "whether", the marker of polar questions. Historically, the meaning of the sentence

(4)   Jesli Ivan doma   prijdu
         if _ Ivan at=home come=.=.=fut.=perf
         "If Ivan is at home, I will come"

is really something like this: "Is it (the case that) Ivan is at home? I will come." As in English, we find a single form (here, the suffix *-li* in *jesli*) with two meanings. It marks polar questions, and is used in compounding with *jest'* to mark the conditional protasis. (To continue the analogy with the usual case of homophony one last step further, it is as though the word /gruša/ in Russian, like /per/ in English, simultaneously denoted both "a couple" and "a kind of fruit".) But the recurrent homophony of conditional and interrogative markers is by no means limited to Indo-European languages, a fact which makes genetic explanations for this homophony irrelevant.

In Turkish, a member of the Altaic family, *if*-clauses are marked by the verbal suffix *-se* as in the sentence

(5)   Ahmed gel-di-yse   zengin ol-acak
         Ahmed come-past-if rich   be-3sg.=future
         "If Ahmed come, he will be rich"

In colloquial registers, this suffix may be replaced by *-mi*, the prototypical function of which is to express polar questions as in

(6)   Ahmed geldi   mi?
         Ahmed he=came whether
         "Did Ahmed come?"

Like subject–verb inversion, like Russian *li*, the Turkish question marker *-mi* has a fundamental meaning: it marks polar questions. In addition to this fundamental meaning, however, it also marks the protasis of conditional sentences (cf. Lewis 1967:265).

In Hua, a Papuan language of New Guinea, the conditional protasis is typically marked, once again, by a suffix on the verb, a suffix which is inflected for the person and number of the subject of the clause. Its basic form is *-mamo*, as in

(7)   Esi-mamo   baigue
        come-if=3sg. I=will=stay
        "If s/he comes, I will stay"

Subject to a number of constraints that do not concern us here, -*mamo* may be replaced by -*ve*, a verbal suffix whose typical use is to mark polar questions, as in

(8)   Esi-ve?
        come-whether=3sg.
        "Will s/he come?"

The homonymy of Hua -*ve*, then, is exactly like that of Turkish -*mi*, or Germanic subject-verb inversion, and similar to that of Russian *li*.

In most of the Uralic languages, hypotaxis was a relatively late development, and conditional clauses were simply in parataxis with their consequent. Following Beke (1919:103–6), it is "widely assumed that the protasis in such sentences was originally an independent interrogative sentence" (Riese 1981:384). Riese points out that "in older Hungarian, the interrogative nature of the protasis was even more apparent" (than it is now) (ibid. 385), as shown in (9–10).

(9)   Vele   kivánsz   lenni(?) ö   tüled   el   nem vál
        with=3sg. you=want to=be? 3sg. from=you away not part
        "If you want to be with him, he will not part from you"

(10)   Töri   a   hátad(?)   vesd le
        breaks the your=back? take=it off
        "If it strains your back, take it off"

Riese also notes that in modern Vogul, conditionals are expressed often by simple parataxis, in which the protasis is treated as an interrogative.

In fact, we could continue to compile an extensive catalog of languages in which the presumably disparate categories of "polar question" and "conditional protasis" are expressed by the same construction of grammatical morpheme(s).

The discovery of such cases of recurrent homonymy, or polysemy as it is more frequently called, is by no means novel, and the fundamental assumption of those investigators who point them out is always the same: identical form, ergo similar meaning. If the categories of polar question and conditional protasis are recurrently expressed by the same forms, it must be because these categories, surprisingly, are semantically related. In many cases, the demonstration of relationship is successful, and in other cases it is not. But this does not reflect on the universality of the assumption made in (11).

(11)   Recurrent identity of form must reflect similarity of meaning

Unfortunately, the truth of (11), like the truth of the assertion that true synonymy does not exist, cannot be proved: one can only multiply examples. Thus, a demonstration of the actual relationship between polar questions and conditionals can be offered only as one example among many which will bear out the heuristic value, at least, of (11).

First of all, we must reject certain traditional notions regarding the meaning of a conditional structure *If S1, S2*. One of these notions, expressed by Jespersen, was that the proposition expressed in *If S1* was necessarily provisional or hypothetical. One of the undesirable consequences of this position, as emphasized by Jespersen himself, was that certain structures such as (12), in which the protasis is not hypothetical, but which nevertheless have the exact form of conditional sentences, must be classified as "pseudo-conditionals":

(12)   . . . in short, I was a terrible carpenter). But, if I was a bad carpenter, I was a worse tailor

The methodological difficulty with this approach is fairly obvious: in the absence of a priori definitions of the meanings of grammatical categories, the only criterion for determining what is an example of such a category is precisely the physical form of the example. To do otherwise is to fail to describe a language "in its own terms", and to risk imposing on it categories which are arbitrary or totally irrelevant to its structure. Later on, the typologist may discover that in fact only English allows non-hypothetical conditionals like (12) whereupon he may be justified in identifying them as anomalous in some way.

But in fact, what he will discover instead is that sentences like (12) are common not only in English but in many other languages as well. He may even discover that there are languages in which conditionals like (12) look more like conditionals than counterfactual conditionals such as (2) or (13).

(13)   If I had known of your arrival, I would have arranged to stay longer

One such language is the Papuan language Hua, already exemplified in sentences (7) and (8). The difference between hypothetical and "given" conditions is not a difference in their conditional morphology – both protasis verbs occur with the suffix *-mamo* – but a difference in their tense alone. The *hypothetical*-conditional verb occurs with the future tense suffix *-si-* (*esimamo=*if s/he comes . . .), and the *given*-conditional verb corresponding to the protasis of (12), without it: *emamo* "given that he came". Counterfactual conditional protases, on the other hand, look very different, the verb ending with a complex suffix *-hipana* as in *ehipana* "if s/he had come . . .".

No one of course would seriously question that counterfactual conditional and hypothetical conditionals belong to the same category in English, since they both are introduced by the same conjunction *if*. The logic of such a classification might not be so apparent to a native Hua grammarian. (As a personal note, I might mention the fact that I was unsuccessful for several months in eliciting counterfactual conditionals in Hua via Pidgin English, and at one point assumed that in Hua there was no distinction between hypothetical and counterfactual conditionals at all. I stumbled across the counterfactual forms at first in a text.) In any event, if we examine conditionals from a cross-linguistic perspective, we cannot insist that they are either provisional or hypothetical in essence.

Another traditional idea, enunciated most forcefully by Ramsey (1931:248), asserts that in a construction *If S1, S2*, there exists some kind of causal connection between the proposition expressed by S1, and that expressed by S2. The extreme statement of this view asserts that *If A, then B* is exactly equivalent to *Because A, B*, where A is known to be hypothetical rather than true. The formal evidence which belies this contention is almost overwhelming:

(14)   I'll get him (even) if it's the last thing I do

The protasis of (14), although formally identical with that of the causal conditional, is concessive in force. The apodosis is asserted to be true in spite of what the protasis would lead us to expect. Nor is English the only language in which concessive conditionals differ from causal conditionals either minimally or not at all.

Compare German *auch wenn*; Spanish *aun cuando*; Latin *etsi* and *etiamsi*; French *même si*; Hungarian *ha . . . is* (= "if" . . . "and"); and Votyak *keno* (= "if+and", Serebrennikov 1963:376); Turkish *-sE dE* (= "if" . . . "and", Underhill 1976:415); Tabasaran *-šra* (= *-š* "if" +*-ra* "and", Magometov 1965:271); Karatin *-bar+el* ("if+and", Magomedbekova 1971:175); Arabic *wa in/lau* ("and if", Reckendorf 1895:726); Vietnamese *thì cũng* ("if and", Hoa 1974:105).

The list above, random as it seems, could easily be extended, but the generalization which emerges already is sufficiently clear. The etymon for "even" is very frequently something like "and" or "also".

The reason for this seems pretty straightforward. In ordinary conditionals of the form *If S1, S2*, the inference is invited that *If not S1, not S2* (cf. Zwicky & Geis 1971). That is, the proposition expressed by S1 is implicitly contrasted with its negation *not S1*, which expresses a condition under which S2 would be less likely to be true. Now, the force of a concessive conditional is precisely to deny the validity of the invited inference, by asserting that *(Even if not S1, (still) S2*, while implying that there would be nothing extraordinary about *If S1, S2*. That is, the force of a concessive conditional is really that of a conjunction, namely

> If S1, S2, *and* if not S1, S2

It is because concessive conditionals are really a kind of abbreviation of such structures that a coordinate conjunction like "and" frequently appears in them.

The presence of the first ellipted conjunct is implied by the remaining coordinate conjunction. It is conceivable that it would be implied by other material as well. In Hungarian, for example, the concessive (conditional) marker is *habár* (where *ha* = "if", and *bár* = "if only"), in effect a reduplication of the conditional morpheme: the presence of the deleted conditional protasis is suggested by the second conditional marker.

It is clear, however, that the morphological near-identity of concessive conditionals and of ordinary conditionals prevents us from assuming that there is a necessary causal connection between protasis and apodosis, or from going even further, as some logicians have done, and asserting that *If S1 S2* is nothing more than the hypothetical counterpart of *Because S1 S2*.

This point is illustrated with particular force in Hua, because the conditional in *-mamo* coexists with other structures which also have conditional force. One of these, we have already seen, is the protasis in *-ve*, which is formally identical with a polar question. Another is the so-called "medial verb" construction, in which the protasis clause is simply conjoined by a coordinating conjunction with the apodosis. That is, if one wishes to translate an ordinary conditional into Hua (or a number of other Papuan languages), one has the choice between using a genuine conditional in *-mamo*, as in (15)

(15)   Esi-*mamo* baigue
        "If s/he comes, I will stay"

or a coordinate structure as in (16)

(16)　　Esi-*gada* baigue
　　　　"If s/he comes, I will stay"
　　　　"S/he will come and I will stay"

The latter option is not always available. Where the protasis is inconsequential with respect to the apodosis, as in If S1, S2, *and* if not S1, S2, *only the conditional* can be used:

(17)　　Esive ʔaʔesive hisi-*mamo* baigue
　　　　"Whether s/he comes or not, I will stay"
(18)　　* Esive ʔaʔesive hisi-*gada* baigue
　　　　"Whether s/he comes or not, I will stay"

The grammaticality of (16) provides the most striking formal evidence that a causal connection between protasis and apodosis is *not* the essential defining feature of a conditional construction.

We should finally take note of the traditional logical definition of conditionals by "material implication", the inadequacy of which is what impelled logicians and linguists to consider the definitions we have just discussed in the first place. Material implication defines conditionals strictly truth-functionally: any conditional of the form *If S1, S2* is valid unless S1 is true, and S2, false. According to this definition, monstrosities like (19–20)

(19)　　If buses in Minneapolis are red, dolphins are mammals
　　　　　　　　　　　　　　　　　　　　(both S1 and S2 true)
(20)　　If MacDonald's serves McDolphinburgers, dolphins are mammals
　　　　　　　　　　　　　　　　　　　　(S1 is false)

are valid, even though the content of S1 is totally irrelevant to that of S2, and no difference in validity exists between (21a) and (21b) since the protasis in each is false.

(21)　　a.　If 2+2=5, dolphins are reptiles
　　　　b.　If 2+2=5, dolphins are not reptiles

Part of what is missing from material implication is a recognition of the fact that protasis and apodosis represent propositions that are mutually relevant in some way.

A much better explication of ordinary language conditionals was proposed by Ramsey (1931) in the same essay to which I have already referred: the speaker asks his interlocutor provisionally to add S1 to his store of knowledge or given information, and then proceed to interpret S2 in the context which S1 provides. That is, the protasis is the given, or framework, or the topic, of the entire sentence.

This analysis of protases or *if*-clauses as topics is compatible with all of the examples cited so far. In each of them, the protasis If S1 establishes a framework within which the apodosis S2 is (perhaps surprisingly) true.

Not surprisingly, there are a number of languages in which the semantic identity of protases and topics is directly reflected in the morphology and syntax of the language itself. In Turkish, for example, *contrastive topics* are marked by the conditional suffix *-se*:

(22)   Ahmed-ise, çok meşgul
         Ahmed-be=if very busy
         "As for Ahmed, he's very busy"   (cf. Lewis 1967:217)

A similar use of the conditional morpheme *kung* "if/whether" to mark contrastive topics is encountered in Tagalog (cf. Schachter 1976:496); in Tabasaran, the verbal suffix *-š* marks protasis clauses, while NP are topicalized by the suffix *-kuru+š* (=*kuru* "say"+*-š* "if", cf. Magometov 1965:271); in Korean, the NP topic suffix is *-(n) un* "as for", but the conditional copula *-(i)myen* may substitute for this topic marker to mark a contrastive topic. Thus,

(23)   Apeci-*nun/myen*   pakk ey se il hayo
         father-*topic cond.* works outside
         "As for father, he works outside"   (Martin & Lee 1969:146, 159).

More frequently, conditional protasis clauses are marked by the topic morpheme in many languages where such a morpheme exists. One such language that we have already looked at is Vietnamese. Topic markers are separated from the sentence that they precede by the marker *thì* (Hoa 1974:103, 341), as in examples (24–6).

(24)   Hồng-Công   thì,   đu   các   thứ   hàng-hoá
         Hong-Kong   topic   all various kind   merchandise
         "As for Hong Kong, it has all kinds of merchandise"
(25)   Anh thì,   anh thiếu gì   tiền
         you topic you much what   money
         "As for you, you have no lack of money"
(26)   Còn ông Hill thì,   bây giờ ông ấy   ở   đâu?
         sir   Hill topic now   sir   that stay where
         "As for Mr Hill, where is he nowadays?"

In Vietnamese, conditional protasis clauses are separated from the following apodosis by means of the same marker *thì*. Consequently, there is a formal parallelism between the structures

> S1 thì S2   "If S1, (then) S2"
> NP thì S   "As for NP, S"

which mark conditional protasis clauses in the first case above, and topic NP in the second, as shown in (27–30).

(27) (Nếu) có   cần thứ gì,   *thì* tôi sẽ   mua ở Hồng-Công
      if   exist need something topic I   will buy in Hong-Kong
      "If you need something, I will buy it in Hong Kong"

(28) Không có   ông *thì*   tôi đã   lạc dường rồi
      not   exist sir *topic* I already lose road   already
      "If it hadn't been for you, I'd be lost

(29) Không có   xoài   *thì*   mua đưđủ   vảy
      not   exist mango *topic* buy papaya thus
      "If there are no mangoes, buy some papayas instead"

(30) (Nếu) ông không thích *thì*   thôi vậy
      if   sir not   like *topic* stop thus
      "If you don't like it, we won't do it then"

Note that in the sentences (27) and (30) above, the subordinating conjunction *nếu* is optional: the constant indicator of a conditional relationship between protasis and apodosis is the topic marker *thì* alone.

Hua is another language like Vietnamese which uses a topic marker to signal conditional protases. The conditional suffix *-mamo* in fact consists of two parts. The first, *-ma-*, is a personal ending on the verb agreeing with the person and the number of the subject, in relative and complement clauses; the second, *-mo*, is a suffix that may occur on any nominal expression which is an immediate constituent of the clause in which it occurs (this eliminates *-mo* on nouns in the genitive case or those used as qualifiers on other nouns in compounds), and which is incapable of acting as a complete utterance by itself (this eliminates nouns in the vocative case, which are utterances, rather than parts of utterances). The distribution of this suffix defines those nouns which are capable of acting as topics in the clauses where they occur (Haiman 1977). Notionally, a potential topic cannot be an entire utterance since a topic, by definition, encodes old shared information, and there would presumably be no point in uttering a sentence which consisted entirely of old information, unless a repetition were intended. Equally unlikely is the possibility that a potential topic could be a qualifier of a noun: generally, objects in a discourse are introduced before the qualities, and are thus old information relative to those qualities. That is, we may talk about a house and then add that it is red; it is relatively unlikely that we would talk first about redness and then associate it with a house.

In Hua, potential topics, whether nouns or deverbal nouns, occur with the potential topic (p.t.) suffix *-mo*, as in (31).

(31)   Fu-*mo*   dmie
        pork-*p.t.* me=gave=3sg.
        "He gave me pork"

So do the protases of conditional sentences, which indeed are often distinguished from relative clauses *only* through the addition of this same suffix *-mo*. The relative clause, which modifies a head noun as in (32), cannot occur with the potential topic suffix.

(32)   D-mi-si-ma-(* *mo*)   fu-mo
        me-give-will-he-rel.-(*p.t.*) pork-p.t.
        "the pork which he will give me"

The conditional protasis, in sharp contradistinction, *must* occur with this suffix, as shown in (33).

(33)   Fu-*mo*   dmisima-*mo*
        pork-*p.t.* which=he=will=give=me-*p.t.*
        "If he will give me pork . . ."

The formal identity of the protasis marker and the topic marker in a number of Papuan languages has been noted in several cases by the grammarians whose work has made them known to us. Thus, Franklin (1971:120) points out that in Kewa, the topic-marking suffix *-re* also follows protasis clauses; Deibler (1976:102–3), that the suffix *-moʔ* in Gahuku has the same dual function; and Scott (1978:98, 131) draws attention to the same polysemy of the suffix *-pa* in Fore. Most recently, Reesink (to appear) notes that in Usan, the particle *eng* marks both topics and conditional protasis clauses.

As well, the morphological markers of condition and topichood are identical in languages as diverse as Lahu (Matisoff 1973) and Egyptian (Gardiner 1957:125).[1] Finally the very etymology of the words *hypothetical* and *condition* indicate that the grammarians of the classical tradition were well aware of the fact that protasis clauses functioned as the topics of the

---

[1] For references to Lahu and Egyptian, my thanks to Ekkehard Koenig and to Joseph Greenberg.

sentences in which they occurred. Although the etymology of learned terms is in itself as suspect as folk etymology in general, it is worth noting that in this case it confirms the morphological evidence furnished by a large number of languages. Literally, a hypothesis is that which is *placed under*, and thus presumably acts as the background or basis for further discussion; a *condition* is something that has been *agreed upon*, and thus also qualifies as the basis for further discussion.[2]

Having established that conditionals are topics, we are in a position to explain why it should be that in some languages the conditional morpheme and the topic morpheme should be identical.

We are apparently no nearer to answering the question we began with, however, which is why conditional and question morphemes should be either identical or interchangeable. But we are at least in a position to rephrase this question:

> Why are *topics* expressed by questions?

For if conditional protases are topics, then that is what is happening (to some extent) in languages like English.

We can indeed find other cases where non-conditional topics are expressed by the same morphology as questions. One such language is apparently Chinese, where the topic markers *a*, *ne*, *me*, and *ba* are all formally equivalent to interrogative markers (Chao 1968:81–2). Another is Hua, where *actual* topics, those nouns which are contrastively stressed, and which the sentence is "about", are followed by the interrogative suffix *-ve*, as in (34).

(34)   Dgaimo-ve ugue
        I-int.   I꞊will꞊go
        "As for me, I will go"

Less formally grammaticalized is a familiar conversational strategy for introducing topics in English, illustrated by (35a).

(35)   a. You know Max, the barber? Well, he died yesterday

Or consider narratives such as (35b), familiar to all parents of preteen children.

(35)   b. There's this girl in my class named Kristin?
           And she used to go to the Open school?
           And she was wearing this really beautiful shirt with penguins on it?
           And I go, . . .

[2] Further implications of the polysemous origins of conditional markers are discussed in Traugott (to appear).

When such examples are considered, the reason for the interrogative structure is transparent enough. In order to qualify as "old information" for both speaker and hearer, a topic must be familiar to both of them. Presumably what the speaker is going to say is already familiar to him or her but when (s)he introduces a new topic into the conversation, (s)he has to make sure that the audience "recognizes" it. It is perfectly natural to seek the assent of the audience by asking for recognition, which is usually indicated by silence. As Havers (1931:21), Chao (ibid. 82), and Jespersen (1940:374) have argued, introducing a topic by a question in effect creates a mini-conversation between speaker and hearer, as in (36) or (37).

(36)   A: You know Max, the barber?
        B: (silence = "yes")
        A: Well, he died yesterday
(37)   A: Is he coming?
        B: (silence = "yes")
        A: Then I'll stay

In (36), the topic that was introduced is *Max*; in (37), it was the proposition that *he is coming*, a conditional protasis in form and meaning in those numerous languages where conditional protases have the form of polar questions.

We now have a functional explanation for the formal identity of conditional protases and questions, the homonymy which was the starting point for our investigation. Two important observations are necessary at this point.

First, it is clear that the relationship between conditionals and topics is very different from that between conditionals and questions. Conditional protases *are* topics (of a sort); but conditionals are not questions. Neither are topics. The formal similarities between conditionals/topics on the one hand, and questions on the other, does not follow from their semantic equivalence. Rather, a topic is established to be such *by means of a question*. The question is the *instrument*, and the establishment of the topic as a given is the *result*. Semantically, there is no more in common between the two than between a spade and the ditch it is used to dig, or between a bullet and a wound. But this uncontroversial observation suggests a question. If a category may be associated with another through semantic equivalence, or *through its use* (that is, pragmatically) are there any limits on the chain of associations whereby any category may be related to others? Ultimately, "da toebone connecta to . . . da headbone". If the association of ideas in language is as open-ended as this, then homonymy, even repeated in many different languages, may violate the isomorphism condition, since toebones and headbones do not have much in common.

So far, of course, the semantic categories that we have been discussing – interrogation, conditionals, and topics – are very few and very closely related. There is as yet no indication that the chain of associations is either open-ended or logically invalid. Yet, if the history of individual words is any indication, chains of association may be both long and illogical, allowing us in principle to get from anywhere to anywhere else step by step. There is, for example, no logical connection between the horn on a cow and the horn in a car, although we can still see the chain of associations whereby non-definitional properties of the first (once again, the *use* to which it was put) gave us the name for a class of objects which made similar noises, irrespective, first, of the substance they were made of, and finally, of the way in which they operate.

1.3 Association

I have seen Robert De Niro in *Raging bull* and now associate the boxer Jake La Motta with the music of Mascagni. Associations like this are not only extra-logical, but entirely personal and thus idiosyncratic. Grammarians may discount idiosyncrasies. What happens, however, when illogical associations are general? Can this happen? And if it does, what are the implications for the isomorphism hypothesis?

The second half of the isomorphism hypothesis maintains that where a single linguistic structure is recurrently associated with the same cluster of meanings, then those meanings are related. But what is at issue is the nature of this relationship. By association, it may be possible for meanings to be related which share no essential properties. And if illogical associations of the same kind are general, then the isomorphism hypothesis will have to be severely modified: repeated identity of form will not always reflect essential similarities of meaning.

In this section, I wish to investigate a widespread tendency for paratactic constructions to be interpreted, and used, as conditional sentences. That is, there are many languages in which the structure *If S1, S2* may be paraphrased by the structure *S1 (and) S2*, in which the two clauses are either juxtaposed without any overt conjunction, or separated by the coordinating conjunction "and". The confusion, like that between conditionals and questions, is reciprocal: less frequently, we encounter cases where a structure of the form *If S1, S2* is used to paraphrase *S1 and S2*, or exhibits some of the syntactic properties of a structure *S1 and S2*.

As was the case before, we shall be able to show why this confusion arises: nevertheless, the semantic categories "coordinate" and "subordinate" clause remain not only distinct, but opposed.

As the givens or topics of their sentences, conditional protases are prototypical subordinate clauses. They are clauses which have no independent illocutionary force, whose content is neither challenged nor denied in the sentence where they appear. Rather, they are (pre)supposed, in the framework of that sentence, to be true, and thus constitute the starting point from which the sentence proceeds.

Typically, although not always, the presuppositions of a sentence are represented overtly by clauses which are embedded within it. The presuppositional status, or modal invulnerability, of a clause subordinated to a principal clause contrasts with the modal vulnerability of a clause which is coordinated with a principal clause. In a typical coordinate structure such as *S1 and S2*, both S1 and S2 are equally open to challenge or denial. In a typical complex structure like *When S1, S2*, on the other hand, S2 may be questioned or denied, but S1 is accepted, by both speaker and hearer, as a given. Thus, one may reply to the sentence

(38)   When I saw you last year, you were only four feet tall

with the indignant response

(39)   I was not!

(denying S2), but scarcely with the response

(40)   You did not!

(denying S1).

Not surprisingly, conditional protases are marked as subordinate clauses in all those languages which make an overt distinction between coordination and subordination, or between principal and subordinate clauses. Thus, in English, the conjunction *if* is a typical subordinating conjunction and an *if*-clause can be identified as a subordinate clause on the basis of a number of syntactic criteria. One property of most subordinate clauses in English is that they may be shifted about the sentence pretty freely. For example, the structure

(41)   It rained a lot *after you left*

allows the subordinate clause, together with its subordinating conjunction, to be shifted to the front of the sentence and yield a grammatical, if not entirely synonymous, sentence

(42)   *After you left*, it rained a lot

In early transformational analyses of English, it was argued that subordinate clauses in this respect resembled adverbs, and the stylistic transformation of subordinate-clause fronting, which converts (41) into (42), is the same as adverb fronting, which converts (43) into (44).

(43)   It rained a lot *last night*
(44)   *Last night* it rained a lot

It seems that *if*-clauses are similar to other subordinate clauses in allowing shifting, although it is at least questionable whether the operation involved is "fronting" or "backing". Greenberg (1966:84) has claimed that the normal order of protasis and apodosis is one in which the protasis precedes, as in

(45)   *If he's right*, they're not adverb clauses

rather than the (presumably "underlying") order of

(46)   They're not adverb clauses *if he's right*

In any case, protases can be moved (at least in English and many other languages) together with their conjunction, while the same liberty of movement is not possible for coordinate clauses. One cannot, for example, paraphrase

(47)   Sammy's mad *and I'm glad*

by the ungrammatical

(48)   **And I'm glad* Sammy's mad

The coordinating conjunction "stays put" between the clauses it conjoins. There is another more subtle difference between coordinate and subordinate clauses that becomes apparent when we convert *S1 and S2* to *S2 and S1*, that is, we simply invert the order of clauses without moving the coordinating conjunction from its grammatical position. The grammatical sentence (47) does not mean the same as

(49)   I'm glad and Sammy's mad

The first sentence suggests that Sammy's anger is the cause of my gladness;

the second, that my gladness is the cause of Sammy's anger. The logical relations between S1 and S2 are different depending on their relative order when they are conjoined by "and" or in unmarked parataxis. The logical relations between S1 and S2 are not affected by their relative order when they are conjoined by "if": in both (45) and (46) the protasis is the framework for judging the validity of the apodosis.

In other Germanic languages, notably German, a syntactic difference between principal and subordinate clauses is their word order. In (most) principal clauses the finite verb is the second major constituent of the clause while in subordinate clauses the (not necessarily finite) verb is shifted to the end of the clause. Contrast the word order in (50)

(50)   Max *liebt* sie nicht
        "Max does not love her"
(51)   . . . weil Max sie nicht *liebt*
        " . . . because Max does not love her"

A clause conjoined with a principal clause by the coordinating conjunction *und* will, like the principal clause, have verb-second order:

(52)   Max liebt sie nicht, und sie *liebt* ihn auch nicht
        "Max doesn't love her, and she doesn't love him either"

A clause joined to a principal clause by the subordinating conjunction *wenn* "when, if", will have verb-final order:

(53)   Max liebt sie nicht, wenn sie ihn nicht *liebt*
        "Max doesn't love her if she doesn't love him"

In other languages, other morphosyntactic criteria distinguish coordinate principal from subordinate clauses. In Hua, and in many related Papuan languages, the verbs of non-final clauses in complex sentences (i.e. those that correspond to S1 in the notation we have been using) will have two opposing kinds of dependent (medial) endings. One set of endings will characterize clauses that are coordinate with the following clause, and another set, those clauses which are subordinate to the following clause. (The coordinate endings are all based on a morpheme which elsewhere in the language functions as the phrasal conjunction "and", while the subordinate endings are based on a morpheme that marks relative and complement clauses.)

In these languages again conditional protasis clauses will occur with the subordinate endings. Not only their static morphosyntactic properties, but also their ability or inability to undergo restricted syntactic processes, mark conditional protases as subordinate clauses. Two diagnostics for determining whether a given clause is coordinate with another one are the possibility of gapping and the coordinate structure constraint. Both processes define clauses as coordinate in different ways. Gapping or, more generally, coordination reduction, is the syntactic operation which converts structures like sentences (54–7)

(54)   Max likes coffee and Hortense *likes* tea
(55)   Max *likes coffee* and Hortense likes coffee
(56)   Max likes *coffee* and Hortense hates coffee
(57)   Max likes coffee and *Max* hates bananas

by deletion of the italicized constituents and regrouping, into the corresponding sentences in (54′–7′).

(54′)   Max likes coffee, and Hortense $\emptyset$ tea
(55′)   Max $\emptyset$ and Hortense like coffee
(56′)   Max likes $\emptyset$ and Hortense hates, coffee
(57′)   Max likes coffee and $\emptyset$ hates bananas

The operation which deletes the leftmost element of a sentence, as in (57), is coordination reduction; that which deletes the rightmost element, as in (56), is right node raising; and that which deletes material from the center, as in (54), is gapping. Arguments of considerable subtlety have been adduced to demonstrate that these three operations are distinct (cf. Hudson 1976), but we shall not be concerned with the differences among them since in the one respect we care about, they are identical: they "apply" only to coordinate structures (ibid. 535).

None of the deletions exemplified in the sentences above is possible if S1 is an *if*-clause, as illustrated in (58–61).

(58)   If Max likes coffee, Hortense (likes/*$\emptyset$) tea
(59)   If Max (likes coffee/*$\emptyset$) Hortense likes coffee
(60)   If Max likes (coffee/*$\emptyset$) Hortense hates coffee
(61)   If Max likes coffee, (Max/*$\emptyset$) hates bananas

The impossibility of deletions indicated in the sentences above is thus a diagnostic for the subordinate status of the protasis relative to the apodosis.

Another famous diagnostic for coordination is Ross' (1967) coordinate structure constraint, according to which no element may be moved out of either element of a coordinate structure. Thus, no extraction operation may move anything out of S2 in the structure *S1 and S2*, exemplified by (62).

(62)   I sent them a cheque and they sent me a plain brown package

Note the ungrammaticality of sentences such as (63–5).

(63)   *What did I send them a cheque and they sent me ____?
(64)   *_Who_ did I send them a cheque and ____ sent me a plain brown package?
(65)   *_Who_ did I send them a cheque and they sent ____ a plain brown package?

in which the interrogative pronoun corresponds to the object, subject, or indirect object of S2.

An extraction operation may move an element out of S2 where S1 is a subordinate clause, however. Corresponding to sentence (66)

(66)   After you send them a cheque, they will send you a plain brown package

we find the awkward but nevertheless acceptable sentences (67–9).

(67)   What, after you send them a cheque, will they send you ____?
(68)   Who, after you send them a cheque, will send you a plain brown package?
(69)   Who, after you send them a cheque, will they send ____ a plain brown package?

Whatever the reason for this difference (and it seems to relate to the fact that subordinate clauses in the examples above may be treated as parenthetical remarks), it is clear that *if*-clauses pattern with subordinate rather than coordinate clauses. Witness the acceptability of (70–7).

(70)   What, if you send them a cheque, will they send you ____?
(71)   Who, if you send them a cheque, ____ will send you a plain brown package?
(72)   Who, if you send them a cheque, will they send ____ a plain brown package?

I have belabored the somewhat obvious point that *if*-clauses are subordinate in order to highlight the disconcerting fact that coordinate structures of the form *S1 (and) S2* very frequently have the force of conditional structures like *If S1, S2*, even in languages where both structures exist. Less frequently, we will find that structures like *If S1, S2* have some of the syntactic properties of coordinate structures (in particular, they exhibit gapping-like behavior), and have the force of coordinate structures.

We are familiar with English sentences like (73–6), all of which may paraphrase conditional sentences.

(73)   Touch that chest, and I'll scream
(74)   You're so smart, you fix it

(75)   Scratch an animal lover, and you'll find a misanthrope
(76)   Smile, and the world smiles with you

Their restriction is limited, inasmuch as S1 is generally going to have to be an imperative. We may be tempted to dismiss the examples above as a marginal peculiarity of English: an idiosyncrasy of a single language. If English differs from many other languages, however, it is only in treating sentences like (73–6) as stylistically marked in any way. In many other languages where conditional and coordinate structures are distinct, coordinate structures or paratactic structures of the form *S1 S2* are regularly employed to express conditional sentences.

One such language is Vietnamese. A "true" conditional sentence has the canonical form

(77)   Nếu S1 *thì* S2
         if   *topic*

As we have seen, the conjunction *nếu* is always omittable. Very frequently, however, the topic marker may also be omitted, with the result that conditional sentences are expressed as *S1 S2*, as illustrated in (78–9).

(78)   Không có màn không chịu nổi
         not   be net not   bear can
         "If there's no net, you can't stand it"
(79)   Nhưng muốn dộn vào, phải sang   nhiều tiền   lắm
         but   want move in   must transfer much money very
         "But if you want to move in, you will have to pay a lot of transfer money"

Nothing formally distinguishes conditional sentences like these from the coordination of two clauses. Their conditional force – in fact, the distinction between given, hypothetical, and counterfactual conditionals – must be inferred from the context in which they are employed. Given the canonical structure of Vietnamese conditionals in (77), it is clear that the existence of structurally homonymous sentences like (78) and (79) cannot be attributed to the morphological impoverishment of the language. Rather, the language provides a means for making a distinction, but does not always make use of it. Jacob (1968:92) notes the same possibility in the contiguous but only distantly related Cambodian language.

Colloquial French is similar to Vietnamese, at least insofar as the structure *S1 and S2* may have conditional force. The counterfactual condition in (80)

(80)   Si tu m'avais averti, je ne serais pas venu
         "If you had warned me, I wouldn't have come"

may be rendered by the coordinate structure in (81)

(81)   Tu m'aurais averti (et) je ne serais pas venu
        "You would have warned me, and I wouldn't have come"

In Cebuano, a Philippine language, the conditional conjunction "if" is *kong*, found in sentences like (82a,b).

(82)   a. Muainum ako og tubaa *kong* aohawon ako
           drink   I the tubaa if   thirsty I
           "I drink tubaa (a drink of fermented coconut milk) when I'm thirsty"
        b. *Kong* latigohun niya ang bata iya langlagpakon sa   samput ang bata
           if hit   3sg. the child 3sg. do it   with hand the child
           "If he hit the child, it was with the back of his hand"

Much more frequently, however, it seems that the conditional protasis is introduced by the versatile particle *og*, whose basic meaning seems to be simply "and", as in (83).

(83)   Akong himoʔon ang ritrato *og* imung paliton
        I   make   the picture *and* you buy
        "I'm making the picture and you will buy it"

Thus, we frequently encounter conditionals like (84–5).

(84)   *Og* imu akong laparohun, muhilak ako
        and you I   hit   cry   I
        "If you hit me, I will cry"
(85)   Tingali mulakaw siya *og* ako siyang ingnum
        perhaps go=home 3sg. *and* I   3sg.   ask
        "Perhaps he will go home if I ask him"

We even encounter concessive conditionals like (86–7).

(86)   Bisan *og* nagdaliʔ kita   maʔolahi gihapon kita
        even *and* hurry   we=inc. late   still   we=inc.
        "Even if we had hurried, we would still have been late"
(87)   Bisan *og* magʔonsay ka diliʔ ako muʔangay ni   Karlos
        even *and* do=what   you not I   like   (name) Carlos
        "No matter what you do, I don't like Carlos"

Perhaps it is unwise to read too much significance into the multiple uses of *og* in Cebuano, for this particle has so many uses that we may be unable to distinguish principled polysemy from random, rampant homonymy. In addition to its "basic" meaning "and", and to its widespread use as a substitute for "if", Cebuano *og* also means "or", as in (88)

(88)   Gahuwat ka   ba kanako *og* waʔ ba?
        wait   you ? for=me *or* not ?
        "Are you waiting for me or not?"

and is used as a complementizer to introduce *indirect* questions. Thus compare the direct question in (89) with the indirect question in (90).

(89)   Nganong gibasa niya?
        why   read 3sg.
        "Why was he reading it?"

(90)   Ako siyang gipangutana *og*   nganong gibasa niya ang libro
        I   3sg.   ask   (*comp.*) why   read 3sg. the book
        "I asked him why he was reading the book"

In fact, we might expect the latter two functions of a particle whose basic function was to mark the conditional protasis.

Recall that conditional protases frequently have the form of polar questions, for reasons we have already described. Polar questions in their turn frequently are marked by a morpheme which is either identical with, or closely related to, the disjunctive marker "or", since one part of the meaning of a polar question is the implicit disjunction between the proposition it expresses and its contradictory. Thus, the question *S?* may be regarded as an ellipsis of *S or not S?* It is consequently not surprising that in languages as diverse as Japanese, Ukrainian, Ono, Lenakel, and Hausa, the interrogative morpheme is identical with the disjunction "or" (Japanese *ka*, Ukrainian *chy*, Ono *me*, Lenakel *ua*, Hausa *ko*). In fact, there are even languages like Hua, in which a single morpheme may express all three categories (disjunction, interrogation, and conditionals) at once, as illustrated in (91a–c).

(91)   a. ... bzama-ve   haguma-ve ...
            sweet=potatoes-or yams-or
            "sweet potatoes and/or yams and/or ..."
        b. E-   ve?
            come-?
            "Did s/he come?"
        c. Gorokamo havisu-ve kogue
            Goroka   I=go=up-? I=will=see
            "If I go up to Goroka I will see it"

Similarly, if it were a function of *og* to signal conditional protases, it would not be surprising to find that this same morpheme was employed to mark subordinate clauses in general, since, as we have argued, conditional protases are a kind of prototypical subordinate clause.

Nevertheless, the fact that a morpheme which serves one set of possibly related functions – to mark disjunction, conditionals, and interrogation – should also be used to mark one which is totally different, that of simple coordination, is a fact which is parallel to the polysemy of parataxis in Vietnamese or coordination in French.

In Gaelic, the coordinating sentential conjunctions *agus* "and" and *ach* "but" occur intersententially: *S1 ach/agus S2*. However, if S2 occurs with its verb in the infinitive mood, these same conjunctions mean "even if" and "if only", as in (92).

(92)   Thioc fadh   Sean agus/ach e   a bheith olta
        would come John and/but him to be   drunk
        "John would come even if/only if he were drunk"

The now subordinate clause may be shifted to the front, yielding the structure *Agus/ach S2, S1*. (cf. Daniel Boyle 1973:223–4).

In a large number of Papuan languages, some of which may conceivably be related to each other, but certainly not to any of the other languages cited here, it has often been noted that structures of the form *S1 and S2*, consisting of a medial and a final clause, are interpretable as *If S1, S2*, although there is a very rigid and pervasive distinction, both morphological and syntactic, between principal and subordinate non-final (=S1) clauses in all of these languages. Hua may serve as one of the extensively documented examples of these languages, others of which are Fore (Scott 1978:131), Wojokeso (West 1973:21–2, 24), Kâte (Pilhofer 1933:154), and Ono (Wacke 1931:197).

In Hua, subordinate clauses (including relative clauses and conditionals) occur with a set of personal desinences on the verb. The unmarked form of this set of desinences, which occurs on verbs in the third person singular, is *-maʔ*, a morpheme which may be related to the "potential topic marker" *-mo* (and in at least one related language, Siane, the two morphemes are identical), a morpheme which follows constituents functioning as nouns in an utterance.

In Hua coordinate S1 clauses, the verb occurs with another set of personal desinences on the verb. The unmarked form of this set of desinences, once again occurring on verbs in the third person singular, is *-ga*, a morpheme which is probably related to the phrasal coordinating conjunction *-gi* – "and". We may easily construct a morphologically minimally contrasting pair of complex sentences *S1 S2*, which differ only in that S1 occurs with the coordinating desinence *-ga* or the subordinating desinence *-ma*, as in (93).

(93) Fumo d-mi-*ma*/-*ga*-da doe
   pork me-give-*sub.*/*coord.*-I I꞊ate

Both may be translated, provisionally, as "He gave me pork and I ate", but there are a number of more or less subtle differences between the coordinate and the subordinate forms.

In contradistinction to the subordinate clause, the coordinate clause (dmi*ga*da) must:

(a) mark "switch reference": whether or not the subject of the S1 is identical with the subject of the S2 is indicated by the deletion or the retention of the desinence -*ga*-. Since the subjects of the two clauses are distinct in (93), -*ga*- appears in S1: if the subjects of the two clauses were identical, this morpheme would disappear. (The subordinating -*maʔ* desinence is never subject to deletion.)

(b) be in the same tense and mood as the following clause: in the sample sentence above, both S1 and S2 are in the non-future tense, and in the indicative, assertive mood. If S1 and S2 were to differ in tense or mood, then only the subordinate S1 form would be acceptable.

(c) observe "tense iconicity": the order of clauses must correspond to the order of events. Note that this constraint is independent of the "same-tense: same mood" constraint, since it is perfectly possible for two events, both occurring in the past tense – that is, before the time of the speech act – to occur in different orders relative to each other.

In short, the morphological distinction between S1 in -*maʔ* and S1 in -*ga* corresponds to both a syntactic and at least two semantic distinctions, in an orderly fashion. The striking flaw in this systematic pattern in Hua, as in each of the other examples presented so far, is that coordinate structures of the form *S1 -ga S2* in the future tense may be interpreted as virtually synonymous with regular conditional constructions of the form *S1 -ma S2*. Both the sentences (94a) and (94b) can be used, apparently interchangeably, to render the English sentence "If he comes, I will stay."

(94) a. Esi-*ga*-da baigue
      come-*coord.*-I I꞊will꞊stay
   b. Esi-*ma*-mo baigue
      come-*sub.des.*-*topic* I꞊will꞊stay

Only the second is a "true" conditional. The literal meaning of the first, as implied by its interlinear gloss, is "He will come and I will stay." In short, the polysemy of the Hua coordinate structure parallels that of the coordinate structures we have examined in Vietnamese, French, English, and Cebuano.

In Mandarin Chinese, conditional protases may be marked as such in a number of ways. They may be introduced by a conditional conjunction *jiărú* "if", *yàoshi* "if", or *zhĭyŏu* "only if", as in (95).

(95)　　*Jiărú* xià　　yǔ, wǒmen jiu　zài wūlĭ　　chī-fàn
　　　　　if　descend rain we　　then at indoors eat-food
　　　　　"If it rains, we'll eat indoors"

They may be followed by a topic marker *me*, as in (96).

(96)　　Tā bu niàn-shū　　*me*, wǒ jiu　bu yǎng　　tā
　　　　　3sg. not study-book *topic* I　then not support 3sg.
　　　　　"If s/he doesn't study, I won't support him/her"
　　　　　　　　　　　　　　　　　　　　(Li & Thompson 1981, 632, 634)

However, it is possible in Chinese to make a conditional statement simply by a juxtaposition of S1 and S2 with no overt indication of the relationship between them, as in (97).

(97)　　a. Nĭ　bu　xiāngxin, wǒ zuò gěi nĭ　kàn
　　　　　　　you not believe　I　do to　you see
　　　　　　　"If you don't believe it, I'll do it for you to see"
　　　　　b. Nĭmen bu　zuò-gōng, wǒmen bu　fù-qián
　　　　　　　you=all not do=work, we　　not pay-money
　　　　　　　"If you all don't work, we won't pay you"
　　　　　　　　　　　　　　　　　　　　(Li & Thompson, 642, 643, 649)

In Spanish, the conditional conjunction *si* may be omitted from the protasis, "so that we find surface strings which are semantically conditionals, but in which the two clauses are juxtaposed or coordinated" (Rivero 1972:209), as illustrated in (98).

(98)　　a.　(Si) muriese el burro, lo enterrariamos
　　　　　　　"(If) the donkey died, we would bury it"
　　　　　b.　Habla se de esta manera, y nadie le escucharia
　　　　　　　"He talks like that, and no one will listen to him"
　　　　OR　"If he talks like that, no one will listen to him"
　　　　　c.　(Si) se enfada el, me enfado yo
　　　　　　　"(If) he gets angry, I get angry"

Finally, it should be noted that early modern English *an* "if" in

(99)　　An please your Reverence, here we are

derives from *and*. In fact, the orthographic distinction *an* ≠ *and*, as the *OED* points out, is a relatively recent convention not observed before *c.* 1600:

(100)　　Now kepe hem wel, for *and* ye wil ye can

While the confusion between "if" and "and" so far has been unidirectional, with "and" acquiring the functions of "if" in a variety of languages, the converse is also attested.

In Xinalug, a Caucasian language of the Soviet Union, the conditional morpheme "if" is a verbal suffix *-ki*: *khiraet-ki* "if 3sg. does", *khiriž-ki* "if 3sg. will do" (Dešeriev 1959:113). Dešeriev notes that, although originally an affix of the conditional mood, *-ki* functions as the coordinating conjunction "and" through a "broadening of its meaning" (ibid. 183), as in

(101) Tmoz aečilmyš-*kij*(a), ej kili ičaeri m'alcyvə
       door opened-*if*   my friend inside entered
       "The door opened, *and* my friend walked in"

Cases of this kind of "broadening" seem to be rare. But there is another sense in which conditional structures of the form *If S1, S2* seem to approximate coordinate structures, and that is that they seem to undergo something very similar to *gapping* or coordination reduction with respect to one deleted element: the marker of their mood.

It is a commonplace that the apodosis of a counterfactual conditional must itself be in the counterfactual mood. Compare the acceptability of (102) with the impossibility of (103).

(102) If it hadn't rained, I wouldn't have taken my umbrella
(103) *If it hadn't rained, I will not take my umbrella

The parallelism is clearly marked in languages like Latin, where both protasis and apodosis of the modal conditional sentence occur with the same verbal modal inflection:

(104) Si Iulia me amav-*isset*,   mihi nups-*isset*
       If Julia me love-*3sg.plpf.subj.* me marry-*3sg.plpf.subj.*
       "If Julia loved me, she would marry me"

But the parallelism is taken to an extreme in those languages where protasis and apodosis are formally indistinguishable: not only are both inflected with the same irrealis particle or verbal desinence, but neither clause has any particle analogous to either "if" or "then".

An example of such a language is Daga, a Papuan language spoken in the Owen Stanley Mountains in the southeast of Papua New Guinea (Murane 1974:259):

(105) Ya wada-nege-*po*, ya anu-*po*
       not say-me-irreal. not know-irreal.
       "If s/he hadn't told me, I wouldn't know"

Other Papuan languages which exhibit the same total parallelism of protasis and apodosis include Maring (Woodward 1973:13), Kobon (Davies 1981:39) and Gende (Brandson mss). Australian languages with the same pattern include Guugu-Yimidhirr (Haviland 1979:15), Pitta-Pitta (Blake 1979:221), and Ngiyambaa (Donaldson 1980:252).

Once again, examples of the formal parallelism of protasis and apodosis clauses in conditionals could be multiplied, but this parallelism needs no elaborate justification: its basis is that the protasis and the apodosis, particularly of counterfactual conditional sentences, do agree in mood. This modal agreement is admittedly obscured in sentences like the following:

(106)   ⎧ you must be rich
       If you're so smart, ⎨ why aren't you rich?
                           ⎩ call him up yourself!

in which the apodosis can be respectively a statement, a question, or a command, although the mood of the protasis, whatever we call it, is identical throughout. But there is a sense in which the mood of the apodosis even in these cases agrees with that of the protasis. The statement "you must be rich" is a hypothetical statement; the question "why aren't you rich?" a hypothetical question; and the command "call him up yourself!" a hypothetical command. They function as statement, question, and command, only if the protasis is assumed or agreed upon. If the protasis is hypothetical they are equally hypothetical, and thus "agree" in mood with the protasis.

Now, the gapping behavior of conditional structures to which I referred earlier consists simply of this: the mood marker which occurs equally in S1 and S2 of a conditional structure is sometimes deleted from one or another of these clauses. That is, the structure $S1 + mood$ $S2 + mood$, realized in languages like Gende and Kobon, is frequently realized as $S1 + \emptyset$ $S2 + mood$ or $S1 + mood$ $S2 + \emptyset$, and the motivation for the deletion is the identity of the two mood markers.

Seldom is this made as explicit by a language, or by its guardian grammarian, as it is by Ono (a Papuan language of the Huon Peninsula), and its brief but pellucid description by K. Wacke (1931:197).

In counterfactual conditionals, Ono employs an irrealis particle *ramo* which marks the protasis as counterfactual, and an irrealis verbal desinence on the verb of the apodosis clause marks the latter as similarly counterfactual:

(107)   Sarimi   *ramo*, edanbe*rap*
        come=3pl.past *count*. I=*would*=have=told=them
        "If they had come, I would have told them"

(108)   Nekone   *ramo*, rapokengem*rap*
        eat=1pl.past *count*. we=*would*=admit=it
        "If we had eaten it we would admit it"

What is crucial in these examples is that the protasis clause without *ramo* does not in itself express the irrealis mood, only the simple preterite tense. The irrealis desinence of the apodosis is, of course, the final suffix *-rap*, which follows the personal endings *-be* "1sg." *-gem* "1pl.", and so on (Wacke 1931:166). The parallelism between protasis and apodosis in Ono is impaired in that the irrealis morpheme *-ra-* occurs with a medial suffix in S1, and a final suffix in S2: but it *is* the same morpheme.

What makes Ono so apparently remarkable, however, is the fact that the irrealis word *ramo* of the protasis is frequently omitted, with the incidental consequence that in Ono, as in French, Vietnamese, etc., a conditional structure looks and sounds just like a coordinate structure:

(109)   Numa maumo,   uwe-*rap*
        way   you=make=med. I-*come*=irreal.
        "You would have made a road, and I would have come"
   OR   "If you had made a road, I would have come"

Wacke explicitly points out that *ramo* can be omitted precisely *because S1 and S2 agree anyway* (ibid. 197).

If this deletion obeys the constraints peculiar to coordination reduction (as opposed to numerous other kinds of "deletion under identity") then we have structural evidence for the coordinate structure of conditional sentences. The criterial property of coordination reduction is that the "direction in which it goes" is determined by the position of the identical elements in the larger constituents of which they are a part. If the identical constituents are left branches of their respective constituents, then it is the leftmost one which remains; if the identical constituents are the rightmost branches of their respective constituents, then it is the rightmost one which remains. In the Ono example above, the morpheme *ra* is arguably the rightmost branch of the verb complex in which it appears in both protasis and apodosis, and accordingly, it is the rightmost one which should remain (i.e. the *ra-* morpheme in the apodosis): and this is in fact the case.

Are there other languages in which this kind of deletion occurs, for which the coordination reduction hypothesis could be tested? Note that by this hypothesis, where the mood marker occurs on a *left* branch of a larger constituent, we should predict that the mood marker remains in the protasis; where it occurs on a right branch, it should remain in the apodosis.

The evidence in favor of the coordination reduction hypothesis, it must be admitted, is quite weak. Whether the irrealis particle is a word or a bound morpheme, there are a number of languages in which it cannot be omitted from either protasis or apodosis (although these languages allow or manifest coordination reduction). An example of such a language is Hungarian. The counterfactual conditional has the verb in both protasis and apodosis in the conditional mood, and the mood marker -*nE* cannot be omitted from either clause:

(110)   Ha jött   *volna*   láttam   *volna*
        if came=3sg. *be=cond.* saw=1sg. *be=cond.*
        "If s/he had come I would have seen him/her"

There are other languages in which the particle may be omitted from either clause, and it is difficult to tell whether the particle is the left branch or the right branch of any larger construction. One such language is Cebuano of the Philippines, where the irrealis particle is *(pa)Ponta*:

(111)   Og ninginum (*paPonta*) siya og tubig, dili (*Ponta*) siya Pohawon karon
        if drunk   (*irreal.*)   3sg. art. water neg. (*irreal.*) 3sg. thirsty   now
        "If s/he had drunk the water, s/he would not be thirsty now"

The irrealis marker may appear on either or both protasis and apodosis (and cannot be totally excluded from both: for some discussion, cf. 3.3.4, below). Finally, there are languages like Ono, in which the irrealis particle (in this case a postverbal auxiliary) is omittable in S1 only, as the theory of coordination reduction predicts.

Summing up, we must admit that the evidence for coordination reduction is less than convincing; but the formal grammatical parallelism of S1 and S2 in conditional sentences is similar to the formal grammatical parallelism of S1 and S2 in coordinate constructions. The assumption that recurrent identity of form must reflect similarity in meaning therefore obliges us to find what meaning is common to coordinate constructions and conditional sentences. There are a number of possible explanations for this recurrent homonymy, and I will begin by disposing of the one that seems to me to be the weakest.

From a purely logical point of view, there is an intimate connection between the logicians' conjunction (S1 $\wedge$ S2), and implication (S1 $\supset$ S2), where the logical symbols " $\wedge$ " and " $\supset$ " are defined in terms of truth tables. *Given p*, the expression p ⊃ q gives q (by modus ponens), whence we have p ∧ q (by conjunction). In this sense the two complex expressions are indeed equivalent; thus, we should not be surprised to find them expressed in the same way. Unfortunately, this begs the question: the givenness of p is the crucial property of conditionals in ordinary language, and is absent in coordinations.

Very well, then, is there any reason to suppose that in ordinary language conjunctions like *S1 S2* there is a sense in which S1 is given (or more given than S2)? There is. An investigation of this reason leads us to a much more plausible explanation for the frequent identity of coordinate clauses and conditionals.

One of Greenberg's word order universals (#14) states that in conditionals the usual order of clauses (and in some languages, the only one allowed) is that in which the protasis precedes the apodosis. This is an iconically motivated universal: S1 precedes S2 as the given precedes the new. But if the linear order of clauses in a conditional corresponds to the order: given–new, then perhaps the same is true of the linear order of clauses in a coordinate structure. That is, in a coordinate structure *S1 S2*, perhaps S1 is given relative to S2 simply by virtue of occurring, or being uttered, first.

There is very widespread evidence that the first of two clauses in a coordination is regarded as a given. This evidence comes from the phenomenon of resumptive clause topicalization, widely attested in a number of oral narrative styles in diverse languages.

Resumptive topicalization is illustrated in the mini-narrative

(112)   He sat down. *Having sat down*, he undid his tie

The second sentence begins by repeating the content of the first. Having once been introduced, the first sentence represents a given. It functions in the second sentence as a topic. There are many languages which seem to use resumptive topicalization very heavily as a narrative technique. What is interesting about them is that many of them express resumptive topicalization in a way that we could model in English rather like this:

(113)   He sat down. *He sat down <u>and</u>* he undid his tie

That is, the repeated (and thus, topical) S1 is expressed as a clause which is coordinate with the "new" clause S2. The status of S1 as a given is sufficiently assured, it seems, merely by preceding S2 in the complex sentence *S1 S2*.

Some of the languages in which this pattern seems to hold are Hua (Haiman 1980:passim), Ono (Wacke 1931:196), Kashaya (Oswalt 1977:52), and Kâte (Pilhofer 1933:132–4). We may take the last, a Papuan language of the Huon Gulf Peninsula, as a representative example. Kâte, like Hua, conjoins clauses by means of the medial verb construction, wherein S1 (and all non-final clauses in multiple-clause sentences) occurs with a distinctive set of medial desinences, while S2 occurs with a distinct set of final desinences. Pilhofer is at pains to state that medial clauses must agree in mood with the following clause (1933:35, 135, 138): whatever the validity or the modal status of S2, it must be shared by S1.

Nevertheless, in head–tail linkages of the form *S1. S1 S2*, in which the second occurrence of S1 represents a given, this second occurrence is rendered by a medial clause whose form is identical with that of the coordinate medial, as in (114).

(114)   Kise fiuc lo-wec. *Lo-lâ*   like-lâ   nâ-wec
yams theft take-3sg. *take-med.* cook-med. eat-3sg.
"He stole the yams. *He stole them*, cooked them, and ate them" (p. 134)

The frequent recurrence of this pattern (particularly in those languages which make a sharp morphological distinction between principal and subordinate clauses) provides some evidence that a clause which is syntactically coordinated with a principal clause may represent a proposition that is treated as a given relative to that principal clause; and that it represents a given by virtue of its position in the chain of clauses of which it is a part.

We have an explanation then, of why *S1 S2* could be interpreted as *If S1, S2*, or, more generally, *Given that S1, S2*. But we do not yet have an explanation for the fact that constructions of the form *If S1, S2* exhibit many of the structural properties of true coordinations: in particular, their symmetry, and the possibility of something similar to coordination reduction with respect to the expression of mood. There is an explanation in the air, however.

Since protasis and apodosis agree in mood anyway, the expression of mood in the first is frequently omitted. This is as Wacke proposed in his description of the fleeting appearance of the counterfactual particle *ramo* in Ono counterfactual protasis clauses (Wacke 1931:197).

Wacke's observation is of particular interest because it illustrates precisely the confusion we are trying to explain. Clearly, there is a tremendous semantic difference between the two sentences (115) and (116).

(115)   If you had come, I would have seen you
(116)   You would have come, and I would have seen you

Yet as we have seen, there are some languages (such as French) in which the second may be used as a colloquial equivalent of the first. And there is a sense, pointed out by Wacke, in which they really are similar: in both constructions, S1 and S2 are both irrealis in mood.

In (115) the protasis creates a set of irrealis worlds and the apodosis represents a proposition whose validity is asserted in the framework of those worlds alone. In this sense – the sense in which the meaning of the conditional protasis has been defined already – the apodosis "agrees" in mood with the protasis. In (116) two separate and (in principle, independent) assertions are made. It happens that they are both irrealis in mood, but neither determines the other, and neither is presented as the framework for the other. Yet it would be incorrect to state that coordinate clauses like those in (116) merely *happen* to agree in being irrealis. There are strong indications that coordinate clauses are constrained to agree not only in mood but with respect to many other features. And there is reason to believe that *necessary* agreement (or parallelism) with respect to these and other features is part of what defines coordinate clauses in general – we will return to this in our discussion of conceptual symmetry in section 2.1.

In the meantime we should note that there are many languages (notably in the "Trans-New Guinea Phylum" of Papuan languages, cf. Wurm 1975) in which modal agreement is precisely what distinguishes coordinate from non-coordinate non-final clauses: thus Kâte (Pilhofer, op. cit.), Chuave (Thurman 1978), Hua, Gimi, and Siane (Haiman 1980), Gende (Brandson mss) and Tauya (MacDonald, to appear and ms). But this structural property of coordinate clauses is no more than a grammaticalization of a universal tendency which is just as well exemplified in English. Examples such as (117) and (118) below may be cited as evidence that clauses which encode different speech acts (and thus are different in mood) can be combined by a coordinate conjunction:

(117)   Stand up and fight, or are you afraid? (S1 imperative; S2 interrogative)
(118)   I live here, and who the hell are you?   (S1 assertive; S2 interrogative)

But these examples are not only highly marked stylistically and prosodically (note the heavy pause before the conjunction in each case); they are also very limited in their privileges of occurrence.

For example, it is impossible to reverse the order of conjuncts in either (117) or (118); it is impossible to conjoin either a question or a command with a following assertion; and it is impossible to conjoin an assertion with a following command. In fact, if we eliminate sentences with the conjunction *or* from consideration, and confine ourselves only to those which are linked by *and*, it seems that the only possibility of linking together clauses which embody different speech acts, is that exemplified by (118). On the other hand, clauses conjoined by *and* may appear in any mood whatever, subject to the general condition that both S1 and S2 are clauses which perform the same speech act (and agree in the formal expression of mood as well):

(119)   a. Close the door and sit down
         b. My grandfather was a democrat, my father was a democrat, and I am a democrat
         c. Who is that woman, and what is she doing in your office?
         d. But, oh, that I were young again, and held her in my arms!

Now, it may be that the operative slogan which allows confusion to arise between conditional sentences like (115) and coordinate sentences like (116) may be simply that *"agreement is agreement"*. Since S1 and S2 are both counterfactual, in both (115) and in (116), the two structures may be interchangeable. Coordinate clauses may be interpreted as conditional sentences; conversely, conditional sentences may exhibit some of the properties of coordinate clauses.

This explanation, if true, offers a good example of what Henning Andersen (1973) has identified as an abductive change: "Abduction proceeds from an observed result, invokes a law, and infers that something may be the case" (Andersen 775). In this case, the "result" is that S1 clauses that are coordinate with S2 clauses agree with these clauses in mood; the "law" is that S1 clauses that are protases agree with S2 clauses that are apodoses; and what may be the case, given this similarity, is that coordinate clauses and conditional clauses are therefore the same.

The identification of S1 as a given (and, hence, protasis) clause in the paratactic construction *S1 S2* on the basis of its relative position is also an example of abductive inference. The "result", in this case, is that S1 precedes S2; the "law" that protasis clauses typically precede apodoses (Greenberg's universal #14); and the inference, that S1 is therefore a protasis.

What is common to both explanations for the confusion of conditionals and coordinate structures (and possibly both explanations play a rôle in creating this confusion) is that, logically, they are false. Both of them are examples, not only of abduction, but of *association*.

Association occurs when two categories are related on the basis of their sharing incidental properties. "True" identification between different objects, or between different categories, is made when they share distinctive, or essential, properties. "False" identification or confusion ensues where different objects or categories are identified as similar on the basis of their sharing incidental properties.

In a coordination or parataxis of *S1 S2*, it is an incidental property of S1 that it precedes S2: after all, linearity entails that the two clauses *have* to occur in *some* order. In a conditional sentence, the relative order of S1 and S2 reflects their difference in givenness: it is therefore at least a distinctive property of S1 that it precedes S2, although not an essential one, given that the protasis is independently marked by a diacritic like "if" or a special grammatical construction of equivalent semantic import. Confusion arises when a property which is absolutely essential to neither category, namely the property of occurring first, is abstracted as the defining property of the "target category", such that another category which shares this property is ipso facto identical with the target category.

A similar confusion between incidental and essential identity is involved in the use of the operative slogan "agreement is agreement". To be sure, there is modal agreement between S1 and S2 in both conditional constructions and coordinate constructions. But there are also crucial differences: in a conditional construction, the apodosis S2 *agrees with S1*, that is, its mood is determined by the mood of S1. In a coordinate construction, all that can be said is that S1 and S2 *are in agreement*. (In fact, in the verb-final Papuan languages where S1 is a medial verb clause, and S2 a final verb clause, the most common idiom for reporting on this agreement is that S1 *agrees with S2*.) This difference accounts for the most striking semantic difference between the structures *If S1, S2* and *S1 (and) S2*: the former makes only one assertion, the latter, two. To overlook these differences is to make a logically unjustified generalization.

It is a familiar principle of lexicography that the properties of any category (or individual word) may be divided into those which are definitional and those which are incidental. The distinction between the two sets of properties is in fact sometimes cited as one of the theoretical bases for the distinction between a dictionary (listing only definitional properties), and an encyclopedia (listing both definitional and incidental properties); cf. Bierwisch and Kiefer (1970).

However, it is a familar principle of lexicography that properties which are "incidental" at one time seem to become "definitional" later on, and vice versa. Darmesteter (1886/1925) refers to the effective mechanism of *enchainement* whereby this transformation allows words to develop meanings that are sometimes the precise opposite, but more generally something entirely different from what they had at first. Originally a W(ord) may denote a referent A with properties "a" and "b"; later, another referent B with properties"b" and "c"; later still, a referent C with properties "c" and "d"; and so on forever. While any two denotata in such a chain of associations will have *some* feature(s) in common, the shared features need not be definitional.

A later, very familiar, discussion of this mechanism is Wittgenstein's treatment of "family resemblances" (1958: sections 169, 219, 373, 441, 464). For other statements in the linguistic literature, cf. Stern (1931:340–1), J. Williams (1975:182), Haiman (1980a,1982).

By *enchainement*, almost any concept may be associated with any other. In the example under extended discussion here, the conditional protasis, in many ways the very model of a subordinate clause, may come to be associated with, and therefore represented by, a coordinate clause. (We shall see in chapter 4 that a converse development, whereby a semantically coordinate clause is represented by a hypotactic construction, is also widely attested.)

It is clear that the existence of association, abduction, or *enchainement*, unless these are constrained, is sufficient to nullify the isomorphism hypothesis. Given this mechanism, recurrent identity of form need not reflect similarity in meaning at all. I would like to propose that, in this case, at least, there may be a constraint on the associations that can be made with the structure *S1 S2*. And this constraint is iconic.

The possible interpretations of *S1 S2* are those – and only those – of which the structure itself is an icon. In the absence of diacritics, the only relationship between S1 and S2 which is signaled by unmarked concatenation is that suggested by their *linear order*. I therefore maintain that there is a constant difference between the analogs of *S1 and S2*, on the one hand, and *If S1, S2* on the other. To wit, conditional protasis clauses marked by a diacritic like "if" may be *concessive conditionals* wherein S2 does not "follow from" S1; conditional protasis clauses that are not marked by such a diacritic cannot be concessive conditionals: conceptually, as well as formally, S2 must follow from S1. That is, conditionals of the form *S1 S2* must satisfy the (narrow, and mistaken) definition of conditionals proposed by Ramsey, wherein *If S1, S2* is equivalent to hypothetical *Because S1 S2*.

Let us at this point eliminate from our discussion those languages like Cebuano or early modern English, where the morpheme "and" has come to have the meaning "if", and concentrate entirely on those languages in which the conditional force of *S1 S2* is expressed entirely by the relative order of the two clauses.

The languages in which this hypothesis is tested and seems valid include English, Chinese, Vietnamese, Hua, Japanese, and Hindi: a representative sample wide enough to encourage optimism that the recurrent polysemy of the structure *S1 S2* is in fact generally constrained as I suggest.

Consider first the English constructions of the form illustrated in (120).

(120)　　a.　No ticket, no laundry
　　　　　b.　Scratch an animal lover, (and) you'll find an misanthrope
　　　　　c.　You keep driving like that, (and) you're going to kill yourself
　　　　　d.　You major in mathematics or physics, (and) IBM will want to hire you

One could argue that the relationship between S1 and S2 in cases of this sort is determined by extra-linguistic context, or by knowledge of the world: given which, the relationship between them could be anything at all (cf. Li & Thompson 1981:641 for an explicit statement of this view). I maintain that there are limits to this possible variation. Specifically, in no case could the sentences of (120) receive an *Even if S1, S2* interpretation, even in cases where such an interpretation did not violate our expectations of what happens in the real world. To appreciate this, consider sentences such as (121a,b).

(121)　　a.　If you major in linguistics or porritology, IBM will want to hire you
　　　　　b.　Whether you major in linguistics or porritology, IBM will want to hire you

We have no real world knowledge of porritology, nevertheless, we know that in (121a) porritology is akin to linguistics in being a subject whose students IBM finds attractive: in other words, (121a) is a causal conditional. In (121b), we know that porritology is as different from linguistics as possible, but IBM is so desperate to hire people they don't care: (121b) is a concessive conditional. Consider now the most likely interpretation of (122).

(122)　　You major in linguistics or porritology, (and) IBM will want to hire you

It seems to me that this sentence, at least with normal intonation, can only be construed as a causal conditional like (121a), and never as a concessive conditional like (121b): and, as we have established, our ignorance of porritology makes it impossible for us to invoke "knowledge of the world" as the explanation for this fact.

With the appropriate contemptuous intonation – a kind of squeal on the word "porritology" – sentence (122) can be made to have an interpretation similar to (121b): but this merely confirms the claim that a structure *S1 S2* can only have a meaning of which the order of clauses is not itself an icon if their true semantic relationship is marked by an additional diacritic. The contemptuous squeal on "porritology", I submit, is this diacritic.

Intonation may act as a diacritic in another class of cases, typified by examples such as those in (123).

(123)　　a.　You're gonna kill yourself, you drive like that
　　　　　b.　He can fix it himself, he's so smart
　　　　　c.　I'll beat the shit out of him, he tries any rough stuff with me

in which the structure *S1 S2* is interpreted in such a way that S2 is clearly the *protasis*, and S1, the apodosis. Again, an order of clauses is not an icon of the semantic relationship between them. Yet the givenness of the protasis is clearly marked, in the most iconic fashion imaginable, by the relative intensity of S1 and S2: the protasis, as befits a clause which expresses a given proposition, is uttered sotto voce relative to the apodosis.

A more or less parallel contrast exists in Hua between *If S1, S2* and *S1 (and) S2*, although the morphological realization of "if" and "and" is very different from that of English (cf. examples (94a,b) repeated below). The difference is in the personal endings on the dependent verb (i.e., the verb of S1), such that *-ga-* of (94a) is "and", and *-ma-* of (94b) is "if".

(94)　　a.　E-si-*ga*-da　　　　　　　　bai-gue
　　　　　　　come-3sg. fut.-*and*-1sg.ant. stay-1sg. fut.
　　　　　　　"3sg. will come and I will stay"　　　　(the literal interpretation)
　　　　　　　"If 3sg. comes, I will stay"　(a possible and common interpretation)
　　　　　b.　E-si-*ma*-mo　　　　　　　bai-gue
　　　　　　　come-3sg. fut.-*if*-p.t. stay-1sg. fut.)
　　　　　　　"If 3sg. comes, I will stay" (no coordinate reading is possible)

Thus, one meaning of the coordinate structure (94a) is the same as the meaning of the conditional sentence (94b): but it is not *exactly* the same. The crucial difference is that only the "true" conditional form in *-ma-* can be used to render a concessive conditional. To express this meaning, Hua makes use of a construction something like *Whether S1 or (not S1), S2* (where *not S1* may be either literally the negation of S1 or some other clause

S3 which can be explicated as mutually exclusive with S1). Both *S1* and *not S1* occur as direct polar questions, as, for example, in (124).

(124)   Fri-si-*ve* (?)   Hava?a bai-si-*ve* (?)
        die-3sg. fut.-*int*. just   stay-3sg. fut.-*int*.
        "Will s/he die? Will s/he live?"

This disjunction is made into a dependent construction by the addition of a resumptive "utility verb" *hu-* "do", which takes all of (124) as its object complement. As the protasis verb, *hu-* may appear only with the conditional marker *-ma-*, never with the coordinate marker *-ga-*. Thus, the contrast between (125) and (126).

(125)   Frisive hava?a baisive hi-si-*ma*-mo,   dgaimo kge?afugue
        (as (124))   do-3sg. fut.-*if*-p.t. I   won't꞊grieve
        "Whether s/he dies or lives, I (for one) won't grieve"
(126)   *Frisive hava? baisive hi-si-*ga*-da,   dgaimo kge?afugue
        (as (124))   do-3sg. fut.-*and*-1sg. ant. I   won't꞊grieve
        "Whether s/he dies or lives, I (for one) won't grieve"

A related difference between (94a) and (94b) in Hua is that in the coordinate structure the order of clauses must correspond to the order of events. In both interpretations of (94a), the action of S1 (s/he comes) must precede the action of S2 (I stay). In the true conditional (94b), on the other hand, the order of clauses does not necessarily reflect the order of events: I may decide to stay *in the expectation of* his/her arrival.

In Mandarin, as Li & Thompson (1981:633) point out, the paratactic construction *S1 S2* may substitute for a number of conditionally marked more complex sentences. Thus, for example, the paratactic sentence

(127)   Bàba qù, wǒ gēn tā qù
        father go I   with 3sg. go
        "Father goes, I go with him"

may be offered as synonymous with any of the following (in which the italicized words are various "linking elements"):

(128)   a. Bàba qù *de huà/me/ba/ne*, wǒ gēn   tā qù
        b. *Yàoshi/Ruguo/Jiǎrú/Jiashi* bàba qù, wǒ gēn tā qù

It is permissible to say, given (127) and (128), that some linking elements may be optionally deleted without doing violence to the meaning of the sentence. But not all of them may be.

As predicted by our hypothesis, those linking elements which specifically indicate a concessive relationship may not be omitted without radically changing the meaning of the sentence. Thus, sentence (129) means something very different from (130).

(129)   *Jiùshi* zhème piányi, tā   *hái* bu mǎi ne
           even=if this   cheap 3sg. *still* not buy response
           "Even if this is cheap, s/he still won't buy it" (s/he just doesn't want it at all)

(130)   Zhème piányi, tā   bu mǎi ne
           this   cheap 3sg. not buy response
           "If this is cheap, s/he won't buy it" (s/he only buys expensive things)

In the same way, it is impossible to retain the meaning of (131) if the linking element *wúlùn* is left out.

(131)   Wúlùn   tā lái   bu lái, wǒmen yào zǒu le
           no=matter 3sg. come not come we   want go currently=relevant
           "Whether s/he comes or not, we must go"

In Vietnamese, *S1 thì S2* "If S1, S2" may be replaced by *S1 S2*; *S1 thì cũng S2* "Even if S1, S2", however, may not be. Thus (132) cannot mean the same as (133).

(132)   (Nếu) có rẻ,   thì cũng phải có tiền   chứ
           (if)   exist cheap topic also must exist money certainly
           "Even if they are cheap, you have to have money"

(133)   (Nếu) có rẻ,   phải có tiền   chứ
           (if)   exist cheap must exist money certainly
           "If they are cheap, you have to have money"

Our discussion of both Hindi and Japanese assumes the near-synonymy of structures like

(134)   a. I raised my arm, and felt the resistance of the water
           b. Raising my arm, I felt the resistance of the water

The extent and limitations of this synonymy are the subject of chapter 4. For now, it is enough to note that sentences like (134b) are found to have paraphrases both as coordinate sentences and as conditionals in both Hindi and Japanese.

In Hindi, (134b) is rendered by *S1-kar S2*, a structure in which *-kar*, a perfective (participial) verbal suffix, replaces aspect and subject markers. The structure basically indicates coordination (Davison 1981: 103), but can also be used to mark causal conditionals:

(135)   Aisee tum kar-*kee* tum   kuursii tooR dẽẽgee
           thus   do-*kar* you=fam. chair break give=fut.=2-fam.
           "If you do that, you'll break the chair"   (Davison 1981:117)

Davison (ibid.) lists the concessive conditional as one of the meanings of *S1-kar S2*, but her examples show that this concessive meaning is only possible if *-kar* is followed by *bhii* "also", the Hindi analog of "even":

(136)   Tum   ustaad hoo-*kar* bhii yah nahíí jaantee?
        you=fam. teacher be-*kar* also this not know=imperf.
        "You don't know this even though you are a teacher?"   (ibid. 111)

Japanese is more interesting because of a further wrinkle. The structure corresponding to (134b) is *S1-te S2*, wherein the gerund suffix *-te* on the verb of S1 replaces tense and mood suffixes. The unmarked meaning of *S1-te S2* is that of simple coordination, as in (137).

(137)   Sono tosi ni wa   Torusútói ga   nakunat-*te* Naitingéeru ga   nakunatta
        that year in topic Tolstoy   sub. die *te*   Nightingale sub. died
        "In that year Tolstoi and Nightingale died"   (Martin 1975:483)

Among the other meanings this same construction may have, however, is that of a conditional, as in (138).

(138)   Sékkusu o   tanosin-*de* náni ga   warúi?
        sex   obj. enjoy-*te* what sub. wrong
        "If one enjoys sex, what's wrong (with that)?"
    OR
        "What's wrong with enjoying sex?"   (ibid. 484)

Another meaning listed by Martin for the same construction is that of the concessive conditional, but the meaning of concession is usually indicated, once again, by a special diacritic, in this case, the focus marker *mo* (ibid. 497):

(139)   Ame ga   hut-*te mo* iku
        rain sub. fall-*te mo* go
        "Even if it rains, I'm going"

So far, Japanese is paralleled by Hindi. Martin observes, however, that the diacritic *mo* – the only morpheme, according to our hypothesis, which can show that the order *S1-te S2* is not an icon of the semantic relationship between the two clauses – may be *omitted*: "this may lead to ambiguity: *hare-te ii* can either mean 'It is nice and clear' = 'It is nice because it has become clear', or (= *hare-te mo ii*) 'It is alright even if it is clear' = 'I don't mind if it's clear'" (ibid. 498).

Our hypothesis forces us to predict that a Japanese sentence like *harete ii* is no more ambiguous than the corresponding English sentence (122). With normal intonation, the conditional will always be interpreted as a causal condition; a concessive conditional reading requires a special intonation which serves as a diacritic to indicate that the order of clauses does not correspond to the temporal or causal order of the propositions or events they describe.

The preceding discussion has established a number of points. First, the isomorphism hypothesis, (11), that recurrent identity of form reflects a similarity in the meanings expressed by it is partially supported, insofar as there is a semantic relationship of identity between conditionals and topics, which is reflected in the recurrent formal identity of the categories themselves.

Second, that formal identity need not always be a reflection of semantic identity, but of pragmatics: interrogative forms are often used to express both conditionals and topics, not because a question is a topic, but because a topic can be established by means of a question.

Third, that association, *enchainement*, or abduction may lead to the recurrent homonymy of categories that are not only unrelated, but in some cases contradictory: paratactic clauses that are formally coordinate may have the force of subordinate protasis (or temporal, or causal) clauses by virtue of sharing with these clauses the non-definitional property of preceding the following clause – a property that is imposed on them by virtue of the linearity of the spoken language.

Finally, however, there is an iconic limitation to the range of possible associations which supply "illegitimate meanings" for such a paratactic structure: only those interpretations are possible for which this paratactic structure itself may be an icon. Having brought into question the validity of the isomorphism hypothesis, and with it, the theoretical status of iconicity, our demonstration that paratactic protases cannot in general have the force of concessive conditionals suggests the prevalence of *motivation* in assigning meanings to linguistic forms.

We have not yet defined motivation in any but the most rudimentary and intuitive way: a diagram is motivated if the relationship among its parts corresponds to the relationship among the referents of these parts. Further discussion of this kind of iconicity will be resumed in the following chapter.

Before proceeding to this discussion, however, I wish to draw attention to the fact that there is a much more familiar way of interpreting limitations on the polysemy of paratactic constructions. We have been illustrating one of the most banal and familiar (but slippery) precepts in all of linguistics, to wit, that there is some kind of functional trade-off between morphology and syntax.

It is often said, but very difficult to prove, that word order tends to be rigid where morphology is absent, but free where morphology is relatively luxuriant. The history of English, for example, suggests that a fairly rigid word order was established before the language lost the rich system of case inflections on nouns (cf. J. Williams 1975:254, citing Saitz 1955).

The reason this precept is difficult to illustrate, and the reason it is hard to show a causal relationship between morphology and syntax in general, is because ideally it requires minimally contrasting pairs within the same linguistic system, and these are relatively difficult to come by. In Old English, for example, nominal inflection distinguished subjects from objects in about half the cases recorded (Williams, ibid.): we should therefore expect that word order was fixed where morphology was ambiguous, and free where morphology was explicit. Saitz showed, however, that word order was equally fixed (subject preceded object in 93% or 94% of cases) whether the morphology was explicit in distinguishing them or not.

In the contrast between *If S1, S2* and *S1 S2*, however, we do find minimally contrasting pairs of constructions within the same linguistic system that illustrate the trade-off relationship quite well. Syntax is the diagram; morphology, the addition of a conditional protasis marker, the diacritic.

There are examples of similar minimal contrast pairs in other areas of language as well. In both Hungarian (Hetzron 1975:37) and the Australian language Guugu-Yimidhirr (Haviland 1979:57) possessive constructions may mark the dependent and the head. In Hungarian, marking the dependent (i.e. the possessor) with the dative case is optional so long as it is contiguous with the head. If possessor and possessum are separated, marking the possessor is obligatory.

(140)   a. a fiu-*nak* a   ház-*a*
            the boy-*dat.* the house-*3sg.=poss.*
            "the boy's house"   (head and dependent both marked)
        b. a fiu   ház-*a*
            the boy house-3sg.=poss.
            "the boy's house"   (only the head is marked)

The expressions (140a) and (140b) are interchangeable so long as head and dependent are contiguous. In (141) however, they are not, and only the morphologically marked (140a) is possible.

(141)   A fiu-*nak* megnéztem a   ház-*á*-t
        the boy-*dat*. I=examined the house-*3sg=poss*.-acc.
        "I examined the boy's house"
(142)   *A fiu-∅ negnéztem a   ház-*á*-t
        the boy I=examined the house-*3sg.=poss*.-acc.
        "I examined the boy's house"

The interchangeability of (140a) and (140b) where syntactic contiguity establishes the identity of the possessor contrasts with the necessity of (140b) where syntax does no such thing. This establishes the functional trade-off between syntax and morphology at least in this tiny but controllable area.

In Guugu-Yimidhirr, where possession is inalienable, both dependent and head are marked with the same case affixes "suggesting that . . . what is true of or happens to a part is also true of or happens to the whole" (Haviland 1979:58). Where possession is alienable only the dependent is marked in general. Thus the contrast between (143a) and (143b).

(143)   a. yugu-wi magil-inh
        tree-loc. branch-loc.
        "on the branch of the tree"
            (inalienable possession: both head and dependent are marked)
      b. bayan ngaahdhu-wi
        house woman-gen.=abs.
        "woman's house"
            (alienable possession: only the dependent is case-marked)

However, when the alienable possessor is *separated* from the possessum, then only the first pattern, that of (143a), is allowed, wherein both possessor and possessum are marked (Haviland 1979:57).

In this example, as in the first, there is a trade-off between the diagram and the diacritics in establishing a certain kind of semantic relationship. Where the diagram fails to establish contiguity between possessor and possessum, then the diacritic of morphological marking must do the work otherwise done by the syntax.

A third area in which the functional trade-off between syntax and morphological diacritics is clearly operative is in the marking of subject and object in a large number of languages. Greenberg (1966) has claimed that if a language is SOV, then it will be likely to have morphological case marking: in an SOV language, as opposed to an SVO language, subject and object are not clearly distinguished by their position on opposite sides of the verb. More interesting is the facultative use of case markers in a fair number of SOV languages.

Many Papuan languages, it has been observed, are superficially ergative in their nominal morphology. The use of the ergative case marker on the subjects of transitive verbs, however, is frequently *optional*, and a number of investigators of these languages have pointed out that whether or not ergativity is marked on the subject of a transitive verb depends on whether or not the sentence would otherwise be intolerably ambiguous: typically, though not always, the ergative marker appears in sentences where the order of constituents is OSV rather than SOV.

Thus in Asaro, the ergative marker *-moʔ* is usually omitted except in cases where the order of constituents is OSV (Strange 1973:90, G. Strange 1975:73).

In the related Fore, a cognate suffix *-ma* may occur on subjects or objects of single-argument sentences, but occurs only on the subject of the transitive verb in two-argument sentences with OSV word order (Scott 1978:108,115). It is also obligatory even in sentences with SOV order, where the subject is inanimate (ibid. 103).

In Kaluli, the ergative or "focussed" forms of the personal pronouns are obligatory in sentences with OSV word order, while the nominative forms are used in the unmarked SOV word order (Voorhoeve 1975:394).

In Kâte, the ergative suffix *-zi* functions as a discriminative marker that may appear on either the subjects of intransitive sentences or the subjects of transitive sentences to emphasize the subject. It is necessary on the subjects of transitive verbs only where the nature of the subject cannot be otherwise unambiguously inferred (Pilhofer 1933:103–5).

In Lower Grand Valley Dani, the ergative suffix *-en* occurs on the subjects of transitive verbs only to avoid ambiguity, which arises typically in single-argument sentences (where the single argument of a verb like "eat", for example, may be plausibly the subject or the object of the activity) and in sentences with OSV word order (Bromley 1981:96–7).

In Hua, the ergative suffixes appear only where ambiguity is created by the word order or the absence of a clearly delimiting context (Haiman 1980:228–31, 360–4).

A somewhat similar state of affairs may exist in a non-Papuan nominative–accusative language, Kanuri, wherein "the nominative and accusative suffixes [*-ye, -ga*] are often omitted; they must be used, however, if the word order would otherwise cause ambiguity ..." (Lukas 1937:17).

In arguing for, and very sketchily illustrating, the "trade-off" principle, I am also arguing for a less familiar point to which I shall return in chapter 3: since all natural languages can express all logical relationships, and since there are languages which are (almost) totally isolating and analytic, it must follow that all semantic relationships may be expressed through word order alone. To say this in the context of the preceding discussion is to say that such analytic languages are more diagrammatic, or more iconic, than languages which have an elaborate morphology. And I shall argue that this is largely true: languages which depend heavily on word order (and these languages include not only isolating languages like Chinese[3] and Vietnamese, but also pidgin languages irrespective of their source) will tend for this reason to resemble each other in being more iconic than languages which do not, cf. section 3.1 below.

[3] The iconicity of word order in Chinese is highlighted in a masterful treatment by Tai (to appear).

2 *Motivation*

In the last chapter, we saw that a possible constraint on rampant polysemy was imposed by the requirement that the interpretation of a diagram be *motivated* by the structure of the diagram itself, in the absence of additional diacritics. We define motivation intuitively as a perceived similarity between the structure of a diagram and the structure of the concepts that it represents.

Operationally, however, we may define motivation through the morpho-syntactic motivation hypothesis:

> Given two minimally contrasting forms and the information that they differ with respect to a single semantic feature, a language learner who is unfamiliar with the forms (or perhaps even with the language) will be able to assign to each form its appropriate meaning. He will be able to do this on the assumption that the difference in form will in some respects be an icon of the difference in meaning.

In phonology at least, the motivation hypothesis is anticipated by the work of Sapir, Jespersen, Köhler, and others on *sound symbolism* (more properly, sound *iconism*, since we find not only that a constant sound is associated with a constant meaning, in defiance of the principle of double articulation, but also that there is a resemblance between the action of producing the sound and the concept to which the sound relates). Given a minimally contrasting pair of words *cìh* and *cùh*, one of which means "here" and the other "there", one does not need to be a speaker of Cambodian to guess correctly that the proximal deictic is the first. Given the contrasting pair of words *nagy* and *kicsi*, one does not need to know Hungarian to know that, if only one of them means "little", it is the second. Given the contrasting pair of made-up words *takete* and *maluma*, subjects with different linguistic backgrounds will associate the first with an angular, and the second with a curvilinear, figure (Köhler 1947: 254–5).

Few languages exploit sound symbolism as a regular, grammaticalized expressive device (but cf. Langdon 1970, Nichols 1971 on sound symbolism in North American Indian languages, and Kim 1977 on sound symbolism in Korean). One of the few in which it is exploited so that sound symbolism is pervasive throughout the language is Rengao, a Mon-Khmer language of Vietnam (Gregerson ms). Gregerson has shown that a complex but regular system of vowel alternations can be used to indicate up to seven different *sizes* for an unlimited range of referents: that is, totally productively. The denoted size is iconically reflected in the sizes of the buccal and the pharyngeal cavities, so that a hierarchy of vowels ranging from the most closed to the most open corresponds to a hierarchy of sizes ranging from the smallest to the largest.

In the realm of morpho-syntax, hierarchies similar to the one postulated for Gregerson's Rengao vowels are frequently encountered. In this chapter, I will investigate two such formal hierarchies and show how they correspond in a fairly straightforward manner to the corresponding conceptual hierarchies.

The first such hierarchy relates to the notion of "conceptual symmetry" and its formal expression in linguistic forms; the second to the notion of "conceptual distance", and its formal expression.

2.1 Symmetry

In concluding section 1.3, we discussed the iconic exploitation of the *linearity* of the linguistic sign, a property which Saussure considered no less essential than its arbitrariness, although determined more clearly by limitations of the medium than arbitrariness is.[1]

Saussure's strictures apply to the spoken word alone. But given the correctness of these strictures, it would seem that symmetry, of all concepts, should be the most difficult for spoken language to express iconically. It seems paradoxical, then, that conceptual symmetry is one of the most easily

---

[1] Linearity is an inescapable property of *spoken* language only. It is interesting that this totally unnecessary property of spoken languages is taken over by media which are not necessarily so constrained, e.g. most computer languages. It is less surprising that written language, insofar as it represents spoken language and is thus parasitic on it, should carry over the same limiting property. Gesture languages like ASL, on the other hand, although arguably once parasitic on the spoken mode, have liberated themselves from the linearity constraint in a number of interesting ways. Not only may aspect and other verbal categories such as deixis be represented simultaneously with the verb; since two hands are often employed in signing, reciprocal constructions are typically produced by the simultaneous indication of the reciprocal predicate with both hands, that is, with non-linear coordination (cf. Hanson & Bellugi 1982:622, 627).

and generally diagrammable ideas in language: devices for expressing balance, parallelism, and antithesis are among the standard tools of rhetoric in all languages. These devices are remarkably similar, as the following discussion I hope will demonstrate.

The thesis of this section is that the asymmetry of any concatenated elements *AB* may be either reenforced or overridden by morphological or prosodic diacritics of two distinct types.

The first type, which I will discuss only briefly now and in the concluding pages of this section, is that of *subordination*. In agglutinative and synthetic languages, morphemes may be either stems or affixes. If we adopt the convention of representing stems by capitals, affixes by lower case letters, the concatenation of 'A' and 'B' may be expressed in a number of ways which either heighten or reduce the asymmetry imposed by their linear order: asymmetry is high in *Ab* and *aB*, and low in *AB* and *ab* (the latter exemplified, perhaps, by expressions like *pell-mell* and other reduplicativa tantum). The relationship between clauses, from the standpoint of symmetry, may be parallel to the relationship between morphemes: asymmetry is high in constructions like *s1 S2, S1 s2* (where lower case *s* denotes a subordinate clause), and reduced in constructions like *S1 S2* and *s1 s2* (the latter exemplified by correlative constructions like *The more I laugh, the more I sneeze*).

Another type of diacritic, which I will concentrate on here, allows us to distinguish between symmetrical and asymmetrical coordination. Given two coordinate clauses *S1* and *S2*, how may they be conjoined? I suggest that schematically, the following possibilities exist:

(1)   S1 x   (and) S2 y
(2)   S1   (and) S2
(3)   S1 x   (and) S2 x

where x and y are arbitrary morphological diacritics (typically, but not exclusively, verbal desinences). My contention is that in any language which has nearly synonymous forms corresponding to (1), (2), or (3), conceptual symmetry will be expressed by (3), and asymmetry by (1): that is, as predicted by the motivation hypothesis, (a)symmetry of form will reflect conceptual (a)symmetry. Constructions like (2) are intermediate: as we have seen in our discussion of paratactic *if*-clauses, their asymmetry may lead to their interpretation as expressions of protasis + apodosis (or often, cause + result, etc.). Nevertheless, particularly in languages with relatively impoverished morphology, the internal structural parallelism of S1 and S2 in (2) may in itself be an icon of some kind of symmetry. The first part of this chapter will deal with the contrast between (1) and (3), while the second part will consider the more general case of (2), or "coordination in general" as an icon of symmetry.

It is fairly clear how (1–3) define a crude hierarchy of *formal* symmetry increasing as we go downwards. Before we continue, it will be necessary to define conceptual symmetry as well. The notion of symmetry has been adequately defined by the logicians: A and B are symmetrical with respect to some relation r, if both $A \; r \; B$ and $B \; r \; A$ are true. The relationship of symmetry may be either necessary or contingent. In sentences like

(4)   Max and Harry are similar

the relationship of *similarity* is necessarily symmetrical: that Max is similar to Harry implies that Harry is also similar to Max. In sentence (5)

(5)   Max and Harry like each other

the relationship of *liking* is only contingently symmetrical: just because Max likes Harry, it does not follow that Harry will necessarily like Max. But both (4) and (5) express symmetrical relationships between Harry and Max.

Where clauses rather than people are defined by some relationship, we may say that they are symmetrical under the following (most frequently encountered) conditions:

(6)   a. They denote events which occur simultaneously.
      b. They denote events which occur in alternation.
      c. They denote events which are mutually dependent.

Two of the devices available in English for expressing symmetry between S1 and S2 are intercalation and fusion. Consider the coordinate construction in (7)

(7)   Max hit Harry and Harry hit Max

which implies that Max hit Harry first. The reciprocal construction, as in (8),

(8)   Max and Harry hit *each other*

is a device whereby the clauses of (7) are fused: we do not have to worry about the temporal succession of S1 and S2 because there is only one clause, S3, with *each other*. All, or almost all, languages have some means of expressing reciprocity without having to enumerate actions by conjunction, as in (7): and at least part of the reason for this, I suspect, is that such a construction is usually necessary to avoid giving rise to the inference of temporal succession. Intercalation is much more exotic. Consider the sentence (9)

(9)   John changed the tire, and Mary walked off for gas

which implies (weakly) that John changed the tire first. The *respectively* construction, as in (10),

(10)   John and Mary changed the tire and walked off for gas, respectively

manages to completely avoid giving rise to this inference: most iconically, it seems to me, insofar as the immediate constituents of S1 and S2 are intercalated. Rather than *NP1 VP1 and NP2 VP2* (as in 9)), we find *NP1 and NP2 VP1 and VP2, respectively*. The *respectively* construction minimizes the linearity of the construction *S1 S2* by shuffling the constituents of S1 and S2 together: *respectively* is the sign that indicates that reshuffling has occurred, so that we interpret (10) as (i) rather than as (ii).

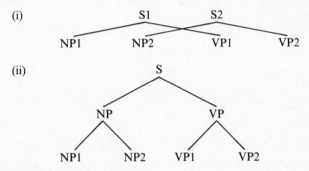

But these are not the usual means for overriding syntactic asymmetry in languages with a richer morphology.

2.1.1 The contrast *AxBy* vs. *AxBx*
The syntactic asymmetry of *S1 S2* is morphologically reenforced in a large number of SOV languages which make a morphological distinction between the *final* or *independent* verb of S2, and the *medial* or *dependent* verb of S1. Such languages are the Papuan languages, which frequently have a different set of personal desinences on medial and final verbs. The following examples are typical of the contrast, whose origins are heterogeneous and largely unexplored:

(11)   *Kâte (Pilhofer 1933)*
         Qatala-*me*   kio-*we?*

deny-*3sg.med.* cry-*3sg.final*
"He denied it and she cried"

(12)   *Kobon (Davies 1981)*
Yad   be   gau   am-*em*   kaj   pak-nab-*in*
I   forest there go-1sg.med. pig strike-fut.-*1sg.final*
"I will go to the forest and kill a pig"

(13)   *Gende (Brandson mss)*
Ya   tuvi-*xo*   ya   pixo   t-*i*
3sg. sit-*3sg.med.* 3sg. story tell-*3sg.final*
"He sat and she told a story"

(14)   *Tauya (MacDonald ms)*
Ne   fofe-*a-te-ra*   ∅-tu-*a-ʔa*
3sg. come-*3sg.-DS-topic* 3sg.-give-*3sg.-ind.*
"He came and she gave it to him"

Given the asymmetry hierarchy (1–3), it is not surprising that compound sentences of this sort, much more strongly than compound coordinate sentences in English, strongly connote asymmetrical relations between S1 and S2. As well as expressing simple coordination, they typically express temporal succession, cause and consequence, and, as we have mentioned in chapter 1, causal conditionals as well. Although there is another means of expressing the conditional relationship, the *medial+final* combination is frequently the only, or at least the most common, way of expressing temporal or causal succession in many Papuan languages: that is, the semantic content of "because" and "after" is expressed by the structure $AxBy$ where x and y are medial and final verb desinences.

We might expect that the symmetry of English coordinations such as

(15)   Many are called; few are chosen

cannot be expressed by the *medial–final* construction exemplified in (11–14). Nor does it seem to be the case that any relationship of conceptual symmetry is expressed by this typical coordinating construction!

What we encounter instead is a heavy use of $AxBx$ construction of various types. While the examples below could be easily multiplied, they are sufficient to show the nature of the phenomenon under discussion.

2.1.1.1 The expression of reciprocity in Kâte

Pilhofer (1933:99) notes that there are two ways of expressing reciprocity in Kâte, which are lexically determined. A small number of verbs form their reciprocal "voice" by deriving a nominal from a reduplication of the first syllable of the verb stem in question. This nominalization is then treated as the object complement of a utility verb *e*- "do", "say", whose subject agreement is with both reciprocal subjects taken together. Thus from *bafiʔke*- "help", *sopeʔke*- "curse", *ba*- "marry", are derived *babafiʔ e*- "help each other", *sosopeʔk e*- "curse each other", and *babaʔ e*- "marry each other". (It may not be farfetched to find in this reduplication the only remnant of a bi-clausal origin of reciprocal constructions for these verbs.)

For other verbs, reduplication is less stingy. The entire verb stem is repeated, the first token with the 1sg. object, the second with the 2sg. object prefix; both tokens are followed by a suffix *-ng*; and the whole derived complex is treated as the nominal object complement of the utility verb *e*-, whose subject agreement, once again, is with both reciprocal subjects taken together. Thus from *le*- "give", *za*- "say", and *pe*- "follow" are derived *na-le-ng ga-le-ng e*- "give each other", *na-za-ng ga-za-ng e*- "say to each other; converse", and *na-pe-ng ga-pe-ng e*- 'follow each other". Note that in these constructions there is a morphological balance between the two reduplicated verbs inasmuch as both are followed by the same suffix *-ng*. The reciprocal construction is therefore an instance of the schema (3) in that both A and B are followed, not by contrasting medial and final verbal desinences, but by the same (nominalizing suffix?) *-ng*.

2.1.1.2 Simultaneity in Kewa

Franklin (1983:43) notes that "the conceptual symmetry of two conjoined clauses may be reflected in their morphological parallelism: both may be dependent on the same final verb" as in (16).

(16)   a. Saa eta   no-∅ agaa lo-∅ pi-pa
           1dl. food eat   talk say sit-1dl.=perf.
           "We two have been eating and talking together"
       b. Ne-me sapi   gusu-∅ nipu-mu ipa   iru-∅ pi-pa
           I-erg. kaukau cook   3sg.-erg. water boil   sit-1dl.=perf.
           "He and I boiled the water and cooked the kaukau, respectively"

The alternative *medial–final* constructions would express some kind of conceptual *a*symmetry, either temporal or focal. Note that in (16), symmetry between A and B is achieved by suffixing each with -∅. The utility verb which takes as its subject the sum of the subjects of the two clauses is (existential) positional verb *pi*- "sit".

2.1.1.3 Simultaneity, balance, and alternation in Tauya

MacDonald (ms) describes four constructions in Tauya that indicate a symmetrical relationship between S1 and S2: I will deal with only two of them here. "To indicate that two events occurred simultaneously, S1 and S2 include medial verbs; the final verb is the verb 'do', which is inflected for the subjects of S1 and S2 . . . [both] medials occur with the [same subject] suffix *-pa* or the [different-subject] suffix *-te*":

(17) a. Pename-ne ?ufiya fei-*a-te*　　?eresiya ni-*a-te*　　?ai-i-?a
　　　　　Pename-erg. food boil-*3sg.-DS* Keresiya eat-*3sg.-DS* do-3pl.-ind.
　　　　　"Pename and Keresiya ate and cooked, respectively"
　　　b. Na-ne ota nono peti-fe-*pa*　　wa?a nono peti-fe-*pa*　　wate
　　　　　2sg.-erg. male child bear-perf.-*SS* female child bear-perf.-*SS* not
　　　　　?ai-e-?1
　　　　　do-1/2sg.-ind.
　　　　　"You didn't have a boy and a girl at the same time"

MacDonald points out that simultaneity is not the only symmetrical relationship expressed by this construction: "it can indicate that S1 and S2 were carried out over and over":

(18) ?　piki-ra　∅-te-pa　　tofi?i ?ai-fe-*pa*　pisi?i ?ai-fe-*pa*　?ai-a-?a
　　　dem. pig-topic 3sg.-get-SS below do-FE-*SS* above do-FE-*SS* do-3sg.-ind.
　　　"(The crocodile) got that pig (in the water) and made it go up and down and up and down and up and down . . ."

Here, the recurrent *x* on both S1 and S2 is the same-subject medial desinence *-pa*, or the different-subject medial desinence *-te*. Again, as in the other examples from Kâte and Kewa, *AxBx* is treated as a nominal complement of a utility verb which may be either medial or final, depending on the rôle that *AxBx* plays in the larger discourse context.

2.1.1.4 *Symmetrical relationships in Hua*

The asymmetry between medial and final clauses is a characteristic of a large number of Papuan languages which may conceivably be distantly related. In Hua (and in a number of other languages of the East-Central and Eastern families of the Eastern New Guinea Highlands Stock), this formal asymmetry between S1 and S2 is even further reenforced as the medial verb occurs not only with a characteristic medial desinence but also with an *anticipatory desinence* that follows it, which agrees with (and thus "points forward to") the subject of the following clause. The structure exemplified by the following Hua sentence is typical of what we find in these languages:

(19)   Kamanibamubo Burobo ebgi-*ga-na*   Burobamubo Kamanibo
            Kamani=erg.   Buro   hit-*3sg.med.-3sg.ant.* Buro=erg.   Kamani
            ebgi-*e*
            hit-*3sg.final*

$$\left\{ \begin{array}{l} \text{``Kamani hit Buro and (then) Buro hit Kamani''} \\ \text{``After Kamani hit Buro, Buro hit Kamani''} \\ \text{``Because Kamani hit Buro, Buro hit Kamani''} \end{array} \right\}$$

As the glosses indicate, a number of asymmetrical interpretations are possible for *S1 S2* in Hua. One interpretation which is clearly impossible is that wherein S1 and S2 are regarded as denoting simultaneous activities.

Given the marked morphological asymmetry of *S1 S2* coordination, Hua avoids this construction for the expression of symmetrical coordination. Among the other constructions that are employed are some that are reminiscent of the symmetrical forms of Kâte, involving reduplication and symmetrical coordination of verbal complexes.

Thus, reciprocity is typically expressed by a repetition of the verb root, each root being followed by the suffix -*ro*, the symmetrical conjunction being treated as the object complement of the support verb *hu-* "do". The structure in (20) is morphologically parallel with the Kâte reciprocals, with *ro* functionally equivalent to Kâte *ng*, and the support verb *hu-* equivalent to Kâte *e-*.

(20)   D-go-ro   k-go-ro   hu-ʔe
            me-look-ro you-look-ro do-1dl.final
            "You and I look at each other"

Back-and-forth activity is indicated by a similar construction. A "round trip" consisting of a single departure and return is rendered by an asymmetrical coordination of the form

(21)   u-ro-*na*   e-*e*
            go-seq.-*3sg.ant.* come-*3sg.final*
            "He went away and returned"

But a repeated round trip, in which coming and going alternate, is expressed by the symmetrical

(22)   u- $\left\{ \begin{array}{l} \text{roʔ} \\ \text{ro-na} \\ \text{goʔ} \end{array} \right\}$ o- $\left\{ \begin{array}{l} \text{roʔ} \\ \text{ro-na} \\ \text{goʔ} \end{array} \right\}$ hi-e
            go   come   do-3sg.final
            "He went back and forth"

in which the symmetrical coordination of the two verb phrases is treated as the object of the support verb *hu-*. (NB: although the three symmetrical suffixes are almost entirely interchangeable, it is absolutely impossible to mix them, thus creating an asymmetrical structure: **u-roʔ o-goʔ hie*, etc.)

For alternating activity involving verbs other than verbs of motion, Hua uses a special verbal desinence, the alternating iterative, for conjoining two clauses. Each of the two verbs denoting alternating actions occurs with the auxiliary *-ro*, and the invariable ending *-hi* – and no personal endings, either medial or final.

(23)   Aumo-vo-*ro-hi*;   hona to-*ro-hi*
        sleep   *alter.it.* fuck   *alter.it.*
        "He slept; then he fucked her; and slept again; and fucked her again; and so on"

Note that the alternating iterative ending is simply ungrammatical on a verb by itself: there must be a pair for the verb which also occurs with the same ending. Thus, the sentence

(24)   *Aumo vorohi
        "He slept, alternating this with . . ."

is unacceptable as it stands. Like its gloss, it suggests a further activity with which the activity of sleeping is alternating.

In the alternating iterative construction, Hua manages to signal the symmetry of *S1 S2* by avoiding the use of medial and final desinences, substituting for both of these a peculiar invariable ending which is common to both S1 and S2.

In the analog of the reciprocal construction which it employs for a handful of extremely common transitive verbs like *habo-* "help", and *ebgi-* "hit", Hua makes full use of the medial desinences in a most ingenious way. As noted in sentence (19), the medial verb of S1 is not only distinct from the final verb of S2; through the anticipatory desinence, the medial verb actually "points forward" to the subject of S2, establishing a diagram something like this:

        S1   S2

In reciprocal constructions, the medial verb of S1 points forward to the verb of S2. But the verb of S2 *is also medial*. Its anticipatory desinence agrees with the subject of S1, and the symmetrical coordination of S1 S2 is treated as the object complement of *hu-*, whose subject is (subject of S1 + subject of S2), as shown in (25).

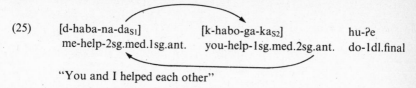

(25) [d-haba-na-da$_{S1}$]   [k-habo-ga-ka$_{S2}$]   hu-ʔe
       me-help-2sg.med.1sg.ant.   you-help-1sg.med.2sg.ant.   do-1dl.final

"You and I helped each other"

This, of course, establishes a diagram something like this:

The anticipatory desinence (which heightens the asymmetry between medial and final verbs in general) is employed on both verbs, establishing not only symmetry, but an actual ring, in which the linearity of the linguistic sign is explicitly replaced by another, symmetrical, geometrical figure, in which anteriority is rendered insignificant.

In actual texts, the structure *S1 S2* is a greatly oversimplified representation of the complexity of compound sentences, which consist of chains of clauses:

S1   S2   S3   S4 ... S$_n$

A widely reported structure in switch-reference marking languages (cf. Longacre 1972, Haiman 1980 for Papuan languages, Gordon 1983, Marlett 1981 for American Indian languages) is one wherein two clauses (say S2 and S3 in a chain such as the one above) will both mark switch-reference to the *same* clause S4. Assuming that the subject of S2 is Fred, that of S3 is Fred, and that of S4 is Joe, we might expect that the verb of S2 is in the same-subject form, while that of S3 is in the different-subject form. What we find instead, very often, is that the verbs of both S2 and S3 are in the different-subject form – inasmuch as the subject of both S2 and S3 is different from that of S4, to which reference is being made. Clearly this establishes a diagram for which two conceptual interpretations are possible.

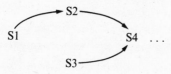

According to the one (suggested by Gordon and Marlett), the fact that S3 is in effect "passed over" is equivalent to the *subordination* of S3: the sentence is removed from the "time line" along which S1, S2, and S4 are strung. Another interpretation, however, is that S2 and S3 are coordinated and symmetrical with each other: the morphological symmetry of S2 and S3 is an icon of their conceptual parallelism. It seems that the latter interpretation is the correct one in cases like (26) in Hua.

(26) a. Ftgegi-ga-na   (S1 verb has 3sg.$_i$ subject and is marked DS)
          coiled-3sg.med.-3sg.ant.
          "he was coiled up and the other . . ."
       b. zuto?   rato?   vobai-ga-na   (S2 has 3sg.$_i$ subject and is marked DS)
          at=home by=fire lie-3sg.med.-3sg.ant.
          "he was lying at home by the fire and the other . . ."

       c. na   aitenemo   vzuvzhuna. . .   ai?e-e. (S3 has 3 sg. $_j$ subject and is final)
          that old-woman crawling   come-up-3sg. final
          "that old woman came crawling up"

If SR marking referred only to the immediately following adjacent clause, then the S1 of (26) would be incorrect, inasmuch as the subjects of S1 and S2 are identical. Clearly both S1 and S2 "look forward" to S3, and the effect of this morphological symmetry of S1 and S2 is to indicate a conceptual symmetry between them as well. Although the clauses S1 and S2 cannot help but occur in a linear order, they do not denote sequential events.

2.1.1.5 Phrasal coordination

Like cause coordination, phrasal coordination may also be either symmetric or asymmetric. By the motivation hypothesis, coordinations of the form $A \times B \times$ will tend to reflect a greater conceptual symmetry or parity of the conjuncts A and B than coordinations of the form $A \quad x B$ or $A \quad Bx$, in both of which the linear asymmetry of "A" and "B" is reenforced by the conjunction "x" which is associated with only one of them. In English, we are led to expect a contrast between "both A and B" on the one hand, and "A and B" on the other. Although relatively subtle, the contrast is at least in part as the motivation hypothesis would lead us to expect. The major semantic contribution of *both* in English, of course, is the indication of set exhaustion: *Tom and Dick* are two men, but *both Tom and Dick* are the *only* two men, in a particular set determined by discourse context. Another contribution, however, is that of diminishing the perceptual or rank asymmetry of the two conjuncts.

Greenberg (1966:103) (and Jakobson 1966:269) observed that the order of conjuncts in expressions like *the President and the Secretary of State* reflected their relative importance, with the consequence that reversing the order of conjuncts, as in *the Secretary of State and the President* creates an odd impression. It seems that this oddness is reduced in *both the Secretary of State and the President*: in this discourse context, these two men are the only ones that "count" – but they count *equally*.

In English, the fact that *both* and *and* are morphologically distinct means that the symmetry of *both A and B* is not between two identical forms, but between two identical meanings which are expressed in different ways in different contexts. A low-level rule of allomorphy converts a structure **and A and B* into the existing form. In languages like French and Turkish, such a low-level rule is lacking, so the symmetry which is somewhat obscured in English is transparent: *et A et B* in French, *A da B da* in Turkish. The semantic contrast between these symmetrical forms and the asymmetric forms *A et B* and *A B da* is very similar to the semantic contrast between the corresponding forms in English.

(27)   Şapkanɨ paltonu   *da* giy
       hat=your coat=your *and* wear=imperf.
       "Wear your hat, and your coat too" (the coat is an afterthought)
(28)   Şapkanɨ *da* paltonu   *da* giy
       hat=your *and* coat=your *and* wear=imperf.
       "Wear both your hat and your coat" (both are equally important)
                                                          (Lewis 1967:203)

2.1.1.6 Testing the hypothesis

Let us assume, simply as a heuristic principle at this stage, that morphological symmetry reflects conceptual symmetry, and see where this assumption leads us. There are a number of cases in natural languages where morphological symmetry is the common pattern. By our hypothesis, there should also be a conceptual symmetry between the constituents which are marked for parity.

Case 1: counterfactual conditional sentences. It has been observed that in a number of languages conditional sentences may have the form of two parallel clauses in parataxis: instead of (the analog of) *If S1, S2*, we encounter *S1 S2*. In most of the languages which exhibit this polysemy of the paratactic construction, *S1 S2* is also the unmarked way of indicating simple conjunction of clauses; and, by the same token, we encounter cases where the superficial structure *S1 and S2* (with the coordinating conjunction explicitly present) serves to render a conditional sentence. However, there are languages in which conditional sentences in general exhibit a formal parallelism between protasis and apodosis which is not found even in typical coordinated clauses. One such language is the Papuan language Kobon, already exemplified in sentence (12) above. In this language, medial clauses have one set of personal desinences on the verb while final clauses have another set of such desinences. The linear asymmetry of S1 and S2 in coordinate constructions is thus reenforced by the morphological asymmetry between medial and final verbs. Conditional sentences do not exhibit this asymmetry: in both hypothetical and counterfactual conditionals, protasis and apodosis are absolutely parallel in form.

(29)   Yad Dusin ar-*nab-in*,   kaj   rɨmnap rau-*nab-in*
      I   Dusin go-fut.-1sg. pork some   buy-fut.-1sg.
      "If/when I go to Dusin, I will buy some pork"

(30)   Yad Dusin ar-*bnep*   kaj   rɨmnap rau-*bnep*
      I   Dusin go-*1sg.irreal*. pork some   buy-*1sg.irreal*.
      "If I had gone to Dusin, I would have bought some pork"
                                       (Davies 1981:39)

My impression, based on an unsystematic survey of languages, is that Kobon is somewhat exceptional in this regard: hypothetical and given conditionals like (29) are not usually characterized by such thorough morphological parallelism between protasis and apodosis in most languages. On the other hand, *counterfactual* conditionals often are. Here (once again) are some languages in which the counterfactual *alone* exhibits the structure of the exemplar (30).

In Latin, both protasis and apodosis verbs occur in the pluperfect of the subjunctive:

(31)   Si Claudia me amav-*isset*,   mihi nups-*isset*
      if   Claudia me love-*3sg.plpf.subj*. me   marry-*3sg.plpf.subj*.
      "If Claudia loved me, she would marry me"

Harris (to appear) notes that this pattern continues to recur in the daughter Romance languages "despite continual denunciation by prescriptive grammarians", and he attributes this irrepressible tendency at least in part to a pressure for "morphological harmony between the two parts of 'modal' conditional sentences".

In Russian, the canonical conditional sentence is *Jesli S1, S2*, but in the counterfactual alone, both S1 and S2 occur with the same irrealis marker *by*, as in (32).

(32)   Jesli *by*   ja byl bogat, ja *by*   kupil   dachu
If   *irreal* I was rich   I *irreal* bought dacha
"If I were rich, I would buy a dacha"

In Hungarian, the canonical conditional sentence is *Ha S1, S2*, but in the counterfactual alone, both protasis and apodosis occur with the irrealis verbal suffix -*nE* as in (33).

(33)   Ha láttad vol-*na*   te   is   megijedtél vol-*na*
if you=saw be-*irreal*. you too get=scared be-*irreal*.
"If you'd seen it, you would have got scared too"
(34)   Ha lát-*ná*-d,   megijed-*né*-1
if see-*irreal*.-you get=scared-*irreal*.-you
"If you were to see it, you would get scared"

In Cebuano, the canonical conditional sentence is of the form *Kong/Og S1, S2*, but in the counterfactual alone, both protasis and apodosis may appear with the same irrealis particle *paʔonta ~ onta*, as in (35).

(35)   Og ninginum *paʔonta* siya og tubig, dili *onta*   siya ʔohawon karon
and ⎰ drunk *irreal.*   3sg. art. water not *irreal.* 3sg. thirsty   now
if ⎱
"If s/he had drunk some water s/he would not be thirsty now"

In all of the languages we have just looked at, a basic asymmetry is maintained between the protasis and the apodosis in all cases: only the protasis is marked with an "if" word. But there are many languages in which the parallelism between protasis and apodosis is complete: they are morphologically indistinguishable.

Thus, Guugu-Yimidhirr (Haviland 1979:145) marks both protasis and apodosis with the verbal suffix -*nda* and distinguishes them only by their relative order; Ngiyambaa (Donaldson 1980:251-2) marks both clauses with the clitic -*ma*. There are no doubt many other languages of Australia which are similar to these two.

Among Papuan languages, we find that Maring (Woodward 1973:13), Siroi (Wells 1979:118-9), Gende (Brandson mss), and Daga (Murane 1974:259) mark protasis and apodosis in exactly the same way in counterfactuals only. Once again, the list is representative rather than exhaustive.

Among African languages, we note Moroccan Arabic (Harrell 1965:241), Hausa (Taylor 1959:57), Kanuri (Lukas 1937:160), Yoruba (Bamgbose 1966:61), and Swahili (Perrott 1957:51-3). One of these languages, Swahili, may be selected to exemplify the pattern that all of the languages just listed evince in conditional structures.

In hypothetical conditionals, the basic asymmetry between protasis and apodosis is clearly marked. The protasis is marked with the durative "identical tense" prefix *-ki-* whose function is to indicate backgrounding in general (cf. Hopper 1979):

(36)   A-*ki*-ni-omba,   ni-ta-m-pa
         3sg.-*dur.*-me-ask I-future-3sg.obj.-give
         "If s/he asks me, I will give him/her some"

In counterfactual conditionals, on the other hand, both protasis and apodosis occur with the same irrealis tense prefixes: *-nge-* "present irrealis", *-ngali-* "past irrealis". An explicit protasis-initial conjunction *kama* "if" is possible, but not essential:

(37)   (Kama) ni-*nge*-jua   ku-soma, ni-*nge*-nunua kitabu
         (if)   I-*irrealis.*-know to-read   I-*irreal.*-buy   sg.=book
         "If I could read, I would buy a book"

The partial interchangeability of coordinating structures *S1 and S2* and conditional sentences *If S1, S2* has been discussed in the last chapter. What has not been approached yet is why the symmetry of protasis and apodosis should be greater in the counterfactual than in the hypothetical conditionals, generally speaking. The motivation hypothesis defended here predicts that there is greater conceptual symmetry between protasis and apodosis in counterfactual conditionals than in hypothetical conditionals.

Unfortunately, this seems to be a case where the hypothesis makes a false prediction: the symmetry of protasis and apodosis in counterfactuals probably has another explanation. It is worth taking a moment to examine some of the possible explanations for the pattern we have just looked at, because they illustrate a problem to which we will return in the final chapter of this book: the problem of competing motivations.

Why are counterfactual protasis and apodosis morphologically symmetrical? The commonsense answer is, of course, that both are counterfactual. QED. This answer is insufficient, however, because it fails to distinguish counterfactuals from hypotheticals. It may be true that protasis and apodosis in counterfactual conditionals are both counterfactual. Unfortunately, protasis and apodosis in hypothetical conditionals are both hypothetical, and so should be morphologically symmetrical also. There are of course languages like Kobon in which that is what they are. But the Kobon pattern does not seem to be widespread.

Another (only apparently) more sophisticated approach is the following. Let us assume, in the teeth of all the evidence, that the semantic relationship between protasis and apodosis in a valid conditional is exactly what is specified by the definition of material implication. That is, a conditional sentence is valid in all cases unless the protasis is true, and the apodosis, false. Then, a counterfactual conditional of the form "If it were the case that p, then it would be the case that q" provides us with two pieces of information. First, $p \supset q$. Second, the extra titbit that *q is false*. By contraposition, p is then also false (given material implication). Therefore, both p and q are false. This is the conceptual symmetry which motivates their formal symmetry. This somewhat more formal explanation is, of course, no more than a restatement of the commonsense answer that in a counterfactual conditional both p and q are counterfactual, that is, false.

In fact, both of these explanations (or, rather, this single explanation) fail for another reason as well. Even in counterfactual conditionals, it is not necessarily the case that the apodosis is false. This contention is most clearly illustrated in concessive conditionals like (38).

(38)   Even if you left me, I'd still love you

In sentences like this, the speaker believes the protasis to be false in fact. ("You haven't really left me.") He imagines a possible world in which it is true. In the imaginary world so created, the apodosis is also true. That is, the situation described in the apodosis is imagined to be true in the (counterfactual) case that the protasis is true. But it does not follow from this that the apodosis is actually false. ("Just because I say that I would love you under certain circumstances doesn't mean I don't love you anyway.") In fact, the force of this sentence is that "I love you in fact and in fiction", as it were. But, if the apodosis is not necessarily false, then we cannot say that both the protasis and the apodosis are false. And we are left with no extra conceptual symmetry between protasis and apodosis in counterfactual conditionals.

It may be that the correct way to look at this problem is from a rather different angle. To wit: even hypothetical conditional sentences exhibit *some* symmetry between protasis and apodosis in that combinations like *If S1 (hypothetical), S2 (counterfactual)* and *If S1 (counterfactual), S2 (hypothetical)* are impossible:

(39)   a. *If you wear a top hat, I would have recognized you
         b. *If you had worn a top hat, I will recognize you

(It has been suggested that sentences like (39a) are perfectly acceptable under a habitual interpretation of the protasis. While conceding that this interpretation improves (39a) it is still, in my opinion, far from acceptable.)

The problem is that a hypothetical apodosis can look like almost anything at all except a counterfactual. It can be a statement, a question, a threat, a promise, an imperative, or almost any other speech act. On the other hand, a counterfactual apodosis can only look like a statement or a question. For example, while the *hypothetical* apodosis can be an imperative; as in (40a), it is impossible to find a *counterfactual* apodosis that is an imperative. In other words, it is impossible to fill in the blank in (40b).

(40)   a. If it rains, *open your umbrella*, you dummy
         b. If it had rained, _____, you dummy

There are hypothetical imperatives, like the italicized apodosis of (40a), but, it seems, no counterfactual imperatives. Why not?

The non-existence of such forms as *would open (imperative) cannot be motivated on semantic grounds, since there are perfectly acceptable paraphrases like *you should have opened*, and so forth. Rather, we are dealing with a morphological impoverishment. And this suggests a banal and obvious answer to our question.

Morphologically, the counterfactual is a highly marked category. In such categories, probably for straightforward economic reasons, many otherwise distinctive oppositions are neutralized. In the (marked) dual number, for example, many Indo-European languages fail to distinguish genitive from ablative, or nominative and vocative from accusative. In the same way, perhaps, languages do not distinguish between the imperative and the assertive in counterfactuals.

If this explanation is correct, then the apparently greater symmetry of protasis and apodosis in counterfactual conditionals is not the reflection of conceptual symmetry, but an artefact arising from syncretism in marked categories generally. More generally, symmetry, like every other formal structure in language, may be motivated by more than a single tendency.

For a much neater fit between the motivation hypothesis and morphological symmetry, we turn now to an entirely different example.

Case 2: independent and conjunct modes in an Algonquian language. In most of the Algonquian languages, finite verbs occur with two distinct sets of personal inflections. Roughly speaking, the *independent* mode is found to occur in independent clauses, while the *conjunct* mode is found in subordinate clauses (cf. Bloomfield 1946:97). But the distribution of these inflections in fact is nowhere near so neat and simple as the (very neat and simple!) distinction between principal and subordinate clauses. The North-West River (NWR) dialect of Montagnais (a language closely related to Cree) is neither more nor less chaotic than the other Algonquian languages in its apparent distribution of these forms.

Starks (ms) notes that in this dialect, complement clauses in general do have conjunct verbal inflections, while independent clauses in general have independent inflections. But this is by no means everywhere the case.

For example, the asymmetric coordination of clauses which observe tense iconicity (i.e. the order of clauses reflects the order of events) is generally rendered (except in the past tense) by the following sequence:

> S1 (independent)   S2 (conjunct)

The linear asymmetry of S1 and S2 is reenforced by their morphological asymmetry in much the same way as in the Papuan languages exemplified in (11–14). Consider the examples in (41–3).

(41)   Nipāsuāu   maskw kuet   tshīuiān
       I=shoot=him bear   and=then I=return
       independent   conjunct
       "I shot the bear and then I came back"

(42)   Niuepamāten unākan kue pikutik
       I=throw=it   pot   and it=breaks
       independent   conjunct
       "I threw the pot and it broke"

(43)   Atusseu   kut nipāt
       3sg.=works   and 3sg.=sleeps
       independent   conjunct
       "He worked and then he slept"

Where S1 and S2 denote simultaneous or concurrent activities, however, we find the following pattern:

> S1 (independent)   S2 (independent)

Consider the following typical examples:

(44)   Atussepan   eku uin nipāpan
       3sg.=worked and 3sg. 3sg.=slept
       independent   independent
       "He worked and/while she slept"

(45)   Tshān utiskuema piminuenua mushuiāshinu māk tūtuenua pakuehikan
       John his=wife 3sg.cooks moosemeat   and she 3sg.=bakes=bread
                       independent   independent
       "John's wife cooks and she bakes"

The denial of tense iconicity is indicated by the symmetrical morphology of S1 and S2.

Symmetry of another sort is involved in correlative constructions, complex sentences where each of the conjoined clauses is dependent on the other. English examples include those in (46).

(46)   a. The more, the merrier
        b. As the twig is bent, so the tree's inclined
        c. Where the bee sucks, there suck I

Basically, correlative constructions in NWR Montagnais are expressed by the formula

      S1 (conjunct)   S2 (conjunct)

as in the sentence

(47)   E-tutamak kue   tshitutet
           past-I=do and then 3sg.=leaves
           conjunct   conjunct
           "When I did it, then s/he left"

It would be misleading to leave a discussion of the verbal morphology of NWR Montagnais with the impression that all the distributional patterns of the independent and the conjunct modes have been accounted for. Starks points out that the neat patterns of the schemata *S1 (independent) S2 (conjunct)*, *S1 (independent) S2 (independent)*, and *S1 (conjunct) S2 (conjunct)* exist, and reflect conceptual symmetry or the lack of it, only where S2 is marked for the *present tense*. Where S2 is marked *past tense*, it may always appear with the independent verbal inflections in any of the constructions we have noted. There are also other complications which we cannot deal with here.

Nevertheless, a significant area of the verbal morphology of this language is illuminated by the hypothesis that symmetry of form reflects symmetry of meaning.

2.1.2 Coordination in general
In discussion up to now, I have focussed on the fundamental asymmetry of conjuncts imposed by the linearity of the linguistic sign, and ways in which this asymmetry may be either heightened or reduced by intercalation or the use of morphological diacritics.

There remains the fact that coordination in itself is frequently taken to indicate a formal and conceptual symmetry between the elements conjoined: thus the standard dictionary definition, and our very means of indicating coordination diagrammatically in syntactic trees. In an important paper, Schachter (1977) has argued for the existence of a *Coordinate Construction Constraint* (hereafter, CCC), which is in effect a requirement that coordinate elements be both syntactically and semantically parallel: "The constituents of a coordinate construction must belong to the same syntactic category and have the same semantic function" (Schachter, 90). Schachter argues that this constraint both replaces and explains the validity of Ross' (1967) Coordinate Structure Constraint (hereafter, CSC) rules, as well as accounting for some cases which are problems for the Ross constraint. Schachter's CCC is superior to the CSC because it accounts for the following:

(a) The difference between chopping out of a coordinate structure (which yields bad sentences), and copying out of such a structure (which yields acceptable ones).

(b) The impossibility of *deletion* out of a coordinate structure, as in **Wilt is taller than Bill is strong and* $\emptyset$.

(c) The possibility of "across-the-board violations" to the CSC. CCC not only predicts that such across-the-board violations are acceptable, but limits their nature to precisely those cases where symmetry is preserved between conjuncts. Thus, across-the-board exceptions are possible where the same element is removed from both clauses, but not where, for example, the subject is removed from one, and the object from another: **It's John who likes Mary and Bill hates.*

I find Schachter's arguments extremely persuasive in demonstrating that coordination in itself is an icon of conceptual symmetry. The problem is to reconcile his observations with the fact that certain formal and conceptual asymmetries indubitably exist between conjoined elements, and to specify the nature and possible constraints on this kind of asymmetry.

Formal asymmetry between conjuncts arises as the result of coordination reduction: $A \ x \ B \ x$ is rendered as $A \ B \ x$. The classical account of coordination reduction assigns the output a symmetrical structure since the constituents brought together are regrouped $(A \ B) \ x$ rather than left as $(A) \ (B) \ x$. But this is not possible with gapping, whereby $A \ x \ B \ \ C \ x \ D$ may be "converted" to the asymmetrical structure $(A \ x \ B) \ (C \ D)$. Nor is it always clear that regrouping takes place.

Conceptual asymmetry between conjuncts, as I have stressed, is a reflection of their order, so that in the structure $A \ B$, A may be interpreted as earlier, more important, or as a cause, while B may be interpreted as later, less important, or as an effect.

Let us consider formal asymmetry first. There are two separate questions which need to be discussed: whether regrouping does in fact take place so that (for example) *A B x* is really represented as *(A B) x* rather than *(A) (Bx)*; and what the conceptual correlates of formal asymmetry might be.

That regrouping is psychologically real in examples like (48a,b) seems reasonably clear.

(48)   a. *John and Mary* love roast chestnuts
        b. *John likes*, and *Mary hates*, roast chestnuts

In (48a), derived in classical accounts by straightforward coordination reduction, *John and Mary* function as a single constituent with respect to a number of transformational operations, for example the passive. In (48b), derived by right node raising (cf. Hudson 1976 for discussion of the differences), intonation clearly marks the italicized conjuncts as parallel units, even though they are not syntactic constituents (at least in the classical tradition: we return to this below). Matters are different in a class of cases where coordination reduction marks switch-reference between clauses. Where *x*, either as a prefix or a suffix on the verbs *A* and *B*, is a person marker of some sort, then the presence of *x* in both conjuncts indicates that their subjects are distinct (cf. the Kâte sentence (11), above), while the absence of *x* in one of them (which one, depends on whether the *x* is a left branch or a right branch, in accordance with the directionality theory of reduction first outlined by Ross 1970), or its replacement by a functionally null-equivalent invariable gerund-like affix, indicates that their subjects are *identical*. Thus, corresponding to the Kâte sentence (11), where the subjects of the two clauses are distinct, we find (49),

(49)   Qatala-lâ kio-we?
        deny-and then
        ²cry-3sg.final past
        "He denied it and cried"

in which the subjects of the two clauses are identical. The phenomenon is widely attested in both Papuan and non-Papuan languages.

There is no phonological or syntactic evidence that regrouping takes place in cases like these: the two clauses which share a single personal verbal

---

² Kâte -*lâ* marks temporal sequence, and may be translated, roughly, as "and then". It may be contrasted with the invariable suffix -*huc* which is translatable as "while". Personal desinences in both same-subject and different-subject medial verbs more or less transparently follow these tense/aspect markers.

desinence are not treated as a single syntactic unit, nor as phonologically parallel intonation units.

It is interesting to observe, however, that this absence of formal parallelism between conjuncts often seems to signal an absence of conceptual parallelism as well. I have in mind not only the linear asymmetries already noted, but also the *auxiliarization* of one or another of the two verbs. Labeling a verb complex *V Aux* rather than *V V* is in part an attempt to formalize, without explanation, the intuition that the two elements are not conceptually symmetrical: one is more important, or more central, than the other.

Given our non-technical understanding of the word "auxiliary", we expect the auxiliary verb to be less important than the "main" verb. We should also therefore expect the auxiliary verb to be reduced in structure relative to the main verb. There are languages in which the auxiliary verb is the one reduced by (what seems to be) coordination reduction. Munro (1983) indicates that Chickasaw may be such a language. A verb which is stripped of its personal endings under identity with the personal endings of a following verb functions as an adverbial conjunct to the main verb, as in (50),

(50)   tali? ish-li-t
        rock take-1sg.-SS
        "take a rock and . . ."

contrasts with the reduced (and auxiliary)

(51)   tali? ish-∅-t
        rock take-SS
        "with a rock"

However, there are also languages in which it is the main verb which is reduced, and the auxiliary verb which retains all the morphological trappings. Hua (Haiman 1982a) is such a language. In Hua (as in many other languages, including English), it is the uppermost (or outermost) auxiliary verb which carries personal desinences, while typically inner auxiliaries and the main verb itself are reduced to the bare verb stem. What makes Hua of particular interest is the fact that there is at least one major verb in the language (the causative or transitivizing verb *to-*) which is in the process of becoming auxiliarized right now, and the source from which it clearly derives is one of clausal coordinate conjunction. Typically, a medial verb with same-subject inflections is followed by *to-* acting as the final verb:

(52)   vo-∅-na³   te-e
          lie-SS-3sg. put-3sg.final
          "3sg. knocked (3sg.) over"

If the transitivizing verb has no prefixes (as above), then the medial verb
may be stripped of its anticipatory desinence, yielding *vo-te-e*, a structure
indistinguishable from *V + Aux + Desinence* structures in Hua generally.
Elsewhere however (even in Hua) the evidence suggests that reduction of
the medial verb is a concomitant of its conceptual auxiliarization. While the
prototypical meaning of *S1 (medial) S2 (final)* is "S1 and S2" there are a
number of specialized meanings of this structure when S1 has been reduced
by coordination reduction: in each of these, S1 may be translated only as an
adverbial adjunct (and never as a conceptually symmetrical conjunct) of
S2.

Medial same-subjects render what are expressed in English by adverbs of
manner:

(53)   Brgefu-∅-na   rmi-e
          quick-SS-3sg.ant. go=down-3sg.final
          "3sg. went down *quickly*"
(54)   Sokohu-∅-na   hi-e
          good-SS-3sg.ant. do-3sg.final
          "3sg. did it *well*"

The medial same-subject verb *Kaso-* "surpass" renders what in English is a
statement of comparison:

(55)   D-gaso-∅-na   brgefi-e
          me-surpass-SS-3sg.   quick-3sg.final
          "3sg. is me-*surpassingly* quick; 3sg. is faster than me"
(56)   P-gaso-∅-na   brikifi-e
          them-surpass-SS-3sg.ant. handsome-3sg.final
          "3sg is more handsome than they are"

Unless the final verb is one of the six basic verbs of motion (in which case
a special auxiliary verb must be used in S1), medial same-subject verbs
render actions carried out simultaneously with, but of less importance
than, the action described in the following or final verb: note the contrast
between (57) and (58).

---

³ The suffix *-na* is an anticipatory desinence typically marked to agree with the subject of the
following verb, and is present in a large family of languages including Hua, cf. Haiman
(1980). Deletion which distinguishes same-subject medials from different-subject medials
affects the preceding *medial* desinence only. For some discussion of the morphology of
medial verbs and medial desinences, cf. section 3.5, below.

(57)   Fofu-∅-na   zumo ri-e
         whistle-SS-3sg. work take-3sg.final
         "Whistling, 3sg.worked"
(58)   Zumo ri-∅-na   fofi-e
         work take-SS-3sg.ant. whistle-3sg.final
         "Working, he whistled"

Both (57) and (58) express cooccurrent activities, but the activity which accompanies, or is less important, is always the one denoted by the first verb.

To summarize the discussion of the last few pages: there is some evidence that the formal asymmetry effected by coordinate clause reduction may cause a structure *(A) (B x)* to be reinterpreted (or simply interpreted) as expressing an asymmetrical (Verb + Auxiliary verb) relationship between verbs A and B. How general this (re)interpretation may be I do not know.

It is tempting to find a similar conceptual asymmetry in structures derived by the putative operation of gapping (which cannot but be formally asymmetrical):

(59)   *John loves cats,* and *Mary, dogs*

I fear this is not possible, however. The italicized conjuncts, for all their formal asymmetry, are semantically parallel clauses. As it stands, example (59) and others like it are counterexamples to Schachter's CCC inasmuch as deletion is permitted to destroy a parallel structure. Yet there is a clear formal difference between examples like (59) and sentences like (60).

(60)   *Wilt is taller than Bill is strong and___

which are disallowed by Schachter's CCC. The difference is that in (59) the deletion site is clearly marked by a pause. In (60) and other sentences like it, the deletion site is not marked by any phonological signal.

Gapping, then, preserves a *rhythmic* symmetry between conjuncts, a symmetry which is apparent in the spoken language, although in writing the deletion site is marked (and sometimes only optionally) by a comma, as illustrated in (61).[4]

(61)   a. A few enlisted from affection, some ∅ from fear, many ∅ from interest, none ∅ from principle
         b. In the prosecution of remote wars, the undertaking became every day more difficult, the event ∅ more doubtful, the possession ∅ more precarious

---

[4] These examples (and those in (74)) are culled from Gibbon's *Decline and fall of the Roman Empire*, an inexhaustible source of symmetrical constructions.

    c. The estates of the Italians were exempt from taxes, their persons ∅ from
       the arbitrary jurisdiction of the governors

    d. Suspicion was equivalent to proof; trial ∅ to condemnation

It is easier by far to hear a beat that falls on a note than one that falls on a
rest. From this self-evident fact, we may derive an explanation for the "No
Ambiguity Condition" noted in Hankamer (1973). Hankamer drew
attention to a transderivational constraint to the effect that a potentially
ambiguous structure like (62)

(62)   Chomsky sent Harris a book, and Halle, some offprints

which, in principle, has two different possible sources before gapping
namely (63) and (64),

(63)   Chomsky sent Harris a book and (Chomsky sent) Halle some offprints
(64)   Chomsky sent Harris a book and Halle (sent Harris) some offprints

can in fact have only one interpretation, namely (63). In general, where a
structure can be derived from two possible sources by gapping, then the one
which is derived by gapping of *peripheral material* is strongly preferred over
the one which is derived by gapping of *central material*.

An explanation for this performance constraint is now available, given
the theory of Generalized Phrase Structure Grammar, hereafter GPSG
(Gazdar 1981, Schachter & Mordechay 1983), and I will sketch it briefly
now. Only the gapping of central material is true gapping, defined as
deletion which creates asymmetry between conjuncts. Peripheral gapping
maintains total symmetry between conjuncts. In cases of true gapping,
symmetry is maintained between conjuncts only by the device of a silent
beat which marks the deletion site. In cases of peripheral gapping, every
beat falls on a "note" – some phonetic material – and the conjoined
structures are more truly symmetrical. The two interpretations of (62)
correspond to (63′) and (64′).

(63′)   *Peripheral gapping: totally symmetrical*
       Chomsky sent . . . (Harris a book) and (Halle some offprints)
(64′)   *Central gapping: imperfectly symmetrical*
       (Chomsky sent Harris a book) and (Halle ∅ ∅ some offprints)

I contend that speakers employ a processing strategy that maximizes the
symmetry of conjoined constituents, namely:

(65)   Given a structure *X and Y*, assign the maximally symmetrical interpreta-
      tion

and this strategy is responsible for Hankamer's transderivational constraint. Like every other analyst before the invention of GPSG, Hankamer analyzed "peripheral gapping" as simple deletion without regrouping, largely because sequences such as *direct object + indirect object* could not be analyzed as single constituents: they were two constituents (NP NP) or *part* of a larger constituent (VP without its main V).

Since in classical generative grammar, no single node may dominate the string consisting of " . . . Harris a book and Halle some offprints", this structure could be represented only as (i).

(i)

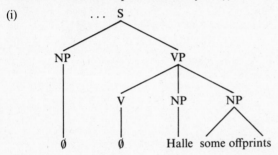

In GPSG, particularly as extended by Schachter & Mordechay (1983), the structures *Harris a book* and *Halle some offprints* may be simply represented as VP/V (verb phrases lacking a verb). The representation of (63) in full is then (ii).

(ii)

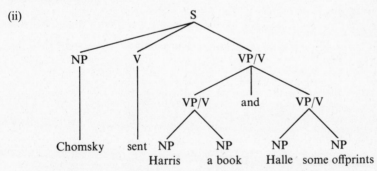

There are two independent pieces of evidence that speakers of English do actually assign a symmetrical structure like the one above to potentially ambiguous sentences like (62).

Consider first sentences such as (66).

(66)   Chomsky sent a book to Harris, some offprints to Halle, a letter to the *New Republic*, an article to *The Nation*, a vita to *Who's Who* and a photograph to his publisher

Each sequence of *direct object + indirect object* in this sentence – including the very first – has exactly the same rhythmic and intonational pattern. Each is treated as a parallel to all the others. This symmetry is captured in the representation provided in the framework of extended GPSG: it is missed by the classical generative representation, in which the repeated sequences of *NP NP* are conjoined not with an initial sequence of the same type, but with an initial S (Chomsky sent a book to Harris).

Within the classical theory, it would have been possible to invoke a "readjustment rule" to mediate between the proposed syntactic structure and the evident prosodic structure of the utterance. But if the only function of such a readjustment rule is precisely to bridge the gap between the attested structure and the abstract structure which is supposed to underlie it, then surely some suspicion is in order.

Consider now sentences such as (67) and (68).

(67)   Chomsky sent Harris a book
(68)   Chomsky sent a book to Harris

Within the classical theory, these sentences are related by a transformation of dative-movement. Leaving aside the question whether such a transformation can be justified in terms of the criterial attributes of transformations, we ask now what interpretation is most likely assigned to a sentence such as (69).

(69)   Chomsky sent a book to Harris and Halle some offprints

There are again two potential "sources" for such a sentence, namely (70a) and (70b).

(70)   a. Chomsky sent a book to Harris and (Chomsky sent) Halle some offprints
        b. Chomsky sent a book to Harris and Halle (sent) some offprints (to Harris)

Hankamer's transderivational constraint implies that only (70a) is acceptable, since it is only in (70a) that gapping is peripheral. However, of those speakers who accept (69) at all, many prefer interpretation (70b). How may this fact be explained?

One possible explanation is that gapping may apply only to such structures that are absolutely symmetrical to begin with, that is, before gapping. Thus, gapping should not be able to apply to such a structure as (70a) at all. Another explanation is that the resulting surface structure is more symmetrical where (69) corresponds to interpretation (70b) than where it corresponds to (70a): speakers therefore assign the reading (70b) to the ambiguous sentence (69) on the strength of the "maximize symmetry" strategy given in (65).

The first explanation cannot be maintained: there are far too many examples of gapping where symmetry before gapping is not absolute. Consider such examples as (71) and (72).

(71)   Max wants to travel, and Hortense (wants) to write a novel about Africa

(72)   Wolfgang thought only of Constance, and Constance (thought) of getting invited to the Archduke's New Year's Eve soiree

The second explanation maintains that it is not the *absolutely* symmetrical, but the *more* symmetrical, interpretation which is preferred: as a putative source for (69), (70b) (which exhibits absolute symmetry) is to be preferred over (70a) (which exhibits less than perfect symmetry).

It is clear from a consideration not only of gapping, but of coordination reduction which involves abstraction of a peripheral element from either the left or the right of a number of conjoined strings, that absolute symmetry between conjuncts is not an obligatory requirement.

(73)   *"True" coordination reduction: abstraction of a left peripheral element*
        a. Max elbowed his way to the front of the crowd and squatted on the sidewalk
        b. He married a tobacco heiress and died rich

(74)   *Right node raising: abstraction of a common right peripheral element*
        a. The mildness of Marcus formed the most amiable, and the only defective, part of his character
        b. The ideal restraints of the senate and the law might serve to display the virtues, but could never correct the vices, of the emperor

Like "peripheral gapping", of course, right node raising creates structures which can only be analyzed as examples of *constituent coordination* within the framework of GPSG: the manifest symmetry of the conjoined structures in (74) provides further evidence for the intuitive rightness of the GPSG analysis.

Summing up section 2.1.2: following Schachter (1977), I find that the relation of coordination is itself one of conceptual symmetry – and in this, we both follow the dictionary definition of coordination as a link between elements of the same rank, order, or importance.

How can this humdrum and totally unsurprising fact be reconciled with the observation of section 1 of this chapter, which suggests that the linear asymmetry of conjuncts reflects temporal, causal, or protasis/apodosis asymmetry?

2.1.3 Coordination and tense iconicity

The temporal asymmetry of structures like *S1 S2* is so marked that it is a plausible explanation for the fact that coordinate structures function as paratactic conditionals; and for the fact that the notion of reciprocity is not generally expressed by a coordination of clauses. We could go even further and suggest that the temporal asymmetry, or tense iconicity, of coordinate structures is one of the things that distinguishes them from structures in which one element is subordinate to the other.

One of the widely accepted criteria for subordinate clauses (cf. inter alia Andersson 1975) is that unlike coordinate clauses, they may be "fronted" without greatly affecting the meaning of the sentence in which they occur. (Allusion has already been made to this property in the discussion of conditional protases as subordinate clauses in chapter 1.) Coordinate clauses and correlative clauses contrast in that the order of clauses reflects causal, temporal, or conditional relations between the clauses that are conjoined. The contrasts between the following sentence pairs in (75–6) are typical.

(75) a. Spike left and got up early the next day
      b. Spike got up early the next day and left
(76) a. The more he eats, the fatter he gets
      b. The fatter he gets, the more he eats

I propose that the *linear* asymmetry of conjoined structures is in effect A CONSEQUENCE OF THEIR CONCEPTUAL SYMMETRY: they can be "lined up", as it were, on a "time line", only on condition that they be of *equal rank*. Conversely, the absence of tense iconicity between S1 and S2 may be a result of the fact that they are not equal in prominence. Typically, where one clause is backgrounded relative to another or subordinate to another, the two clauses are not necessarily on the same time line, and may thus express *simultaneous* events or events whose relative order is the opposite of the order of the clauses that represent them.

Evidence in favor of this contention is provided by those languages in which the formal morpho-syntactic device for expressing simultaneity is identical with the device for expressing subordination in general. An obvious candidate is the -*ing* verbal form and its participial and gerundial counterpart in other languages, to which we will return in chapter 4. The argument that durative or simultaneous verbal aspect is typically an index of backgrounded clauses is made in Hopper (1979) and developed in Hopper & Thompson (1980).

We witness in the polysemy of *-ing* morphemes another example of the process of association, already exemplified in chapter 1. In this case, the categories that are associated are those of *backgrounding* and of *simultaneity*.

A partial explanation, at least, for this association, may be the fact that languages (for all the notorious linearity of the linguistic sign) iconically model not one, but two dimensions along which the relations of symmetry and asymmetry may be expressed. These two dimensions are the dimensions of temporal succession or simultaneity, on the one hand, and prominence, on the other. Coordination with neutralizing diacritics (*AxBx* structures) represents symmetry of prominence and symmetry of time as well. Coordination without such diacritics (*AB* structures) or with reenforcing (*AxBy*) diacritics may represent asymmetry of time, but symmetry of prominence. Subordination (*Ab* or *aB* structures) entails asymmetry of prominence: such asymmetry does not necessarily entail temporal symmetry or the lack of it. But since asymmetry of prominence allows the inference of simultaneity, the marker of subordination may be interpreted as the marker of simultaneity. Conversely, since simultaneity allows the inference that one event is less central than the other with which it is concurrent, the marker of simultaneity may be interpreted as a marker of subordination.

Diagrammatically, the correlation between temporal succession and equal rank may be represented as in the figure below:

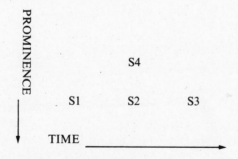

S1, S2, and S3, of equal prominence, are tense-iconic. S4, backgrounded, need not be, and may denote events or states that are simultaneous with any of S1, S2, or S3. Since simultaneity and backgrounding are equivalent in removing S4 from the time line, the morphological expression of the two categories may be identical.

Conclusion: symmetry and the motivation hypothesis

Given the linearity of spoken language, one would expect, perhaps, that the iconic representation of symmetry is precluded by one of the "limitations of the medium" to which reference was made in the introduction. In fact, however, spoken language is capable of modeling symmetry in not one, but two dimensions: first, by distinguishing between coordination and back-grounding, and second, by overriding the temporal asymmetry of coor-dinately conjoined elements through the use of parallel diacritics of various types. The recognition of this ability of language to express balance or parallelism is nothing new, dating back to the classical rhetoricians (cf. Scaglione 1972:21–2 for a summary account).

The one-dimensionality of speech *is* responsible for some limitations in its expressive power, to which we will return in chapter 6. But first, let us turn to another conceptual dimension for which the speech chain is ideally adapted, the dimension of distance.

2.2 Conceptual distance

If a linguistic utterance were definable phonetically, the "linguistic distance" between two expressions would be equivalent to the time interval between them. Even this very crude criterion allows us to distinguish between the members of the English minimal contrast pairs in (77–9).

(77)   a. lighthouse keeper
       b. light housekeeper
(78)   a. 40 Ninth Street
       b. 49th Street
(79)   a. How much is 100 and (*'n'; *$\emptyset$) 22?
       b. One hundred and ('n'; $\emptyset$) twenty-two

Bolinger & Gerstman (1957) pointed out that the semantic difference between the examples of (77) did not correspond to the relative *stress* of the three morphemes, but rather, as the orthography indicates, to the relative *time intervals* between the first and second, and the second and third. The examples of (78), pointed out to me by Bolinger (pc), are self-explana-tory – once Bolinger has pointed them out. The sentences of (79) constitute a conversation with my five-year-old daughter, who posed the question (79) without realizing that the sum of the two numbers 100 and 22 was itself the name of the number she wished to know. Note that the name of the number, expressed as a single entity in (79), allows reduction and deletion of the conjunction *and*, while the sum of two different numbers, as in (79), does not. Grammarians only rarely bother to state the obvious, but there are some honorable exceptions.

By far the most careful and comprehensive discussion of the iconic function of the pause (at least, that I have seen) is Gilbert Rappaport's (1979) examination of "detached' and "non-detached" adverbial participle clauses in Russian.

The minimal contrast is between sentences like (80a) and (80b).

(80)   a. Vanja vyšel   (pause) posvistyvaja   (detached)
        b. Vanja vyšel   ($\emptyset$)   posvistyvaja   (non-detached)
          Vanya went out   whistling

Rappaport shows that whereas non-detached reduced clauses (like *posvistyvaja* above) must have the same subject as the subject of the matrix clause, detached reduced clauses are subject to no such restriction. Thus the contrast between (81a) and (81b).

(81)   a. Vozraščajas' domoj, (pause) menja zastal dožd'
          returning   home   me   caught rain
          "As I returned home, the rain caught me" (= "I was caught in the rain")
        b.*Menja zastal dožd' ($\emptyset$) vozraščajas' domoj
          (same translation) (ibid. 61,98)

Further, the time reference of a non-detached reduced clause must be simultaneous with that of the matrix clause. The time reference of a detached clause may be to an earlier or to a later time. Thus the contrast in acceptability between (82a) and (82b).

(82)   a. Ja sklonen   doverjat' etomu čeloveku $\begin{cases} \text{pause} \\ \emptyset \end{cases}$ znav

          I am=inclined to believe this   person   having-known
          ego v molodosti
          him in youth (ibid. 123)

Detached reduced clauses may be what Rappaport terms "focus limited operators" (142), or new information, while non-detached clauses cannot be. Thus the contrast between (83a) and (83b).

(83)   a. Vanja vyšel $\begin{cases} \text{pause} \\ \emptyset \end{cases}$ posvistyvaja
        b.*
          Vanya went=out   whistling   (ibid. 142)

in response to the question *Kto vyšel?* "Who went out?"

Non-detached reduced clauses may not be within the scope of negation on the matrix clause. In contradistinction, non-detached reduced clauses may be within the scope of such operators. Thus the contrast between (84a) and (84b).

(84) a. Vitja stoit   v koridore, no on ne stoit   tam $\left\{ \begin{matrix} \emptyset \\ \text{pause} \end{matrix} \right\}$ posvistyvaja
　　b.*
　　　　Vitya stands in corridor but he not stands there　　　　　whistling

In (84a), negation is understood to apply to the non-detached clause *posvistyvaja*; in (84b), this is impossible, and the only possible reading of the sentence is a contradictory one: Vitya is both standing in the corridor, and not standing in the corridor (ibid. 153). In conclusion Rappaport observes that detachment "may be viewed as a prosodic means of iconically marking the relative isolation of a constituent" (257).

The preceding summary does no more than skim off some of the most striking insights in Rappaport's masterful treatment. All of his other observations, however, serve to confirm even further the validity of his conclusion. Nor is Russian the only language in which the pause has the iconic function of marking conceptual distance. In Japanese, the sequence *V1-te V2* has in principle two interpretations:

(85)　　a. V1 and V2
　　　　b. V1 + auxiliary

The verb *simau* means "puts (stores) away" or "shuts up completely" and it may be used after a gerund (=*V1 + te*) in its basic meaning, which can be cued by careful phrasing: Huyumono o zenbu aratte (sorera o) simatta "I washed the winter clothes and put them away". But, especially with the juncture reduced, the final verb in such a sentence can also be taken as an auxiliary "I finished washing all the winter clothes" (Martin 1975:533).

The verb *miru* means "looks at" or "sees" and it can retain its basic meaning following a gerund, as you can sometimes tell from the juncture: Hon o totte mimasita "I took the book and read in it." But, especially with the juncture reduced, the final verb may be taken as an auxiliary: "I tried taking the book (to see what the result or effect would be . . .)" (ibid. 541).

That is, a pause after -*te* signals the meaning (85a), while the absence of such a pause tends to signal (85b).

In the Papuan language Siroi, Wells (1979:79) distinguishes between "closely knit" and "loosely knit" merged sentences of the form *S1 S2*. In both the subjects of S1 and S2 are identical. But in closely knit merged sentences there is no phonological break between S1 and S2, and "the focus is on the composite process rather than the individual actions":

(86)   Mbanduwang   ngur-mba   buk-ng-ina
         bow   break-SS   throw-class.-3sg.past
         "He broke and threw away the bow"

In loosely merged sentences there is an optional phonological break between S1 and S2, implying " a series of actions by one actor in which each is a separate entity":

(87)   Sai-k-a   kile   kil-mba, wande   nguel-ning-ig
         cut-class.-SS now take-SS   house   roof-3pl.obj.-1pl.imperf.
         "We cut the rafters and now collected them, and built the roofs of the houses"

In other words, once again a pause denotes a temporal separation. But the iconic representation of conceptual distance can also exploit the fact that language is hierarchically structured. The linguistic distance between expressions is reflected not only in the number of milliseconds that elapse between them, but also in the nature and number of the morphemes that lie between them. If they are contiguous, it may depend on the nature and number of the non-segmentable boundaries between them. The linguistic distance between X and Y diminishes as we proceed downwards along the following scale:

(88)   Diminishing linguistic distance between X and Y
         a. X $\#$ A $\#$ B $\#$ Y
         b. X $\#$ A $\#$ Y
         c. X $+$ A $\#$ Y
         d. X $\#$ Y
         e. X $+$ Y
         f. Z

(88d) represents analysis; (88e) agglutination; and (88f) synthesis of the morphemes X and Y into a single morph – which may be, but is not necessarily, identical with either X or Y.

While the scale shown in (88) is (presumably) unexceptionable, it is still rather crude in recognizing no boundaries other than the word boundary $\#$ and the morpheme boundary $+$. Nor does it take note of any dimension other than that of *distance* between morphemes, thus ignoring the conceptual asymmetry between root and affix in agglutinative structures, or between dependent and head in analytic structures.

The isomorphism hypothesis predicts that where nearly synonymous expressions exist in a given language (corresponding, for example, to the various "rungs" on the hierarchy given in (88)), they will differ in meaning *in some way*.

The motivation hypothesis, however, makes a further prediction, namely that the difference in form will correspond in some way to the difference in meaning. Specifically here, the greater the formal distance between X and Y, the greater the conceptual distance between the notions they represent. Our aim in this section will be to show how this prediction is borne out by the facts in a variety of languages.

The notion that formal distance corresponds to conceptual distance is not a new one. Although Behaghel (1932:4) is credited with the first explicit statement of the principle, Scaglione (1972:243) argues that it was first adumbrated by Condillac's *Essai sur l'origine des connaissances humaines* of 1746. Jespersen (1949:56) speaks of a principle of cohesion, that "ideas that are closely connected tend to be placed together." Bolinger (1975:137) speaks of the same principle in his introductory textbook, *Aspects of language*. The idea has been effectively "rediscovered" in several recent papers, for example Bybee, to appear; Haiman 1983a,b; Lambrecht 1984; where attempts have been made to associate the principle with fairly extensive bodies of data.

On the face of it, there are two major problems with this principle. The first problem is the existence of glaring and irrefutable counterexamples. The central (and, in some versions, the only) transformational rule recognized in generative grammar is the rule of *wh*-fronting, which removes an interrogative word from the clause in which it plays a grammatical rôle, and moves it over an arbitrarily long string to the head of the sentence, for example:

(89)   *Who* did you say Max had told you it was likely the committee would finally select ____?

Whatever the definition of "conceptual closeness", it would seem that the interrogative pronoun *who* is conceptually closer to the verb *select*, whose direct object it is, than to any other word in the sentence. Yet it is further from this than from any other word. The second problem is that "conceptual closeness", although intuitively a plausible notion, has never been explicitly defined in such a way as to exclude ad hoc appeals.

I will postpone discussion of the first objection until chapter 6, where I will deal with competing motivations in a limited medium. The first step in giving some theoretical rigor to the idea of conceptual distance is to attempt a definition for it, and to show some of the data for which it provides a satisfactory account.

Two ideas are conceptually close to the extent that they

(90)   a. share semantic features, properties, or parts;
          b. affect each other;
          c. are factually inseparable;
          d. are perceived as a unit, whether factually inseparable or not.

A common diagrammatic representation of (90a) is the Venn diagram, wherein two sets which share common members are represented by overlapping circles; sets which are disjoint are represented by separate circles; and sets which include other sets are represented by circles which contain smaller circles within them.

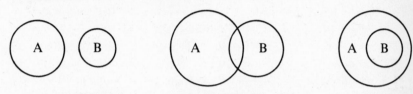

A and B are disjoint   A and B overlap   A contains B

(90b) is diagrammatically represented in sociograms and organizational charts, whether of institutions or machines. Typically, units that affect each other or that interrelate are joined by lines, while units that are independent of each other are not so joined. Units which are indirectly connected through intermediaries or "common acquaintances" are marked as such by lines that link each of them with the intermediary, but not with each other.

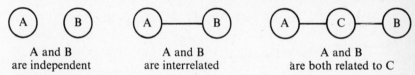

A and B   A and B   A and B
are independent   are interrelated   are both related to C

(90c and d), for linguistic purposes may be treated as identical, since what determines linguistic fact is not objective reality, but the way in which this reality is perceived and conceptualized. Inseparable ideas are typically represented by diacritics *on the same symbol* (e.g. nasalization, tone, and timbre on the same orthographic symbol, positive and negative poles on the symbol for a power source), or by similar or identical symbols (e.g. the brackets surrounding this example) or by a single undecomposable sign (e.g. any sign representing male or female, however graphic, need not specify *all* properties which together constitute the definiendum).

    In the expression of such common semantic categories as coordination, causation, transitivity, and possession, languages often match the formal distance between X and Y with the conceptual distance between them, as suggested in (88).

2.2.1 Causation

The transformation of "predicate raising", first proposed in McCawley 1968, is a syntactic operation that matches a dictionary definition with a complex concept. Whereas a dictionary may define *kill* as *cause to die*, predicate raising (in the spirit of the Katz–Postal hypothesis that transformations do not change meaning), will derive *kill* from this syntactic source.

Arguments against predicate raising have focussed on the well-known fact that lexically frozen causatives are not in fact synonymous with the sources from which predicate raising attempts to derive them (cf. among others Fodor 1970, Shibatani 1972, Song 1978, Wierzbicka 1980).

My concern is to show how the often noted and incontestable differences in meaning between expressions like *kill* and *cause to die* are in fact motivated, not only in English, but perhaps in all languages where the distinctions exist between coexisting forms.

Shibatani has noted that lexically frozen causatives, in contradistinction to causatives formed by productive derivation, tend to signal direct physical contact between causer and causee. For this reason, he has termed them *manipulative* causatives (cf. also Comrie 1980). Further contrasts, noted by Fodor, and summarized by Wierzbicka, include the fact that in the frozen causative construction, cause and result occur at the same time and the same place.

Two further often noted facts may be viewed as consequences of this twofold distinction. First, where the causee is inanimate or unconscious, the analytic causative either suggests that the causer has magical powers, as in (91),

(91)   a. I caused the tree to fall
        b. I caused the chicken to die
        c. I caused the cup to rise to my lips

or, in many cases, the analytic or productive causative is impossible in such cases:

(92)   ?I caused the books to leave the room

The imputation of magical powers in (91) is a natural consequence of the fact that indirect causation is signaled by the separation of the morphemes denoting cause and result. The only indirect causation which such inanimate causees are subject to is telekinesis. The restriction that the causee of a productive causative construction must be *animate* (noted for Japanese by Shibatani, and for Korean by Song) is, I would suggest, a consequence of the same constraint: unlike inanimate causees, human (and conscious) causees may be subject to indirect causation effected through *commands*. In fact, the irrelevance of the animacy constraint in itself is clearly revealed by the fact that where the causee is *unconscious*, the analytic or productive causative is just as peculiar as the cases where the causee is totally inanimate; and by the fact that even starred sentences like the Japanese one in (93) and the Korean one in (94)

(93)   *Taroo-wa   nimotu-o   ori-sase-ta
        Taroo-topic baggage-obj. come=down-caus.-past
        "Taroo caused the baggage to come down"
(94)   *Mary ka   sopho lul   ka-key   ha-ess-ta
        Mary sub. package obj. go-comp. cause- past
        "Mary caused the package to go"

are judged acceptable if a magical reading is allowed: that is, the stars denote not the impossibility of indirect causation in general with inanimate objects, but the impossibility of the unmarked indirect causation, which is effected by verbal comands, addressed to sentient and reasoning creatures.

It is noteworthy that the contrast between causatives in Japanese (unlike English and Korean) is between a form $X + Y$ on the one hand, and Z on the other. The only significant generalization which describes the facts in all three languages is that greater linguistic distance between cause and effect in each case signals greater conceptual distance: indirect causation, with the possibility that cause and effect occurred at different times and at different places.

Since the facts in English and Japanese at least are virtually a cliché of grammatical description now, they are not worth repeating. However, it is worth pointing out how widespread the distinction is in other languages.

In Diyari, an Australian language of South Australia (Austin 1981:159–60), the manipulative causative (Verb + *ipa/ma*) contrasts with a periphrastic causative (*nanka* "cause" . . . Verb) where the causee is animate, such that the periphrastic construction can only be used where indirect causation is indicated.

In Cebuano, an Austronesian language of the Indonesian group, a number of verbs form two causatives: $pa + V$, where pa = "cause"; and V, where the causative morpheme is fused with the verb. Thus (*pa*)-*undang* "stop", (*pa*)-*balik* "put back", (*pa*)-*saka* "bring up", and (*pa*)-*kanaʔug* "bring down" (Wolff 1967:297). The agglutinative form, unlike the synthetic, is grammatical in Cebuano (as in Korean and Japanese) only where the causee is animate – that is, able to respond to the normal indirect causation of a verbal command:

(95)   Gi-(*pa)-undang   ang bula niya
        obj.foc.-(caus.)-stop topic ball 3sg.
        "He stopped the ball"

Compare the grammatical (96), in which the causee is animate.

(96)   Gi-(pa)-undang kami   niya
        obj.-(caus.)-stop us=topic 3sg.
        "He stopped us"

In Tauya, a Papuan language of the Madang-Adalbert Range subphylum of the Trans-New Guinea Phylum (Wurm 1975), a handful of verbs distinguish between direct and indirect causation (MacDonald, to appear). Intransitive verbs are made transitive or causative by a causative verb *fe*: ʔumu "die", ʔumu + *fe* "kill". Indirect causation may be signaled for a small number of these by the interposition of an object pronoun between the intransitive verb root and the causative verb: ʔumu + *object pronoun* + *fe* "kill by sorcery". The formal contrast $X + Y : X + A + Y$ corresponds to the conceptual contrast, direct : indirect causation.

There is at least one language in which the contrast between direct and indirect varieties of causation is signaled by the *reduction* of a bound affix: both forms can only be represented as $X + Y$ in the schema of (88), but fusion is farther advanced in the form which represents direct causation.

In Mixtec, an Otomanguean language of Oaxaca (Hinton 1982), the causative morpheme is a verb *śaʔá* "make", which may be reduced to a prefix *sá-* or even further reduced to a prefix *s-* in causatives of various types. With verbal roots, *śaʔá* contrasts with *s-*: *śáʔá . . . kee* "make someone eat; prepare food for someone to eat", *s-kée* "feed someone; put food in someone's mouth". With adjectival predicates, *sáʔá* contrasts with *sa-*: *sáʔá . . . kwaʔa* "make someone red; cause someone to blush", *sá-kwaʔa* "paint someone red". In each case, the bound form is opposed to the free form of the causative verb such that $X \# Y$ signals indirect causation, and $X + Y$ signals direct causation. Hinton further suggests that the contrast *sa + Adjective* vs. *s + Verb* is iconically motivated in that where the predicate is verbal, the result is coterminous with the cause in time. Where the predicate is adjectival, the result may persist after the cause has ceased. The contrast between $X + Y$ and what we may represent as $x + Y$ is then an iconic grammaticalization of different amounts of temporal overlap between X and Y.

The data presented above are undoubtedly fragmentary, but sufficiently typical of a general pattern that we may conclude that the linguistic distance between cause and effect is motivated by the conceptual distance between cause and result, and the conceptual (or in some cases, physical) distance between causer and causee.

Whether or not this conclusion is an "interesting" one is purely a matter of taste. What can be debated, however, is whether it is *independent*, in the sense that it does not follow other axioms or theorems, whether currently fashionable or otherwise. I believe that it *is* independent, and that no other generalization is compatible with the familiar data we have been reviewing here.

2.2.2 Coordination and complementation

The motivation hypothesis predicts that conceptual distance between elements that are linked by a coordination "and" is greater than the conceptual distance between elements that are side by side without a connector. This contrast exists, of course, only within languages or registers in which both constructions coexist.

Where the elements are *clauses*, the conceptual distance between them will be greater if they have different subjects or different topics; denote different events (rather than aspects of a single event); or represent events that occur at different times (rather than simultaneously). Conversely, the conceptual distance between them will be diminished if they share a common subject or topic; common tense, mood, or aspect; denote the same event; or two simultaneously occurring events. There are a fair number of unrelated languages in which the formal contrast *X and Y* vs. *X Y* is an iconic reflection of the contrast between greater and lesser conceptual distance of this sort.

In Turkish, the conjunction *da* "and" derives from *dahi* "too, also" (Lewis 1967:207) and, as we have already seen, is the equivalent of "both . . . and . . ." (cf. above, p. 83). Where two clauses with a common subject are conjoined, the use of *da* after the first "marks a break between the action of two verbs: this is particularly common where the second verb is negative, but the first one is not" (Lewis, 179). Thus, Lewis notes the contrast between (97a) and (97b).

(97)   a. Zengo-yu görüp *de kork-ma-mak* imkânsizdi
          Zengo-acc. see   *and* fear-not-inf. was=impossible
          "It was impossible to see Zengo, and not fear him"
    b. Zengo-yu görüp Ø   kork-ma-mak imkânsizdi
          "It was impossible not to see and fear Zengo"

That is, verbs separated by *da* have different polarity while verbs that are not separated by *da* have the same polarity. It is important to note that this is not specifically the "meaning" of *da*: in fact, it is possible to juxtapose identical verbs without *da* so that they differ *only* in polarity, as in (98).

(98)   Kendisini sevip sev-me-diğimi   bilmiyorum
            him   love love-not-my=doing I=don't=know
            "I don't know whether I love him or not"

That is, "if a positive stem with *-ip* is followed by the same verb in the negative, . . . the sense is of a choice between the positive and the negative" (Lewis, 178). Clearly, the general function of *da* is to increase the conceptual distance between clauses, a function whose general nature is rendered all the more apparent by the contrast between (99a) and the nearly identical (99b).

(99)   a. Ne   yapacaksın, eve   gidip *de*?
           what you=will=do home go   *and*
           "What will you do, *after* you go home?"
    b. Ne yapacaksın, eve gidip ∅?
        "What will you do *when* you go home?"

Here, the *da* marks a *time lag* between going home and doing something (Lewis, 179).

In the Parkeri dialect of Gujerati (Johnson ms), progressive reduction of the conjunction *ʌn* between verbs may result in a corresponding diminution of the conceptual distance between them to the point where the second verb is a mere aspect marker on the first:

(100)   a. Ue kadho *ʌn* gyo $(\cong X \mathbin{\#} \text{and} \mathbin{\#} Y)$
            he ate *and* left
    b. Ue khae*n* gyo $(\cong X + \text{'n} \mathbin{\#} Y)$
            "Having eaten he left"
    c. U khaegyo $(\cong X + Y)$
            "He ate it up"

In Ono (Wacke 1931:171,196), medial verbs denote actions which are either simultaneous with, or which precede, actions denoted by the following verb. The distinction between simultaneous and sequential medials is formally the difference between $Verb + \emptyset$ and $Verb + so$, where *so* is the coordinate conjunction "and":

(101)   a. ŋauk   ne-∅ arimaike
            tobacco eat 3sg.=be=going
            "He went along smoking"
    b. ŋauk ne-*so* arimaike
        "He had a smoke and then went along"

In Usan, another Papuan language, Reesink (ms) notes that a number of nearly synonymous sentences may render the complex sentence "They will cut the fenceposts and erect them"

(102) a. Qoren su-ab ugab wogub ne nagsiorubor
    post cut finish cease and they=will=erect
   b. Qoren suab ugab ∅ ne nagsiorubor
   c. Qoren suab ∅ wogub ne nagsiorubor
   d. Qoren suab ∅ ∅ ne nagsiorubor
   e. Qoren suab ∅ ∅ ∅ nagsiorubor

While cautiously conceding that the differences in meaning among these five sentences are anything but clear, Reesink ventures the observation that (102a) conveys a definite sense of a time lapse between the actions of cutting and erecting, while the maximally different (102e) suggests that the second action will follow immediately after the first. The diminution of the linguistic distance between the verbs (effected only in part by the elimination of the conjunction *ne*) signals a diminution of the time elapsed between their performances.

In Feʔfeʔ Bamileke (Hyman 1971), a Grassfields Bantu language of Cameroon, coordinate clauses may be either juxtaposed or separated by the coordinate conjunction *nī* "and". When the clauses are merely juxtaposed, there is a strong implication that the events described in those clauses took place at the same time. When they are separated, the implication is that the events described by the two clauses are separated by a time lag, just as they are in Turkish. Thus

(103) a. à kà gén ntēe njwēn lwàʔ
    he past go market &buy yams

"definitely implies that yams were bought at the market" (Hyman, 43 fn.). On the other hand,

(103) b. à kà gén ntēe *nī* njwēn lwàʔ
    he past go market *and* &buy yams

yields a meaning that is slightly altered: the overt conjunction, in Hyman's terms, "disassociates the conjuncts" with the resulting implication that the subject bought yams at a later date (and a different place).

One may be tempted to assume in cases such as the above, that the specific meaning of the "and" word is really something like "and *then*". There are two reasons for doubting this. The first is that "and" comes to mean "and then" in a number of languages, but not because of any properties of the conjunction itself. Rather, because coordination is asymmetric, the sequence *S1 S2* even without any overt conjunction will tend to represent a sequence of events (recall Julius Caesar's *vēnī, vīdī, vīcī*).

The second reason that this suggestion is implausible is that, as we have already seen in at least one of the Turkish examples, the generalized function of the conjunction is not so much to signal a temporal disassociation between conjuncts as just *any* disassociation: clauses separated by *da* contrast with clauses that are not separated in that they differ in polarity, as well as in the time of the event.

We may observe now that in a number of other languages, the presence of the conjunction signals yet other kinds of conceptual disassociation between coordinate clauses.

Thus in Aghem, another Bantu language (Anderson 1979:114), consecutive verbs which share a *common subject* do not repeat this subject on the second verb (just like English) as illustrated in (104).

(104)   Ò   mɔ̀   zɔ́m mám kɨbɛ́
         she past sing cook fufu
         "She sang and cooked fufu"

Consecutive verbs which do not have a common subject, not surprisingly indicate the nature of the second subject (just like English) by specifying the subject pronoun. Moreoever, they indicate the lack of a common subject by the interposition of a "consecutive marker" which Anderson consistently glosses simply as "&":

(105)   Ò   nàm kɨbɛ́   gháʔ   ʔyía zɨ
         she cook fufu we=exc. &   eat
         "She cooked fufu and we ate it"

The use of a coordinating conjunction to signal a change of subject between clauses is widespread among those areally related languages where such switch-reference is a grammaticalized category. Prominent among such switch-reference marking languages are the Papuan languages of New Guinea. In many of them, the formal distinction between same-subject (SS) and different-subject (DS) medial verbs is that between *Verb* + $\emptyset$ and *Verb* + *"and"*. Examples are Maring, where "and" is the medial suffix *-k* (Woodward 1973); Chuave, in which it is *-go* (Thurman 1978); Daga, in which it is the separate word *amba* (Murane 1974); and Koita, in which it is the suffix *-ge* (Dutton 1975). (There is the strong possibility that *-k*, *-go*, and *-ge* are actually cognate as well as synonymous in Maring, Chuave, and Koita.) It should be noted that in these and many other Papuan languages, the SS ≠ DS distinction is completely grammaticalized. The presence vs. the absence of the coordinating conjunction is the obligatory signal of the category of switch-reference.

A somewhat different example of disassociation is offered by Barai, a Koiarian language very closely related to Koita (Olson 1981:134–7). Medial clauses that are juxtaposed must share a common *thematic topic*: it is impossible to introduce a new topic in S2 that is absent in S1. Thus, the ungrammaticality of (106a).

(106) a.*Na Devidi kua, kofu sosaeti ije fu samuake
        I David spoke, coffee society topic 3sg. will=look=after
        "I spoke to David, and, as for the coffee society, he will look after it"

Where the medial clause, however, is followed by either of the coordinating conjunctions -*ro* "and", or -*ga* "and" (the latter very possibly cognate with Koita -*ge* "and"), the requirement that S1 and S2 share a common thematic topic is relaxed, and we derive the grammatical example in (106b).

(106) b. Na Devidi ku-*ga*, kofu sosaeti ije fu samuake

Yet another kind of semantic disassociation is signaled by the coordinating conjunction *a* "and, but" in Mokilese, a Micronesian language (Harrison 1976:244–9). The conjunction is employed when the coordinate clauses "have no necessary logical connection with each other" (ibid. 245), and therefore may be glossed as "but". Contrasting with *S1 a S2* is the "implicational construction" *S1 S2* "where two clauses seem to form a single event, because the second is the logical result of the first" (ibid. 247). One may be tempted, again, to ascribe the semantic difference between *S1 a S2* and *S1 S2* to the meaning of *a*: "but". Further constraints on the distribution of *a*, however, indicate that the semantic disassociation between S1 and S2 is of a more general nature than this. As in Barai, omission of *a* is possible only if S1 and S2 share a *common topic* (ibid. 248); moreover, when both predicates of an implicational construction are transitive, the omission of *a* is possible only if the predicates have both subject and object in common (ibid. 249).

Up to now I have only dealt with cases where the identity of the morpheme of disassociation is totally uncontroversial. Where agglutination and sandhi have contributed to the phonetic erosion of this morpheme, its identity with the coordinate conjunction, while still reconstructible, is superficially (and, I would guess, psychologically) obscured.

An interesting example of a language in which such erosion has taken place is Gende, a Papuan language of Madang Province in Papua New Guinea (Brandson mss); the same morpheme *ko* may appear between clauses *both* as a coordinating conjunction *and* (in other constructions) as a suffix on the verb of the first clause. In the former case, #*ko*# between clauses indicates that they describe separate events; in the latter, the suffix *-ko* on the first verb indicates that the two clauses have different subjects.

The string *brene nae*, literally "hit=3sg.medial eat=3sg.final" describes a single action – the verb "kiss". The string *brene ko-no nae*, literally "hit=3sg.medial and-3sg.medial eat=3sg.final" means exactly " hit and eat". Where the two verbs share a common subject, the first verb occurs with the following personal endings:

1sg. *-o*, 2sg. *-o*, 3sg. *-ono*, 1dl. *-ori*, 2dl. *-iri*, 3dl.-*ini*, 1pl. *-o* 2pl. *-i* 3pl. *-ini*

where V1 and V2 do not share a common subject, the medial desinences on V1 are:

1sg. *-oxo*, 2sg. *-anigo*, 3sg. *-ixo*, 1dl. *-orixo*, 2/3dl. *-arixo*, 1pl. *-onigo*, 2/3pl. *-axo*

Synchronically, the SS and the DS desinences are distinct: nevertheless, a plausible origin for the DS desinences can be reconstructed if we abstract from their paradigm the only recurrent partial they contain: a final syllable *-xo* or *-go*, identical with the postvocalic form of the conjunction *ko* "and".

In each of the cases we have looked at, the conceptual distance between clauses or verbs separated by "and" is greater than the conceptual distance of clauses that are simply juxtaposed.

A point which I have already made, but which cannot be overstressed, is that the meaning of the morphological material between clauses is not "directly" responsible for the difference in meaning between *S1 S2* on the one hand and *S1 "and" S2* on the other in that "and" does not (at least originally) mean "different time", or "different event", or "different subject" or "different topic" or "different polarity".

One may certainly wish to claim that in the present stage of Daga, for example, the morpheme *amba* has become grammaticalized as "different-subject", and so forth. However, this merely impels us to wonder why a morpheme whose initial meaning (as the etymological evidence makes clear) and whose principal current meaning (as the investigators of the languages describe it) is simply that of coordination, should come to have the various meanings that it does. There is only one meaning that is common to all the coordinate morphemes: disassociation, or conceptual distance. There is one formal property they all share: phonological bulk separating S1 and S2.

Before leaving the contrast *and* ≠ ∅, we should note, if only in passing, that it may be employed in cases where the conjuncts are not clauses but other constituents. Recall the English example (79) at the beginning of this section: while one hundred *and* twenty-two may be either two numbers or the name of their sum, the minimally contrasting expression one hundred $\emptyset$ twenty-two can only be the name of a single number. We should also note the contrast between adjective sequences like

(107)   a. naïve (and) sentimental lover
           b. sweet (and) sad song

in which a conjunction between the adjectives is optional or avoided, and other sequences like

(108)   a. black and white dog   (*black white dog)
           b. good and bad news   (*good bad news)

in which this conjunction is obligatory. While the facts are complex, it is always the case that when the adjectives are incompatible, as they are in (108), the conjunction *must* be present.

I have encountered one example of a contrast between *NP NP* and *NP and NP* in which apparently the semantic distinction is the opposite of what we should expect. The language is the Australian Diyari. Austin (1981:231) notes a tendency for the conjunction to be present where both NPs denote members of the *same sex*, and to be absent where the NPs denote members of *different sexes*. A cursory survey of Austin's texts indicates that the conjunction is absent in precisely those cases where the NPs denote a married couple (e.g. "elder sister and brother-in-law"), presumably conceptually close by virtue of being a culturally recognized unit.

The linguistic distance between members of a coordinate construction may be affected not only by the contrast between coordination and asyndeton, but also by means of coordination reduction, first proposed as a possible transformation by Chomsky (1957:37). The formal contrast is between a structure *XAY and XBY* and *X (A and B) Y*. The latter structure is in part economically motivated, insofar as one does not repeat what is already known. But one of the properties of the latter construction is that *A* and *B* are closer together here than they are in *XAY and XBY*.

The isomorphism hypothesis predicts that where these two constructions coexist in a language they cannot be totally interchangeable: and this point is made in great detail in Wierzbicka 1972, 1980. The motivation hypothesis, moreover, makes the point that the difference in meaning will correspond to the difference in form: specifically, that the conceptual distance between A and B will be less when the linguistic distance between them is less. Below are given some of the classic, and some less familiar, examples of non-synonymous constructions that are allegedly related by a transformation of coordination reduction. In each case, it is transparently clear how the conceptual distance between the italicized elements A and B covaries with their linguistic distance from each other.

(109)   a. red ribbons and white ribbons
        b. *red* and *white* ribbons (colors may occur on the same ribbon)
(110)   a. We can do it quickly, and we can do it well
        b. We can do it *quickly* and *well*

(A Soviet bureaucratic joke asserts (110a) and then denies (110b) without contradiction, inasmuch as the grouping in (110b) forces the inference that the italicized attributes are realizable on the same occasion, while the structure of (110a) allows the inference that the attributes are realized on different occasions, and are in fact mutually exclusive.)

(111)   a. John Smith and Mary Smith are employees of the CDC Corporation
        b. *John* and *Mary* Smith are employees of the CDC Corporation

(Wierzbicka 1980 points out that in (111b), there is a stronger implication that John and Mary are related, that is, that they belong to the same family.)

(112)   a. All a's denotes $a1$, and $a2$, ... and a_n
        b. Every a denotes $a1$, and denotes $a2$, ... and denotes a_n

(Russell 1964:59 attempted, as a naïve speaker of English, to explicate the difference between the universal quantifiers *all* and *every* as in the definitions above. He was exploiting the intuition that where the "a's" were all together, as in (112a), they would be understood as belonging to the same group; where the "a's" were listed separately, as in (112b), they would be understood as individuals that were not part of the same group.)

(113)   a. the ability to read and to write letters
        b. the ability to *read* and *write* letters

(Bolinger 1977:7 points out that in (113b) the two verbs are more likely to share a common object *letters*, while in (113a) the more likely inference is that the object of *read* is unspecified.)

(114)   a. Frank Osterflood had the build of a professional wrestler and the mentality of a professional wrestler
        b. Frank Osterflood had *the build* and *the mentality* of a professional wrestler

(While (114b) is utterly banal, (114a), which occurs in the novel *The Diceman* by Luke Rhinehart, elicits a chuckle. The humor of (114a) lies in the fact that the formal separation of *build* and *mentality* prepares the reader for a contrast between them – which fails to materialize, of course.)

"Classical" generative grammar, which still posited a transformation of coordination reduction, accounted for the difference in meaning between the (a) and (b) forms of (111–14) by recognizing *two* sources for the (b) forms: on one reading, they were derived from the (a) forms by coordination reduction, and hence, synonymous with them. On another reading, they were generated directly by phrase structure rules. I see two major problems with this attempted solution.

In effect, this approach associates an iconicity of exactly the sort we are discussing with the putative deep structure that underlies the actually occurring forms. But there is no need to impute to a hypothetical deep structure the very iconicity which the surface forms display. In fact, the proposal makes empirically untenable claims, when all but the simplest examples are considered. The great descriptive advantage of the generative proposal is that it accounts for the ambiguity of the reduced form (which has *two* possible deep structures), while predicting that the full, or (a) form, which has only one syntactic source, will manifest no comparable ambiguity. In fact, however, when we compare the non-reduced (a) forms in all cases above but the very first, we find that these are *also* ambiguous.

What needs to be explained, then, is that the more likely interpretation of the (b) form is one in which the conjuncts are conceptually close, while the more likely interpretation of the (a) form is one in which they are distant. We are dealing with tendencies rather than hard-and-fast rules, and they are tendencies which are determined by surface structure. Where a semantic contrast is so perspicuously displayed on the surface, appeals to a hypothetical deep structure are not only factually incorrect but a priori redundant. Here, if anywhere, is one of those places where things are truly what they seem to be.

Although the claim that coordination reduction is a meaning-preserving operation should be refuted by examples such as (111–14), there is a sense, perhaps, in which one may still be tempted to dismiss them as "stylistic" variants: the semantic contrast is not rigidly grammaticalized. Moving farther afield, however, we can encounter a large class of cases where coordination reduction is grammaticalized; deletion of material under identity signals one meaning, while the retention of this material signals another. And in every case we shall examine, deletion signals conceptual closeness of the remaining constituents.

Non-final or medial verbs in many Papuan languages, as we have already noted above, often mark switch-reference: they indicate through some kind of affixation whether they share a common subject with the following verb. In some of these languages, noted on p. 114, the same ≠ different subject contrast is signaled by the absence vs. the presence of the coordinating conjunction. In many more of these languages, the same semantic contrast is signaled by coordination reduction. The different-subject medial verb typically consists of the verb stem followed by personal agreement suffixes, while the same-subject verb consists of the verb stem followed either by zero, or by the functional equivalent of zero, an *invariable* affix.

In Kâte (Pilhofer 1933:35–6), the same-subject perfective medial verb "eat" consists of the root *nâ-*, followed by an aspect marker *ku-*, followed by zero; the different-subject medial verb in the same aspect consists of *nâ+ku*, followed by personal endings (1sg.-*pe*, 2sg. -*teʔ*, 3sg. -*me*, etc.). In the closely related Ono language (Wacke 1931:171–2), the same-subject simultaneous action medial verb consists simply of the bare verb stem: thus *ne* "eat". The different-subject medial verb consists of the same verb stem, followed once again by the personal endings (1sg.-*we*, 2sg. -*nom*, 3sg. *ki*, etc.).

In Kewa (Franklin 1971, 1983), the same-subject medial consists of the verb stem followed by an invariable aspect marker: thus *piru* "eat" +*a* "tense/aspect". The different-subject medial consists of the verb stem followed by personal endings: 1sg. *pirano*, 2sg. *piraina*, 3sg. *pirina*, etc.

In Usan (Reesink ms) the same-subject medial verb consists of the bare verb stem followed by a verb-class marker which does not vary for person: thus *su-* "cut" +*-ab* "class marker". The different-subject medial verb consists again of the verb stem followed by a set of personal endings: 1sg. *su-ine*, etc.

In Tauya (MacDonald, to appear), the same-subject medial verb consists of the verb stem followed by a same-subject suffix -*pa*: thus *yate* "go" +*pa* "same-subject". The different-subject medial consists of the verb stem, followed by personal endings and the different-subject suffix -*te* (which has an allomorph -*tefe* in the 2sg.): *yate-e-te* "go-1/2sg.-different subject", *yate-a-te* "go-3sg.-different subject", etc.

The contrast is less rigidly grammaticalized in some Papuan languages like Telefol (Healey 1966:26), where the deletion of the personal desinences on the medial verb is an *optional* way of signaling same-subject reference (but deletion is impossible for different-subject medial verbs).

There is some speculation that the Papuan languages enumerated above may be distantly related, but their sharing this common structural feature can certainly not be taken as evidence for their relationship, since, as we shall see, the same contrast marks essentially the same semantic contrast in other indubitably non-Papuan languages as well.

One such language is Turkish (Lewis 1967: 177–8) where, if V1 and V2 in a compound sentence "have identical suffixes", the suffixes of V1 may be replaced by the invariable suffix *ip* (originally a past participle). Thus sentence (115a) may be reduced to (115b).

(115) a. Gid-eyim   şehirde çalis-ayim
           go-1sg.subj. city=in work-1sg.subj.
           "Let me go and work in the city"
     b. Gid-*ip*   şehirde çalişayim

It is clear that more than formal identity of the suffixes is involved in this reduction, however, as we can see from the semantic contrast between (116a) and (116b).

(116) a. gel-en-ler   ve gid-en-ler
           come-part.-3pl. and go-part.-3pl.
           "those who come and those who go"
     b. gel-*ip* ve gidenler
           "those who (both) come and go"

That is, the -*ip* suffix is possible only where the subjects of the two verbs with identical endings are the same.

In Ancash Quechua (Cole 1983) adverbial S1 clauses mark switch-reference very much as they do in Tauya. The same-subject adverbial clause verb consists of the stem followed by a tense/aspect marker followed by zero: *uyra* "work" + *shpa* "aspect", "while working". The different-subject adverbial clause consists of the stem followed by a different-subject suffix -*pti*, followed in its turn by a set of personal agreement endings: *uyra-pti-i* (1sg.), etc.

Lynch (1983) has shown a parallel marking of switch-reference in the Austronesian language Lenakel, in which the personal affixes which are used to mark person–number agreement are *prefixed* rather than suffixed to the verb form. As the theory of coordination reduction would predict (cf. Ross 1970), in Lenakel it is the *second* of the two coordinate clauses which will then be reduced. Lynch points out that different-subject final verbs have a personal prefix to mark subject–verb agreement; same-subject final verbs have an invariable "echo-subject" prefix *m*- (which, Lynch suggests, may derive from an original conjunction).

In the examples we have considered up to this point, deletion of "X" marks *identity with respect to X*, and one might argue that the motivation for such deletion is therefore in all cases purely economic. We shall now turn to a set of cases where deletion of "X" does not mark identity with respect to X, but rather identity with respect to some other feature "Y". The importance of these cases is in demonstrating that the generalized function of such deletions is in all cases to signal the diminution of conceptual distance, and is not specifically limited to the economic function of avoiding repetition.

In Kâte (Pilhofer 1933:135, fn.2) same-subject medial verbs consist in general of the verb stem followed by an aspect marker: for example *wale-lâ* "come" + "sequential", *lo-huʔ* "take" + "simultaneous". However, this aspect suffix is not always present. Pilhofer suggests that the semantic import of such deletion is to signal either the rapidity of the succession of events, or their close connection with each other.

In Menya, an Angan language of New Guinea (Whitehead ms), two kinds of non-final verb are distinguished: *medial* and *close-knit*. Medial verbs consist of the verb stem followed by an aspect suffix, followed by personal endings. Close-knit verbs consist of the verb stem, followed directly by the personal endings. In contradistinction to medial verbs, close-knit verbs tend to merge with the following verb semantically to denote one single complex event. Thus *t-qang-i* "say-aspect-3sg." + *i-* "do" means "3sg. said and did . . ." But *t-∅-a* "say-∅-1dl." + *i-* means "we two *thought* . . ." (That is, in close-knit verbs, the lexemes denoting *say* and *do* have become lexicalized to form the single verb meaning "think".)

Another contrast in Menya involves the contrast between $V1 + person$ and $V1 + ∅$ on medial verbs: again, the contrast does not signal the difference between SS and DS forms, but between two separate actions and one single action. Thus the contrast

(117)   a. Yaqueqä ä-ma-*äqe*   ä-yap-qäqä-i
        pig   mood-get-3sg. mood-come=up-3sg.past-ind.
        "He got the pig and then came up (perhaps without the pig)"
        b. Yaqueqä ä-ma-∅   ä-yap-qäqä-i
        "He brought the pig up"

Munro 1983 notes a similar auxiliarization or lexicalization of stripped down non-final verbs in Chickasaw, a Muskogean language of Oklahoma. Chickasaw happens to be a switch-reference marking language, but switch-reference is marked not by the presence or the absence of personal desinences on the verb of S1, but by a pair of equipollent suffixes (SS-*t*,

DS-*N*) which follow the personal desinences. The structure of a non-final verb in Chickasaw is therefore *Stem+person+SR suffix* as in (118a).

(118)   a. Tali? ish-*li*-t   isso-li-tok
         rock take-1sg. SS hit-1sg.-past
         "I took a rock and hit (him)"

Deletion of the personal desinence on V1 "reflects conceptual closeness to the point where a two-clause paraphrase is impossible":

(118)   b. Tali? ish-t   isso-li-tok
         rock take-SS hit-1sg.-past
         "I hit him with a rock"

The stripped verb "take" functions in effect as an instrumental case in effect: as in Menya *V1 V2* (where V1 is stripped) denotes a single complex event rather than two.

In Swahili, a Bantu language of East Africa (Hinnebusch 1979), as in Lenakel, personal desinences appear as prefixes on the verb, and we should therefore expect that in Swahili, as in Lenakel, reduction should occur on the second of two coordinate clauses This is indeed what we find. Once again, however, the formal contrast $\emptyset+Verb$ vs. *personal affix+verb* is used not only to signal identity of subjects but another kind of conceptual closeness. In Swahili, where subjects are identical and the tense prefixes are also identical, the complex *subject prefix+tense prefix* on the second verb may be replaced by the invariable (infinitival) prefix *ku-*:

(119)   a. Juma a-li-imba   na *a-li*-piga   ngoma
         Juma 3sg.past-sing and *3sg.-past*-play drum
      b. Juma a-li-imba   na *ku*-piga   ngoma
         Juma 3sg.-past-sing and *inf.*-play   drum

Both sentences (119a) and (119b) mean that Juma sang and played the drum, but they are not entirely synonymous. As Hinnebusch points out (ibid. 250), "the infinitive *ku-piga* is reduced: there is no subject marker, and no tense marker, and this is why there is a strong implication that the drumming goes together with the singing, *as a single act*" (my emphasis).

In Menya, Hua, Chickasaw, and Swahili, reduction of the form of a verb signals its semantic fusion with another verb to the point where the two verbs tend to denote a single act. This kind of correlation between reduction and conceptual fusion is of course quite typical not only of auxiliary verbs but of the so-called "serial verbs" in many African languages (cf. Stahlke 1970, Lord 1973, and, in particular, Givón 1979a).

Recall that exactly the same kind of conceptual closeness between clauses was signaled by the absence of a coordinating conjunction in Fe?fe? and Gende. The formal and semantic parallelism between deletion of the coordinating conjunction and reduction of the verb is further highlighted by the fact that in some languages the two occur together to signal the same conceptual contrast.

In Chuave, a Papuan language of the Central Highlands of New Guinea (Thurman 1978), same-subject and different-subject medial verbs contrast according to the schema given in (120).

(120)   DS = Verb + personal endings + *goro* (a different-subject marker)
         SS = Verb + $\emptyset$ + *ro*   (a same-subject marker)

The different-subject marker looks very much like *go* + *ro*: the first syllable *go-*, which is what is distinctively "different-subject", looks suspiciously like the coordinating conjunction meaning "and" attested in a number of other Papuan languages: Maring *-k*, Hua *-gi*, Fore *-ki*, Kanite *-ke*, Gende *-ko*, Gahuku *-go*, Gimi *-ga*, Siane *-ge*, and possibly even Koita *-ge* and Barai *-ga*. If this identification is correct, then (120) indicates that the SS ≠ DS distinction is signaled by presence vs. absence of both personal desinences and coordinating conjunction.

Recall now that in Aghem (cf. Anderson 1977:112–14), "consecutive verbs" also distinguish between same- and different-subjects. Same-subject consecutive verbs "delete all subjects but the first" (Anderson, 112). Different-subject consecutive verbs have both a subject pronoun and a consecutive marker which derives etymologically from a demonstrative but which is invariably glossed as the conjunction "&" (ibid. 114). Again, the SS ≠ DS distinction is doubly marked.

What is common to both deletion of the conjunction and deletion of affixation on the verb is the diminution of linguistic distance between verbs. The fact that this structural result consistently reflects the same kind of shift in meaning means that we cannot dismiss it as an accidental fact.

Having looked at deletion and reduction of various types, we may now look at another kind of reduction that is manifested in English, and which has attracted considerable attention in recent years. Larry Horn pointed out that the low-level rule of phonetic reduction which converts *want to* to *wanna*, etc., has semantic consequences in minimal pairs like (121a,b).

(121)   a. Who do you *want to* succeed?
         b. Who do you *wanna* succeed?

In (121a) two meanings are possible:

> A. For which person x do you want to succeed x?
> B. For which person x do you want x to succeed?

In (121b), only one of these meanings is possible, namely A.

The explanation given for this fact in current generative grammar, as is well known, is "trace theory". The logical structures of the two meanings of (121a) are as given in A and B. The interrogative pronouns *who* have been moved out of the embedded sentences in A and B, where *x* marks the spot from which they have been moved. When an element is moved by a transformation, it leaves a phonologically empty but psychologically real trace in its place. This trace intervenes between *want* and *to* in B. Contraction of *want to* to *wanna* is blocked when anything intervenes between the two words *want* and *to*. Therefore, the meaning B cannot yield the sentence (121b), which is the required result.

A number of very significant theoretical consequences have been deduced from trace theory (cf. Chomsky 1981). However, the empirical basis for this theory itself is still quite slender, and I think it is fair to say that Horn's observation is still the most cogent empirical justification for it. There are, however, significant problems for this theory in accounting for the facts of sentences like (122). Postal & Pullum (1979, 1982) have drawn attention to a number of these, under two headings: first, contraction is often blocked even where no movement of any element has taken place; second, it is not certain that there is no element between *want* and *to* in the underlying representation corresponding to A.

Consider first some cases where contraction is blocked even where no movement has removed any element from between *want* and *to*:

(122)   a. What does a girl need to *have, to* (*hafta) be popular?
        b. I won the raffle, so I *got to* (*gotta) go to Hawaii last winter
        c. You don't need to *want, to* (*wanna) be eligible for an old age pension

Postal & Pullum argue that contraction never takes place in sentences like (122a) and (122c) where the embedded sentence is a purpose clause rather than a complement clause, and they therefore propose that contraction is only possible where *to* initiates a complement clause. This proposal does nothing to account for (122b), a sentence noted by Bolinger (1961:25). Bolinger's explanation for the failure of contraction in (122b) can be generalized to (122a) and (122c), however: the length of an utterance (or of a word used in an utterance) depends on the speaker's degree of familiarity with it: "condensation is tied to familiarity" (ibid. 27), and a "loss of analyzability is a concomitant of reduction" (ibid. 31).

I believe that Bolinger's observation is optimally explained by an appeal to "familiarity" à la Zipf. For further discussion, cf. chapter 3. In any case, it should be noted that it relates to the less serious of Postal & Pullum's objections to trace theory, since this objection in itself involves no more than *adding* an additional rider to trace theory. Making a distinction between purpose clauses and complement clauses does not in itself challenge the validity of trace theory; nor does marking a distinction between familiar and unfamiliar combinations. These distinctions merely indicate the need for further constraints on contraction.

More serious is Postal & Pullum's contention that there is an intermediary constituent between *want* and *to* in the structure *A*: this constituent is one which Chomsky recognizes as *PRO*, another phonologically null category bound by or coreferential with "you" (cf. Chomsky 1981). (In earlier versions of generative grammar, the gap between *want* and *to* in these cases was created by coreferential complement subject deletion, cf. Postal 1970.) They argue, I think convincingly, that the distinction between two null elements is strained and ad hoc, and propose as a much more direct and realistic description of the contraction phenomenon the general constraint that it can apply only if the subject of the "semi-auxiliary" (*want, have, got, used*) and the subject of the embedded infinitival complement are the same. In other words, they are proposing that English, like a host of other languages in exotic parts of the world, *grammaticalizes* switch-reference: thus *want to* is ambiguous between same-subject and different-subject readings; *wanna* is unambiguously same-subject.

There are two reasons why this explanation is attractive. The first is that it immediately relates observations about a relatively peripheral and isolated fact in English to similar observations concerning very similar facts in a large number of other languages. Not only is the semantic distinction (same vs. different subject) a familiar one, but the morphological expression of this distinction is familiar in that a reduced or contracted version signals conceptual closeness (same subject), while a non-reduced version signals conceptual distance (different subject). Contraction then joins deletion of the conjunction and deletion of verbal affixation as a functionally related device for reducing both the linguistic and the conceptual distance between verbs.

The second reason for finding the explanation congenial is that it allows us to explain another apparently unrelated fact about English. A familiar and apparently idiomatic fact about English is that another contraction, that of *let us* to *let's*, like the contraction of *want to* to *wanna*, has semantic correlations.

(123)   a. Let us go
          b. Let's go

As is well known, (123a) is ambiguous, having the possible interpretations

(124)   a. us = you and me
          b. us = third person(s) and me

But (123b) is not ambiguous, and can only have interpretation (124a). Moses addressing Pharaoh, for example, intending (124b), could not utter (123b).

Trace theory cannot explain this fact: ergo, trace theory is not even interested in it. Presumably, the semantic contrast between (123a) and (123b) is simply dismissed as idiomatic. Idioms are a pervasive fact of life, and there is nothing implausible about dismissing any fact as an arbitrary one. Nevertheless, the formal unity of the phenomenon of contraction in English is so striking, and the semantic parallelism between these two cases is so neat, that one might wish for a unified analysis of (121) and (123).

The understood subject of any imperative in English is *you*. In the first interpretation of (123a), *us* is inclusive, and therefore the subjects of *let* and *go* are *non-distinct*, both including *you*. Therefore, a same-subject (reduced, contracted) form *let's* is possible. In the second interpretation of (123a), on the other hand, *us* is exclusive, and it follows that the subjects of *let* and *go* must be entirely distinct. Therefore the same-subject form *let's* is impossible.

This analysis may seem suspect in treating *non-distinctness* of *you* and *you and me* as *identity* (both non-distinctness and identity motivating the same-subject form). In fact, however, there is a fair body of comparative evidence that suggests the correctness of precisely this approach. That is, in languages which mark switch-reference as a clearly defined grammatical category, cases of overlap or inclusion between subjects are typically treated as "borderline" cases where often both same-subject and different-subject forms are possible (cf. Longacre 1972, Langdon & Munro 1979, Haiman 1980, Austin 1981, Comrie 1983, Franklin 1983). The ambiguity of (123a) is exactly parallel inasmuch as the non-distinct interpretation, (124a), may be rendered by either *let us*, as in (123a) (the different-subject form) or *let's* as in (123b) (the same-subject form).

Once again, harking back to the promise in p. 3, an analysis of linguistic data is possible here: according to this analysis, things are *exactly what they seem to be*. A contraposed generative analysis posits two null elements with different properties and explains less data. Unless one has a predilection for mystery, the choice between contending explanations, in this case at least, seems reasonably clear.

An early statement of the position that "to-contraction" in English is a function of identical subjects in two clauses is made by Frantz (1977), who argues, as I have done, that this analysis is not at all ad hoc if data from a wider range of languages is taken into account. Frantz notes that the phenomenon of *clause union* (cf. Aissen & Perlmutter 1983), which is well-attested in a wide range of unrelated languages, occurs only where the two clauses that are fused share a common subject. Thus, Isleta, a Tanoan language of New Mexico (Frantz 1977:73):

(125)   a. Te-na-beow-a ti-diru-tuwi-hi-ʔi
              I-ʔ-want-pres. 1→3-chicken-buy-fut.-sub.
              "I want to buy the chicken"
          b. Te-na-beow-a a-dire [sic]-tuwi-hi-ʔi
              I-ʔ-want-pres. 1→3-chicken-buy-fut.-sub.
              "I want you to buy the chicken"

Sentence (125a), in which the subjects of "want" and "buy" are coreferential, corresponds to a reduced, fused structure (125c).

(125)   c. Te-na-diru-kum-beow-a
              I-ʔ-chicken-buy-want-pres.
              "I want to buy the chicken"

In (125c), the verb "want" is auxiliarized and appears as a suffix on the (suppletive) root *kum* "buy". No corresponding reduced structure exists as a near-synonym of (125b), in which the subjects of "want" and "buy" are distinct. Frantz argues that the familiar phenomenon of "clitic climbing" in Romance languages exemplifies the same type of clause union, inasmuch as "dependents of the complement verb clearly become dependents of the matrix verb" (ibid. 74). Thus the Spanish example given in (126a).

(126)   a. *Te los*   quiero mostrar
              you them I=want to=show
              "I want to show them to you"

In (126a), both *te* and *los* are understood as object complements of the verb *mostrar*. They may in fact appear as postverbal clitics with *mostrar*, as in (126b).

(126)   b. Quiero mostrar*telos*
              "I want to show them to you"

In a valuable study, Napoli (1981) has shown that in one Romance language at least, namely Italian, the analogs of (126a) and (126b) are not in fact totally interchangeable. The clitic climbing which characterizes (126a) occurs pari passu with the *auxiliarization* of the higher verb: the less the upper verb is used to denote an independent fully specified activity, and the more it signals a grammaticalized dependency on the lower verb, the more acceptable clitic climbing becomes. Inasmuch as auxiliarization signals a conceptual fusion between two verbs to the point where they no longer describe separate activities, this result is also compatible with, and predicted by, the motivation hypothesis that linguistic fusion reflects conceptual fusion.

An analogous phenomenon is also encountered in Hungarian, where the elements that may "climb" are directional/perfectivizing verbal prefixes, and object agreement verbal suffixes. The principal relevant condition, as in Spanish and Italian, is that the subject of the upper and lower verbs be identical.

(127)   a. Fel-hiv-t-alak
           up-call-past-1sg.subj.→2 obj.
           "I called you up"

Where sentence (127a) is embedded as the object complement of the verb *akar* "want", different structures result, depending on whether the subject of "want" is identical with that of "call up". In Hungarian, as in Italian and many other languages, the following general pattern obtains:

Subject of S1 = Subject of S2:   S2 verb appears as subjectless infinitive
Subject of S1 ≠ Subject of S2:   S2 appears as full sentence with "that" complementizer

Thus, where the subjects are different:

(127)   b. Akar-t-a,   hogy fel-hiv-j-alak
           want-past-3sg. that up-call-sub.-1sg.→2
           "He wanted me to call you up"

The lower verb appears in the subjunctive mood, and with its perfective/directional prefix *fel-*, and with its subject–object agreement marker *-alak*. The higher verb *akar* takes the 3sg. definite object agreement marker *-a* (indicating that its subject is 3sg., and its object, the entire clause S2, is definite). Where the subjects are identical:

(127)   c. Akar-t-alak   fel-hiv-ni
           want-past-1sg.→2 up-call-inf.
           "I wanted to call you up"

Note that the subject–object agreement marker -*alak* is now affixed to the higher verb *akar*, while the lower verb *hiv* occurs with the infinitive suffix. This movement is obligatory, as infinitival affixes and agreement markers are mutually exclusive, and thus cannot both occur on the lower verb. An optional variant of this sentence is (127d), in which the directional prefix has also traveled upstairs.

(127)   d. Fel-akar-t-alak   hiv-ni
            up-want-past-1sg.→2 call-inf.
            'I wanted to call you up"

Sentence (127d) is analogous to the Spanish sentence (126a) in that, here too, dependents of the complement verb become adjuncts of the matrix verb. And here too, clause fusion or clause union may occur only where the two clauses share a common subject.

2.2.3 Alienable and inalienable possession
Differing conceptual distance will also exist, under different circumstances, between *possessor* and *possessum*. Languages will frequently codify or grammaticalize a distinction between *alienable* and *inalienable* possession. It seems intuitively clear that conceptual distance is greater when possession is *alienable* than when it is not: possessor and possessum are not indissolubly bound together where possession is alienable, either in fact or in the perception of speakers. Typically, inalienable possession is indicated when the possessum is a body part, a kinsman, or a personal attribute: all of these denotata are viewed as permanently associated with the possessor.

The motivation hypothesis now predicts that where the distinction between alienable and inalienable possession is grammaticalized, inalienable possession will be indicated by the structure in which the linguistic distance between possessor and possessum is *less*; alienable possession will be indicated by the structure in which the linguistic distance between possessor and possessum is *more*.

For the most part, this hypothesis is borne out by the facts, though there are certain systematic problems which I shall point out. First, let us see where the hypothesis is simply confirmed.

In Hua, body parts and kinsmen, and some other possessa (including sweat, semen, personal names, and quasi-kin relations such as *namesake*, *agemate*, and *enemy*) indicate the person of the possessor with a pronominal prefix: *d-ruʔ* "my thigh", *k-noguʔ* "your maternal uncle", *r-vari* "our sweat", *p-varuʔ* "their agemate", and so on. Alienably possessed possessa cannot indicate possessors by this prefix, but by a free-standing noun or pronoun in the genitive case: *dgaiʔ ruʔ* "my axe", *kgaiʔ bodoʔ* "your loincloth", *rgaiʔ fu* "our pig", *pgaiʔ zuʔ* "their house", etc. Although the pattern is complicated by phonological conditions (some inalienably possessed nouns cannot occur with the pronominal prefixes), to the extent that the distinction corresponds to a semantic distinction at all, we have the formal contrast $X + Y$ (inalienable possession) vs. $X \# Y$ (alienable possession).

A similar contrast is observed in a wide range of languages in the Austronesian family. For example, in Nakanai (Johnston 1981:217), the inalienable possessor is indicated by a pronominal suffix on the possessum: *lima-gu* "hand-my", *tama-mulua* "father-1dl.exc.", etc. The alienable possessor is indicated by a free-standing pronoun: *luma taku* "house my", *luma tamulua* "house 1dl.exc.". Again, the formal contrast $X + Y$ vs. $X \# Y$ corresponds to the conceptual contrast inalienable possession vs. alienable possession.

The same type of contrast is overlaid with an insignificant complication in Mekeo, another Austronesian language spoken on the Gulf coast of Papua New Guinea. Inalienable possession is indicated, as in Nakanai, by a pronominal suffix: *aki-u* "my younger brother", *aki-mu* "your younger brother", *aki-ʔa* "our (inclusive) younger brother", and so on. Alienable possession is indicated by a free-standing pronoun which *precedes* the possessum: *eʔu ngaanga* "my canoe", *emu ngaanga* "your canoe", *aʔa ngaanga* "our (inclusive) canoe", etc. Here, the formal contrast $X + Y$ vs. $Y \# X$ corresponds to the conceptual distinction between inalienable and alienable possession. The word order permutation does not affect the fact that the alienable possessor is separated from the possessum by a word boundary, while the inalienable possessor is separated by a word-internal morpheme boundary only.

Many Australian languages also grammaticalize a distinction between alienable and inalienable possession: typically, the alienable possessor occurs with a genitive–dative suffix, while the inalienable possessor is juxtaposed with the possessum. The formal contrast $X + gen. \# Y$ vs. $X \# Y$ corresponds, as predicted, with the semantic contrast alienable vs. inalienable possession.

In Yidin^y, the basic – and "always possible" – method of expressing possession is by means of the construction *possessor + genitive possessum* (Dixon 1977:363): *waga:l-ni guda:ga* "wife-genitive dog". But possession involving a "part–whole relationship, where the possessum is a body part or name, or one's bodily secretions or smell may be expressed by simple apposition" (ibid. 357; cf. also 360, 361): *bama dungu* "person head", *nganyany gurga* "I neck". Thus, the construction *NP+gen. NP* is ambiguous between alienable and inalienable readings, while *NP NP* is reserved for a subset of inalienable nouns, typically (body) parts. (Kinship terms notably pattern with *alienably* possessed nouns.)

In Maung (Capell & Hinch 1970:60–1), most nouns take independent possessors which occur with the same articles/classifiers/gender markers as the nouns they qualify: *dja injanad dja jangali* "article her article bag". The possessor is, however, prefixed to "certain nouns, mostly those indicating certain relationships and certain parts of the body or part of an object" (ibid. 61): *ngal-agbiridj* "my-mouth", *ngad-ingan* "my-brother". The formal contrast *article NP article NP* vs. *NP NP* correlates roughly with the conceptual distinction alienable vs. inalienable possession.

The Bantu languages of Africa typically contrast alienable and inalienable possession in much the same way as Yidin[y]: *NP+gen. NP* vs. *NP NP* is the linguistic distinction with the predictable semantic correlation. Thus, in Kinyarwanda (Kimenyi 1980:44–6), a morphological contrast is possible between *umwaana umusatsi* "child hair" and *umusatsi wa uumwaana* "hair of child". The more natural reading of the latter construction is the alienable meaning, where "hair" is the hair of a toy animal belonging to the child, for instance (ibid. 46). For extensive discussion of the same morphological contrast in Swahili, cf. Hinnebusch & Kirsner (1980).

Kpelle offers a very striking example of the grammaticalization of the possessive contrast, since it is realized in different ways where the possessor is a noun or a pronoun. In each case, the motivation hypothesis makes the correct predictions. Where the possessor is a *pronoun*, the distinction between alienable and inalienable possession is that between $X \# Y$ and $X + Y$: *nga pérɛi* "my house" vs. *m+pôlu* "my back". Where the possessor is a common noun, the formal contrast is between *NP+gen. NP* (for alienable possession) and *NP NP* (for alienable possession): *ɓkaloñg nc pérɛi* "chief's house", as opposed to *ɓkaloñg pôlu* "chief's back" (Welmers 1973:279). It is noteworthy that the common distinction between alienable and inalienable possession in Kpelle is one that can be stated only in terms of "linguistic distance" as set out in the hierarchy in (88). No other generalization seems to be possible.

For another example of almost exactly this type we turn to (Moroccan) Arabic (cf. Harrell 1965:168, 178). Once again, we must distinguish between pronominal and nominal possessors. Where the possessor is a personal pronoun, and the possessum is a kin term, a body part, or (optionally) one of a small number of alienably possessed monosyllabic nouns like *ḍar* "house", the possessor is indicated as a suffix on the possessum: *šɛăr-ha* "hair-her", *m̂m̂-ek* "your mother", *ḍar-ek* "your house". Where the possessum is inalienably possessed it is always possible (and, in most cases, obligatory) to suffix the possessive marker on a marker of alienation *dyal-* ~ *d-*: *s-sarut dyal-hom* "key alien-their", *l-konnaš dyal-i* "notebook alien-my", *ḍ-ḍar dyal-ek* "house alien-your". Where the possessor is a full noun phrase, inalienable possession is indicated by the "construct form" *NP NP* : *ḍheṛ l-weld* "back boy", i.e. "the boy's back". Alienable possession, on the other hand, requires once again the use of the particle of alienation *dyal*, which separates possessor from possessum.

In Acooli (Crazzolara 1938:46–7) the formal contrast is between *NP NP* for inalienable possession, and *NP pà NP* for alienable possession. Only body parts are counted as inalienably possessed. Crazzolara cites the interesting minimal pair *eém leè* "thigh animal", i.e. the body part of the animal, and *eèm pà là cɔ̀ɔ̀* "thigh belonging to man", i.e. the man's portion to be eaten.

There are as well a number of American Indian languages which grammaticalize the distinction along the same lines. In Tunica (Haas 1940:37) the formal contrast is between *possessive prefix + NP* for alienably possessed nouns, and *possessive prefix + hk + NP* for alienably possessed nouns, typically kin terms and body parts. The enlargement *-hk-* may be partly phonetically motivated as well as semantically used to mark conceptual distance. Compare *ʔu-esiku* "3sg.('s) father" and *ʔu-hk-iyu-tʔeku* "3sg. ('s) hog".

In Chiricahua Apache (Hoijer 1946:75), a distinction can be made between alienable and inalienable possession of body parts by the use of a particle of alienation *-ʔì-* that may be inserted between possessor and possessum: *bi-ci* "his head", vs. *bi-ʔì-ci* "his head", i.e. his war trophy.

In Papago, as in Maung, the formal contrast between alienable and inalienable possession is grammaticalized by the interposition of a nominal classifier between possessor and possessum in the former case (Saxton 1982:186–7):

(128) a. hihi-j g haiwañ
           "the cow's gut"
       b. hihi-j-*ga*-j g huan
           "Juan's tripe" (i.e. the guts he has to eat)

Note the repetition of the genitive suffix -*j* after the classifier -*ga*- which further increases the distance here between possessor and possessum.

In Seri (Marlett 1981:112–19), inalienable possession is indicated by a series of pronominal prefixes on the possessum, e.g. *ʔ-ɬit* "my head", *ma-nya:k* "your older brother". Alienable possession is indicated by a relative clause meaning literally "which (possessor) owns" (ibid. 118). Thus *kanoatax ʔioya:t koi* "boats which=we=own the", or "our boats".

Languages which simply do not make a distinction between alienable and inalienable possession, such as English, do not pose a problem for the motivation hypothesis which predicts only that *if* a distinction exists, it will be compatible with the hierarchy in (88). Other languages, however, do pose problems.

Languages of the Micronesian group of the Austronesian family pose a minor problem. The general pattern in these languages, attested in Puluwat (Elbert 1974:55–61), Aroma (Lynch 1973:78), Woleai (Sohn 1975:57–9), and Mokilese (Harrison 1976:114–29), is reminiscent in some ways of the pattern in Papago: alienable possession is marked by an additional nominal classifier associated with the possessum. Unlike Papago, however, in which the classifier is interposed between the possessor and possessum, these languages manifest the contrast

> Alienable: Classifier + possessive suffix possessum
> Inalienable: Possessum + possessive suffix

Thus Puluwat *nay-iy hamwol* "classifier-my chief" vs. *pay-iy* "hand-my"; Woleai *ya-ai babiyor* "classifier-my book" vs. *babiyor-oi* "book my" (a book *about* me); Mokilese *nima-a penok* "classifier-his coconuts" vs. *rioa-mw* "brother-your"; Aroma *ga-ku gage* "classifier-your leg" (e.g. the chicken leg you are eating) vs. *gage-ku* "leg-your" (your own body part). Although the classifier is not interposed between the possessor and the possessum in alienable constructions, it is still the case that the linguistic distance between possessor and possessum is greater in the alienable construction. The formal contrast *Classifier + X # Y* vs. *Y + X* is still one in which greater linguistic distance between X and Y reflects greater conceptual distance between them.

More upsetting is the pattern manifested by Mandarin Chinese, and perhaps by other languages as well. In Mandarin, there is a formal contrast between possession expressed by a nomino-adjectival particle *de* and simple juxtaposition: *NP de NP* vs. *NP NP*, where, in each case, the first NP represents the possessor. The motivation hypothesis predicts that the first pattern is used where possession is alienable. What actually seems to be the case, however, is that *NP de NP* expresses the relationship of possession where the possessum is anything but a kinsman: thus "my hair" and "my house" pattern in one way, and "my uncle" in another (cf. Li & Thompson 1981:115,161).

One could maintain, à la Whorf, that Mandarin simply conceptualizes the *alienable/inalienable* contrast differently. We cannot, however, accept this. Although we may expect languages to conceptualize categories in different ways (and this is the essence of both the linguistic relativity hypothesis and the emic principle), there must be universal limits to this variation, or the cross-linguistic validity of the category labels simply disappears. In this particular case, we cannot wish to characterize as an example of the *alienable/inalienable* distinction a contrast such as the one that exists in Mandarin, and treat kin as "less alienable" than arms, legs, or hearts.

An essentially similar point is implicit in the recent literature on "hierarchies" (cf. Keenan & Comrie 1977, Silverstein 1976, Givón 1979a, 1983): given a universal hierarchy which languages will subdivide in different ways, we may expect variation in the location of the "cutoff points" along this hierarchy, but the hierarchy itself is fixed and immutable. Intuitively, the hierarchy of "alienability" is: body parts less alienable than kinsmen; kinsmen less alienable than artefacts. Languages which make no overt distinctions among these categories (like English) are not problematic for this hierarchy; neither are languages which oppose kinsmen and body parts to artefacts (like Hua, Mekeo, or Arabic); nor, again, are languages which oppose body parts to both kinsmen and artefacts (like Yidin[y] and Acooli, cf. Crazzolara 1938:46–7). The only variable in all of these cases is the location of the "cutoff point" between alienable and inalienable possession with respect to the immutable hierarchy.

Mandarin violates the hierarchy, and is not alone in doing so. That is, there are other languages in which, by the morphological evidence, the hierarchy of alienability is: kinsmen less alienable than body parts; body parts less alienable than artefacts.

One such language, apparently, is Menya, a Papuan language of the Angan family (Whitehead ms). In Menya, kin terms are possessed by pronominal prefixes: *t-apiqu* "your-father". But all other nouns, including body parts, require the interposition of a genitive/possessive suffix between possessor and possessum: *t-qä angä* "you-gen. house", *t-qä hanguä* "you-gen. shoulders".

Another such language is Mokilese, although the evidence is comparatively subtle. As Harrison (1976:115) points out, Mokilese distinguishes three degrees of "tightness" of possession: kin terms and body parts allow the direct suffixation of the possessive affix onto the possessum, while other NPs require a classifier, as outlined above. However, there is a distinction between kin terms and body parts with respect to the nature of the suffixes they take. Harrison distinguishes between what he calls tightly inalienable possessa (body parts) which take suffixes 1sg. *-ioa*, 2sg. *-mwen*, etc., and loosely inalienable possessa, which take suffixes 1sg. *-i*, 2sg. *-mw*, etc. For example, *mijoa-ioa* "face-my" vs. *joamoa-i* "father-my".

The motivation hypothesis predicts that the more fused (and reduced) an affix, the greater the conceptual fusion between denotata of the affix and the root. In this case, it is clear that the suffixes of "loose inalienability" are reduced versions of the suffixes of "tight inalienability". Harrison's nomenclature (and ours) to the contrary, Mokilese really seems to be treating body parts as *more* alienable than kinsfolk, though in a fashion less blatant than Mandarin or Menya.

The extent of this phenomenon is unknown. However, it seems unlikely to me that my cursory survey should have uncovered the *only* three languages in the world which violate the hierarchy of alienability: most probably, there are quite a few others. Assuming that both hierarchies are represented in languages of the world, we can only hope to salvage as a universal a much cruder hierarchy:

$$\left\{ \begin{matrix} \text{kinsmen} \\ \text{body parts} \end{matrix} \right\} > \text{artefacts}$$

and predict that there will be no language in which the linguistic distance between possessor and possessum is greater for terms on the left than it is for terms on the right of this two-stage hierarchy.

2.2.4 Distance between verb and object

Yet another dimension wherein differing distance may be expressed is that of transitivity. Intuitively, the conceptual distance between a verb and its object complement is going to covary with the transitivity of the verb. Where the transitivity of the verb is *high* (and the object is more likely to be affected, or more deeply affected), the conceptual distance between the verb and its object complement will be *small*; where the transitivity of the verb is *low* (and the object is less likely to be affected, or is less deeply affected), the conceptual distance between the verb and its object complement will be relatively *great*.

In the following discussion, we shall make use of the global definition of transitivity proposed by Hopper & Thompson (1980), according to which the transitivity of a clause is higher to the extent that

    (a) the object is individuated (definite, distinct from agent)
    (b) the object is animate
    (c) the verb is punctual rather than progressive or habitual in aspect
    (d) the entire object (rather than a part of it) is affected

There is a well-established and by now familiar correlation between the case marking of an object, and the transitivity of a verb. In Spanish, for example, Hurst (1951), Bolinger (1956) and Brewer (1970) have all drawn attention to the fact that the accusative case is favored when the object is directly affected, the dative case when it is not. Thus *contestar la pregunta* "answer the question(acc.)" means to *succeed* in answering the question. The transitive counterpart *contestar a la pregunta* "answer the question (dat.)" means to *attempt* to answer the question, but not succeed. "The transitive member of the pair has taken on the meaning of 'really doing' the act in question (saturating the object with it, so to speak) leaving the less earnest meanings to the intransitive member" (Bolinger 1956).

This contrast has been generalized by Moravcsik (1978) to include not only nominative–accusative languages like Spanish, but nominative–ergative languages as well. The verb is transitive where the object occurs in a direct case (accusative or absolutive), and intransitive where the object occurs in an oblique case (dative, partitive, or instrumental, among others).

I wish to draw attention here to a probably universal (or nearly universal) property of the formal contrast between direct and oblique cases:

> In no language will the morphological bulk of a direct case affix *exceed* that of the oblique case affixes, as a general rule. There will be languages, however, in which the morphological bulk of oblique case affixes exceeds that of direct case affixes.

Thus, we may expect to find languages like Spanish, where the contrast $\emptyset : a$ corresponds to the contrast *direct : oblique*; languages like Latin, where the contrast *-um : -ō* corresponds to the contrast *direct : oblique*; but no languages in which the contrast *x : y* (where x exceeds y) corresponds to the contrast *direct : oblique*. For morphological bulk, let us read *syllables*. The languages for which this hypothesis is tested include many for which the contrast between direct and oblique cases is *not* employed to signal

Table 2

Language	Direct case marker	Oblique case marker	Contrast reflects degree of transitivity	Source
Diyari	∅ (absolutive)	ni (locative)	Yes	Austin 1981:154
Eskimo	-q (absolutive)	mik (instrumental)	Yes	Sadock 1980
French	∅ (accusative)	a (dative)	Yes	Hyman & Zimmer 1976
Guugu-Yimidhirr	∅ (absolutive)	wi (dative)	Yes	Haviland 1979: #304
		ni (locative)	Yes	Haviland 1979: ##305–6
Hungarian	(V)t(accusative)	vel (comitative)	Yes	Comrie 1980:156
Kalkatungu	∅ (absolutive)	ku (dative)	Yes	Blake 1982
Pitta-Pitta	∅ (absolutive)	ku (dative)	Yes	Blake 1979:207
Spanish	∅ (accusative)	a (dative)	Yes	Bolinger 1956
Walbiri	∅ (absolutive)	ki (dative)	Yes	Hale 1973
Yidin^y	∅ (absolutive)	nda (dative)	Yes	Dixon 1977: chapter 3

differences in transitivity. But where the contrast *is* used, it is used as Moravcsik has predicted, such that oblique cases signal low, and direct cases, high, transitivity (see Table 2).

Following a suggestion made by Hyman & Zimmer (1976:193), Comrie (1980:166–7) has proposed another area in which conceptual distance correlates with the case of an object complement: the case of the causee in a causative construction varies depending on whether causation is direct or indirect. Where causation is *direct* (and the causee is physically manipulated or physically forced to perform the caused activity), the causee appears in the direct case. Where causation is *indirect* (and the causee is typically persuaded rather than forced to perform the caused activity), the causative appears in some oblique case.

Hyman & Zimmer draw attention to the minimally contrasting sentences

(129)   a. Je *l*'ai fait   préparer la mayonnaise   (causee is accusative)
        b. Je *lui* ai fait préparer la mayonnaise   (causee is dative)

and note that they are not entirely synonymous: "In [129a], causation is more direct, or may involve forces or pressure. As such, it is adequately translated as 'I *made* him prepare the mayonnaise'. In [129b], on the other hand, the causation is indirect, and the translation 'I *had* him prepare the mayonnaise' is more accurate."

Comrie cites the (quite untypical) Hungarian contrasting pair shown in (130a,b), which reflects the same correlation between case and degree of affectedness of the object-causee.

(130)   a. Köhög-tet-t-em   a   gyerek-*et*
          cough-caus.-past-1sg. the child-*acc.*
          "I made the child cough" (e.g. by hitting him on the back)
        b. Köhög-tet-t-em a gyerek-kel
          (as (130a))   *comitative*
          "I made the child cough" (e.g. by asking him to do so)

Assuming that the contrast between direct and indirect cases may be represented as $NP+x$ vs. $NP+y$, where the number of syllables in x is equal to or less than the number of syllables in y, this result is compatible with the motivation hypothesis only in those cases where the expression of case *intervenes* between the verb and its object complement.

That is, the result is compatible for the VO languages if case is expressed as a prefix or a preposition, for then we have a formal contrast:

> Direct: V x NP
> Indirect: V y NP

Similarly, the result is compatible with the hypothesis for OV languages if case is expressed by a suffix and/or postposition, for then we have a formal contrast

> Direct: NP x V
> Indirect: NP y V

There is indeed a statistical correlation between OV and postpositions or suffixes (cf. Greenberg 1966:78–9), a correlation for which there may be a diachronic explanation (cf. Hetzron 1980:178). But there is no such correlation between VO and prepositions/prefixed case affixes: indeed, as our examples from French and Hungarian make clear, there are violations in both directions.

In French, where the object complement is a pronoun, as in (129), the order is OV: yet if *lui* is analyzed as *à le*, the preposition appears before the object complement, yielding a structure x NP V vs. y NP V. In the Hungarian sentences of (130), the order is VO: yet the case is expressed as a suffix in both instances, yielding a contrast V NP x vs. V NP y. In neither instance does the expression of case intervene between the verb and its object.

We may recall that a similar lack of "cooperation" characterized word order in the expression of possessive relations in the Micronesian languages: alienable possession was marked by a nominal classifier on the possessum, but this classifier did not intervene between possessor and possessum. Rather, in these languages, there exists a contrast between *possessum + possessor* (inalienable) and *classifier + possessor possessum*.

It may be that there are reasons for postulating a more abstract, or historically prior, stage, where the order of constituents was more or less that which the motivation hypothesis would predict. We are then forced to postulate a possible change whereby the motivation of superficial (actual) linguistic structure could be obscured.

In the case of *possession*, the change would be

$$\text{*possessum classifier} + \text{possessor} \overset{?}{>} \text{classifier} + \text{possessor possessum}$$

In the case of *transitivity*, the comparable change would be

$$\text{*V x NP} \overset{?}{>} \text{V NP x}$$

Assuming that independent evidence could be provided for the prior reality of such a stage as that which is marked with an asterisk in the conjectured developments above, the problem still remains that motivation could be overridden by other factors.

What, if any, are the limitations on such overriding factors? We shall return to this question in the second part of our study. For the time being, it is important to note that a correlation does seem to exist between degree of transitivity and the phonological/morphological bulk of the complement case affix: and that this correlation is of the sort that the motivation hypothesis would predict for us.

We turn now to a related but distinct conceptual dimension that is expressed in the formal contrasts of figure (88) on page 105: the dimension of conceptual *individuation* or *independence*.

2.2.5 The expression of conceptual independence

By individuation, I mean the following intuitively related ideas:

> A separate *word* denotes a separate *entity*; a bound morpheme is less likely to do so.
> A separate *clause* denotes a separate *event*; a reduced clause is less likely to do so.

The correlation between the meaning and the form of *clauses* was explored in a pioneering article by Talmy Givón (1980). He showed that the reduction of a complement clause corresponded roughly to the degree to which its truth (or rather, the truth of the proposition it expressed) was implied by the matrix clause. The less the degree to which the validity of the clause was implied by its context, the fuller the expression of that clause.

The conceptual independence of a proposition was then iconically reflected in the linguistic "binding" of the clause which expressed it.

We may illustrate Givón's principle with an example he did not consider, but which we have already looked at in another context: the causative in Korean. We may formalize the notion of conceptual independence by using the notion of entailment. Given two propositions P1 and P2, P1 entails P2 if whenever P1 is true, P2 is also true. Where P2 is entailed by P1, it is clearly less independent conceptually of P1 than if it were not entailed by P1. Given now a language which expresses the category of *causation* in various ways as schematized in the figure in (88), and given that these ways may differ semantically with respect to the expression of entailment, the motivation hypothesis predicts that the degree of linguistic fusion corresponds to the degree of entailment.

English is clearly *not* a language in which different kinds of causative constructions differ with respect to the degree of entailment of the result. We may see this by attempting (and failing) to contrast the two sentences in (131).

(131)   a. I caused the tree to fall
         b. I felled the tree

Neither sentence can be followed (without contradiction), by the continuation

(132)   . . . but it didn't fall

That is, both *cause to fall* and *fell* entail the truth of the proposition that the tree actually fell.

Korean, on the other hand, *is* a language in which different causative constructions differ with respect to the degree of entailment of their result complement. Patterson (1974) has pointed out that both *Verb # ha-* and *Verb + I* are causative constructions: that is, both *ha-* "do" and the verbal suffix *-I-* "cause" function as causative morphemes. The same *Verb* expresses the complement or result in both cases:

(133)   Ku-ka na-eykey kimchi-lul *mek-key ha*-ess-ta
         he-sub. I-obl.   kimchi-obj. eat-comp. do-past-decl.
         "He caused me to eat kimchi"

(The complementizer *-key* corresponds in some constructions to the adverbial suffix *-ly* in English, so the sentence could be expressed as "He did (I=eat=kimchi)-ly".)

(134)   Ku-ka na-eykey kimchi-lul   *mek-I-*ess-ta
         he-sub. I-obl.   kimchi-obj. *eat-caus.*-past-decl.
         "He fed me kimchi"

To make both (133) and (134) concessive clauses, the final ending -*ta* is replaced by the adversative suffix -*una* "although". Now (133), thus altered, may be followed, without contradiction, by

(135)   . . . na-ka mek-ci   an(i)-ha-ess-ta
         . . . I-sub. eat-comp. not-do-past-decl.
         " . . . I didn't eat (kimchi)"

That is, the causative verb *ha*-, although it strongly implies the truth of the complement clause, does not entail it absolutely. The combination (133 + 135) suggests that he put me into the position where I *had* to eat kimchi (perhaps he made me an offer I could not socially refuse), but nevertheless, I was able to weasel out of it somehow. Sentence (134), however, may not be followed by (135). The combination (134 + 135) is as ungrammatical in Korean as the English (131 + 132), and for the same reason: the causative morpheme -*I*- absolutely entails the validity of its complement. Linguistic fusion signals conceptual fusion; linguistic independence signals conceptual independence.

The same, or a closely parallel kind of contrast, is evident when we consider the semantic correlates of the linguistic fusion of *nominal expressions*. We are dealing here with the familiar linguistic phenomenon of *noun incorporation*, which has an extensive literature.

Our concern is with the possible semantic distinctions between *Verb # Object* (object is not incorporated) and *Verb + object* (object is incorporated) in those languages where both expressions are permitted to coexist. The isomorphism hypothesis maintains, of course, that the two expressions will not be synonymous; the motivation hypothesis in general, that the difference of form will correspond to the difference in meaning. Characteristically, the incorporated nominal object is non-referential, incapable of appearing in focus, and incapable of bearing contrastive stress (cf. Sugita 1973; Mardirussian 1975; Merlan 1976; Hopper & Thompson, to appear).

Hopper & Thompson (to appear) have pointed out that an incorporated object is grammatically *less of a noun*: it appears with fewer of the "morphological trappings" of a typical noun, such as case, gender, number, or definiteness markings. It is conceptually less of a noun also, inasmuch as it fails to denote a single readily identifiable time-stable entity. Instead, the incorporated noun tends to denote a class of possible objects, and the *Verb + object* combination denotes a kind of activity. Compare *shot a duck* with *(went) duck-shooting*: in the first, a specific duck is shot, but in the second this is not so.

A very similar semantic contrast between separate and incorporated objects shows up where the object is a *reflexive* morpheme. There are a number of languages, among them Russian, Turkish, and Hungarian, where forms *Verb # Reflexive* and *Verb + reflexive* coexist. The incorporated reflexive morphemes, like incorporated objects in general, do not refer, do not bear contrastive stress, and cannot appear in focus. In addition, the combination *Verb + reflexive*, like the combination *Verb + object* in general, exhibits syntactic intransitivity.

Thus consider for example the contrast in Hungarian between (136a) and (136b):

(136)   a. Meg-mos-t-am   *mag*-am-at
           perf.-wash-past-1sg. *self*-my-acc.
           "I washed myself"
        b. Meg-mos-*akod*-t-am
           perf.-wash-*refl.*-past-1sg.
           "I washed"

In (136a) the reflexive object is a separate pronoun *mag(amat)*; in (136b) the reflexive morpheme is the suffix *-akod-*. Only (some permutation of) sentence (136a) is possible as a grammatical response to the question *Kit mostál meg?* "Whom did you wash?", or as the translation of "I washed *myself*": that is, in those cases where the object of the verb is in focus.

There is in addition a less striking semantic contrast between the reflexive pronoun and the reflexive affix in languages like Hungarian. Traditional descriptions to the contrary, I contend that

(137)   Reflexive pronouns tend to denote an entity conceived of as in some way
        distinct from the antecedent; reflexive affixes, like incorporated objects
        generally, do not refer, and do not denote such a distinct entity.

Principle (137), if true, will account for an otherwise puzzling distinction between independent and incorporated reflexives in languages where the two cooccur.

It is a truism that reflexive constructions in a large number of unrelated languages come to have a passive meaning. Langacker & Munro (1975:801) and Haiman (1976:34) have suggested that the semantic motivation for the formal identity of the passive and the reflexive constructions is that *in both constructions, subject and object are nondistinct*.

It is also notable, however, that in languages where both independent and incorporated reflexives are found, *only incorporated reflexives can express the passive voice*. The point is explicitly noted in Bhat (1978:26,35), with a variety of examples: we may add that Hungarian, Russian, and Turkish exemplify the same contrast. The construction *Verb+reflexive* may have passive force; the concurrent construction *Verb # Reflexive*, never. Given the traditional analysis of reflexives, this contrast is totally unexpected: by the traditional definition, subject and object are identical in all reflexive sentences. Either this analysis is wrong, or Langacker & Munro's explanation for the polysemy of the reflexive is wrong. In my opinion, Langacker & Munro are correct, and the traditional analysis of reflexive constructions needs to be superseded by something along the lines of principle (137). In general, the reinterpretation

Verb # Reflexive > Verb + passive

fails to occur because the independent reflexive does not (exactly) denote a referent identical with, or non-distinct from, the subject of the verb, or the antecedent in general.

I will try to demonstrate the correctness of (137) now, by showing how *Verb # Reflexive* constructions are used to describe *two-participant* activities: *Verb+reflexive* constructions, in contradistinction, are used to describe *one-participant* activities.

I contend that the two participants of a reflexive clause are interpreted as the mind and body, or perhaps as the two halves of the divided self, of the agent. Consider such a simple example as (138a) and compare it with the almost identical (138b).

(138)   a. Newton was proud of *himself*
         b. Newton was proud

There is a sense in which Newton stands outside himself in (138a): self-admiration implies alienation from the self to some extent. So too does any kind of self-awareness. In (138b) where the reflexive object is incorporated into the verb (to the point of disappearance), this self-awareness or alienation from the self is lacking.

Jespersen (1949:330) made the observation that "there is an element of volition or exertion in the reflexive form" (i.e. in sentences like (138a)) which is absent in the incorporated form (i.e. in sentences like (138b)). We may observe the contrast in sentences like those in (139).

(139)   a. He proved (himself) to be a brave soldier
         b. The rope snagged (itself) in the briars
         c. Superclusters don't seem to have enough gravitation to hold (them-
            selves) together

Jespersen argued that his element of volition explains why "it is impossible
to add the reflexive pronoun in cases . . . where the subject is not a living
person", citing (140), a sentence which contrasts minimally with (139a).

(140)   The assertion proved (*itself) to be true

Dwight Bolinger (who drew my attention to (139b) and (139c)) has pointed
out that Jespersen overstated his case, since both of these latter sentences
with their inanimate subjects are acceptable with the reflexive pronoun.
One could argue, however, that the presence of the reflexive pronoun has
the effect of imputing animacy to ropes and superclusters. The rope in
(139b) is personified when the reflexive pronoun is added: the speaker is
more likely to be *angry with* it than if he had omitted the reflexive. So it may
be that Jespersen's observation is basically correct. The significance of this
is that the use of the reflexive immediately suggests precisely the kind of
mind/body dualism in reflexive sentences which allows these to describe
two-participant events.

Similar semantic contrasts, considerably less subtle in many cases, exist
in other languages where a free reflexive contrasts with a bound (but not
null) reflexive affix. In Russian, the two morphemes are *sebja* and *-sja*.
(Russian is the only language we discuss in which the two morphemes are
actually cognate and thus lend direct support to Faltz' contention (1977)
that all bound reflexive affixes originate as free-standing words.) The verbal
affix *-sja* is no longer a true reflexive, but a derivational morpheme whose
Gesamtbedeutung is to signal the derived intransitivity of the preceding
verb (cf. Babby 1975). This is, of course, a characteristic result of
object-incorporation in general (cf. Mardirussian 1975).

There are a number of verb stems in Russian which allow either *sebja* or
-sja, among them *utixomirit'* "pacify", *utomit'* "exhaust", and *bit'* "hit".
When these are used as transitive verbs with reflexive pronoun objects, they
denote a mind-originated activity which affects the body of the agent.
When they are derived intransitive the verbs denote spontaneous (i.e.
unwilled, non-volitional) events. In other words, *Verb ǂ sebja* denotes a
two-participant event, while *Verb + sja* denotes one with only one prota-
gonist. Thus *bit' sebja* "hit oneself" contrasts with *bit' + sja* "bump into

(accidentally)"; *utomit' sebja* "exhaust oneself (on purpose)", with *utomit' + sja* "grow weary (spontaneously)"; *utixomirit' sebja* "(force oneself to) calm down", with *utixomirit' + sja* "settle down". In each case, the reflexive pronoun *sebja* denotes a second participant in the event, while the incorporated reflexive does not: a separate participant.

In Latin, Flobert (1975) and Baldi (1975) agree that the analytic *se* reflexive and the incorporated (deponent) reflexive are apparently interchangeable in a number of instances. Yet Flobert points out (387) that "on appelera 'reflexif' un verbe pronominal dont l'objet, en principe à l'accusatif et accessoirement à un autre cas est tonique et constitue une détermination commutable avec n'importe quelle autre et cumulable, e.g. sē atque aliōs alunt. Le procès reflète *une volonté délibérée de soi sur soi*; le reflexif est donc *dualiste*" (my emphasis).

In the same vein, Flobert adds that the analytic *se* passive/reflexive (as opposed to the deponent in *-r*) is motivated by "un souci de personnification ou plus précisément d'animisation" (389). In other words, there is a parallel between Latin reflexives in *se* and English sentences like (139b,c), where the use of the reflexive pronoun imputes animacy to the subject of the sentence.

In Hungarian the morphological contrast is between the reflexive pronoun *mag* (literally, "seed") and the reflexive/intransitive suffix *-kod-*, *-koz-*. The semantic contrast between *üti mag-át* "3sg. hits 3sg. + self" and *üt=köz-ik* "3sg. bumps into" is exactly parallel to the contrast between the Russian *bit' sebja* and *bit' + sja*: the subject is purposely mortifying himself in the first case, and the victim of an accident in the second.

In Turkish, the contrasting morphemes are the reflexive pronoun *kendi* "self" and the reflexive suffix *-In-*. Like Hungarian, Turkish has very few words which allow both expressions, but these few contrast in the predicted fashion. *Kendini bürüdü* "3sg. dressed (3sg.'s body) in mourning" contrasts with *bürü-n-dü* "3sg. was in mourning", the latter denoting a psychological state rather than an action performed on one's body; *kendini dövdü* "3sg. hit 3sg.'s self" contrasts with *döv-ün-dü* "3sg. felt guilty". The former describes a two-participant event, the latter a state with a single experiencer.

While all of these examples show that the reflexive word, unlike the reflexive affix, denotes an entity distinct from the subject of the verb, the question might arise whether morphemes such as English $\emptyset$, Russian *-sja*, Latin *-r*, Hungarian *-kod-*, or Turkish *-In-* are properly identified as reflexive morphemes at all, rather than simply as markers of derived intransitivity. The latter identification would account for the fact that these bound morphemes do not refer. It is true that they do not: but in this respect, they behave in exactly the same way as bound or incorporated objects do in general, cf. Mardirussian (1975).

The main reason, however, that all the incorporated affixes are identified as reflexive is that they are used with reflexive meaning. The fact that they do not refer is precisely what calls for an explanation, as does the fact that incorporated reflexive morphemes so often come to acquire passive force and the more general meaning of "derived intransitivity".

A common explanation for this fact is "valence reduction": where the subject and object of a verb are identical, as they are in a reflexive construction, the number of distinct arguments associated with the verb is only *one*, and thus a reflexive verb is like an intransitive. This explanation makes no distinction, however, between *Verb # Reflexive* and *Verb + reflexive* constructions: valence should be equally reduced in both constructions. And yet the fact remains that only the latter construction is reinterpreted as a passive or intransitive form. For this fact, only (137) provides a possible explanation. The truth of (137), in turn, provides evidence for the correction of the motivation hypothesis: the lexical independence of a word reflects the conceptual independence of the entity that it represents.

2.3 Some further uses of morphological bulk

Sections 2.1 and 2.2 have shown how the interposition of material between morphemes may reflect conceptual distance between their denotata. Another incidental difference among the rungs on the hierarchy in (88) is that the morphological bulk of the entire message diminishes as we go down from the first rung (X#A#B#Y) to the last (Z). Given the limitations of the medium of spoken language, it is not surprising that this contrast, incidental to the examples we have already discussed, should be used to signal yet other conceptual contrasts.

In this section I will very briefly discuss two that are very well known: the iconic expression of conceptual complexity, and the iconic expression of social distance through euphemisms and gobbledygook.

2.3.1 The iconic expression of "complexity"
"Formal complexity corresponds to conceptual complexity." A somewhat more familiar but not entirely equivalent expression of this relationship is that morphological markedness corresponds to semantic markedness. If

both statements were true, and equivalent, then this would be another clear example of the iconic usage of morphological bulk. It is clear, however, that they are not.

Morphological complexity and morphological markedness are the same: the morphologically marked exponent of a categorial opposition is the one which has the extra morpheme(s). Semantic complexity and semantic markedness, on the other hand, are *not* identical. It is true that a concept (and the corresponding form) may be marked because it is relatively complex: most compounds exemplify this relationship, e.g. *room, bedroom, master bedroom*. On the other hand, it is also true that a concept may be marked because it is relatively unfamiliar or infrequent, and, conversely, a concept may be unmarked because it is relatively familiar. The morphological distinction between *mare* and *female hippo* does not correspond to a difference in relative complexity, but to a difference in familiarity, as grammarians since at least the time of Varro have noted.

As factors which motivate morphological reduction, frequency and conceptual simplicity intersect so often that it is difficult to factor out and keep distinct purely *semantic* complexity from *pragmatic* infrequency. As a case in point, consider the classically unmarked third person singular form, which seems, in almost every language but English, to be morphologically unmarked. The iconic motivation for this, it is generally agreed, is perfectly straightforward: the "non-person" (relative to the speech act) is represented by the non-desinence. Yet even here, non-expression of the person may be discourse conditioned. There are cases in colloquial English, for example, where the *first* person is unmarked (e.g. *Gone fishin'*), and others where the second person is unmarked (e.g. *Been fishin'?*) (John Lyons, pc.), and the same may hold for other standard "unmarked" categories as well.

The best evidence for the inseparability of semantic and pragmatic markedness is the phenomenon characterized by Andersen (1972) as "markedness assimilation" and by others since then as "local markedness". In Andersen's view, semantic markedness is at least in part a relationship between a form and its (purely linguistic, biological, or cultural) context, rather than simply a property of the form in itself, cf. Shapiro (1983:92–4).

For a simple example, consider the contrast *singular/plural*. Morphologically, the plural is nearly always marked, and once again the semantic motivation is apparently straightforward: "more is more". Nevertheless, there are some objects which *we* typically think of primarily as occurring in groups: and for these objects, the plural may well be the unmarked form.

Noss (1979:176–7) presents some intriguing data from Fula, an African pidgin language in which the singular/plural distinction of Fulani has been suppressed for all nouns in favor of a single invariant form. Since in effect Fula is neutralizing the contrast singular/plural, and since it is the unmarked form which appears in positions of neutralization, we might expect that the invariant Fula form derives in all cases from the singular Fulani form. And yet, as Noss has shown, this is not the case. Given in Table 3 are some singular/plural paradigms for Fulani common nouns: the italicized form represents the form which has been borrowed into Fula as the invariant form.

Table 3

Singular	Plural	Gloss
hoore	koʔe	"head"
horre	*koode*	"star"
yiitere	*gite*	"eye"
gertogel	gertoâe	"rooster"

We think of heads and roosters primarily as individuals, but of stars and eyes primarily as groups. For some more examples of such "local markedness", cf. Tiersma (1982).

Witkowski and Brown (1983) review some cases of markedness shift or "markedness reversal" in effect keeping pace with cultural developments in a variety of languages. One example will serve for many.

In Tenejapa Tzeltal, a Mayan language spoken in the Mexican state of Chiapas, one reversal has involved the relative cultural importance of native deer and introduced sheep . . . [A]t the time of the Spanish conquest, deer were designated *cih*. When sheep were introduced, they were equated with deer and were labelled *tunim cih* "cotton deer" (in this expression *tunim* "cotton" is the overt mark). Today, however, the Tenejapa term for sheep is *cih* while deer are labelled by the overtly marked expression *teʔtikil cih* "wild sheep". (Witkowski and Brown 1983:571)

Similar are cases where *guns* are first designated as "iron bows", and then become the unmarked weapon through cultural contact, so that *bows*, a cultural oddity, come to be designated as "wooden guns" and the like.

All of these cases are familiar as examples of what may be called the "iron horse" phenomenon. Languages tend to have complex periphrastic means of expressing notions that are unfamiliar. Downing and Fuller (1984) present some beautiful examples from Hmong which speak for themselves (see Table 4).

Table 4

Hmong form						English equivalent
daim	ntaub	npog	xwb	pwg		"shawl"
classifier	cloth	cover	only	shoulder		
daim	ntawv	qhia	kev	roob	hav	"map"
classifier	paper	tell	way	mountain	valley	
daim	ntauw	hla	ciam	teb		"passport"
classifier	paper	cross	boundary	country		

It is therefore clear from even the briefest consideration, I feel, that morphological complexity is not only an iconic measure of semantic complexity, but an economically motivated measure of pragmatic familiarity. Reduced form (and the concomitant morphological opacity that is almost always associated with it, cf. Frei 1929:111–13) is economically motivated in the sense made famous by Zipf (1935): there is a powerful tendency in languages, no less than in other diagrams, to give reduced expression to the familiar and predictable. We return to this correlation, one of the most well-attested in human language, in chapter 3 below.

But there is also another factor which perturbs the simple and idealized iconic relationship between morphological and semantic markedness. That is the tendency of the unmarked form to come to assume what Greenberg (1966a) has called its "par excellence" meaning: that meaning which *only* the unmarked form can have.

Ideally, the morphological contrast $A + \emptyset$ vs. $A + "X"$ does not correspond to "A without xx" and "A with x". Rather, as Jakobson and others have insisted, the form $A + \emptyset$ can mean, indifferently, either "A with x" or "A without x". Thus, theoretically, unmarked words like *cow* can mean either "male cattle" or "female cattle", unmarked categories like the *singular* can denote either "singular" or "plural", and so on. In fact, however, the situation is always complicated by the tendency for the unmarked term to be associated chiefly with the one meaning for which no other term is available. Once this has occurred, the morphological contrast $\emptyset : x$ corresponds to the semantic contrast *"minus x": "plus x"*: no longer then is it possible to say that "more is more". Instead, "more" is simply "different". A classic and familiar example of this tendency is the development of the *stative/active* opposition in Indo-European languages.

Originally, *stative* was "active" or "passive", while *active* was only "active". Recurrently and independently, *stative* morphology has become specialized in Indo-European for the expression of the passive voice (cf. Kuryłowicz 1964: chapter 2).

It is worth noting, incidentally, that in the opposition *stative/active*, it is *stative* which is marked: and that one of the indices which operationally defines markedness – greater syncretism – is indistinguishable from one of the indices which operationally defines unmarkedness – greater range of possible meanings. The tendency for an ambiguous form to acquire as its principal meaning its "par excellence" meaning, however, is the same whether the original ambiguity is attributable to syncretism or to lack of specificity.

And this tendency results, in either case, in an erosion of the iconicity of morphological marking. Consequently, we cannot maintain that formal complexity corresponds to conceptual complexity. A tendency for such a correspondence does exist, and may even be said to be pervasive: but it is complicated and weakened by at least the two other tendencies briefly presented here.

2.3.2 Social distance

In his oft-anthologized discussion of linguistic etiquette in Javanese, Clifford Geertz (1960:250) drew attention to a probably universal speech phenomenon: the use of different registers for saying the same things to different people under different circumstances. The "non-linguistic" or conceptual dimension along which distinctions are made is usually identified as that of *politeness* or *familiarity*, and this dimension corresponds almost universally, it would seem, with the "linguistic" or formal dimension of *length* in accordance with principle (141).

(141)   The more polite the register, the longer the message

A reader totally ignorant of Javanese, but able to count syllables, will be able to use principle (141) to sort out the five versions of the sentence "Are you going to eat rice and cassava now?" from the most polite to the most familiar, as given in (142).

(142)					
	a. Menapa	pandjenengan	badé	ḍahar	sekul kalijan
	b. Menapa	sampéjan	badé	neḍa	sekul kalijan
	c. Napa	sampéjan	adjeng	neḍa	sekul lan
	d. Apa	sampéjan	arep	neḍa	sega lan
	e. Apa	kowé	arep	mangan	sega lan
	are	you	going	to=eat	rice and

a.	kaspé	samenika?	(22 syllables)
b.	kaspé	samenika?	(21 syllables)
c.	kaspé	saniki?	(17 syllables)
d.	kaspé	saiki?	(16 syllables)
e.	kaspé	saiki?	(15 syllables)
	cassava	now	

All of the sentences of (142) could be spoken by urbanized, somewhat educated persons. According to Geertz, peasant dialects include only c, d, and e, the relative politeness of which is the same as for urban dwellers.

The same kinds of correlations are attested in other languages, albeit in comparatively wan, attenuated forms. Stevens (1965) demonstrates essentially the same kind of contrasts, compatible with (141), in the closely related language Madurese.

Samuel Martin (1964), and Roy Miller (1967:283) draw attention to a survey-finding in Japanese, that "the longer an utterance, the more polite it is felt to be". Miller points out that in Japanese, respect for the *addressee* is grammaticalized somewhat differently from respect for the *referent*, but that the relationship between the length of the message and the degree of honor accorded to the addressee or referent is once again compatible with (141) (ibid. 270, 271).

Miller identifies three different points along the "axis of address" which are grammaticalized in affixes on the verb and expressions of the copula, as shown in Table 5. He identifies five different points along the axis of reference which are grammaticalized in the same categories, as shown in Table 6. The choice of form, not only in these categories but in others, is determined by extremely delicate considerations. (Miller notes that "it is clearly possible to say the same thing in Japanese in a virtually unlimited number of ways" (ibid. 290).)

Classical Nahuatl (Hill & Hill 1978) is another language which grammaticalizes etiquette to a remarkable degree. There are four different levels of address, the first three ranging from familiar to polite, and the fourth a register employed between "compadres". The relationship between compadres is characterized on the one hand by enforced intimacy, on the other by extreme competitiveness and presumably hostility. As predicted by our hypothesis, the morphological complexity/prolixity of a message increases as we proceed from the most familar to the most polite register. The fourth register, used by compadres, is, like the relationship for

Table 5

	Plain	Deferential	Polite
Verbs	-(r)u	—	-(i)masu
Copula	da	—	desu
Formal copula	de aru	de gozaimasu	de arimasu

Table 6

	Humble	Neutral	Respectful	Elegant	Exalted
Verbs	o-suru	-(r)u	-(r)areru	o- -ni naru	o- -asobasu
Copula	—	da	—	de irassharu	—

which it is employed, ambivalent: in terms of length of expressions, it seems to be "hors de série".

Haviland (1979a) notes that the "taboo language" corresponding to everyday Guugu-Yimidhirr in Australia is another highly marked formal language whose raison d'être seems to be the avoidance of "verbal assault" on respected *alters*. The language is characterized by its users as "sideways" or "crosswise" talk (ibid. 369), its lexicon the moral equivalent of speaking "softly and slowly", and the language as a whole the verbal equivalent to the physical gesture of "turning away". The fact that the taboo language evinces a particular richness of terms for body parts (ibid. 392) further suggests that its function is in part euphemistic. Haviland does not, in this valuable study, provide comparative wordlists of the taboo language and the everyday language. But in each of the examples he provides, the taboo language word is of the same number of syllables as, or more than, its everyday language equivalent:

(143) a. *Everyday language* Ngayu mayi   buda-nhu
       b. *Taboo language*   Ngayu gudhubay bambanga-nhu
                             I   food   eat-purposive
                             "I want to eat"

We need not look so very far afield to find the same principle at work: baroque embellishment is a characteristic of higher, more formal, polite register, in all languages which make the familiar *tu/vous* distinction.

The polite form of address is distinct from the familiar form in one universal way: whereas the familiar form of address identifies the addressee as what s/he is, namely 2sg., the polite form of address identifies him/her as *something else*. This alone is sufficient to identify the *vous* (V) form as one of "embellishment". But there is a more direct motivation for the actually occurring V forms than the overarching fact that they are lies.

The 2sg. is rendered in polite speech either as a *third person* (thus Italian, Hungarian), or a *plural* (thus French, Turkish), or as both third person and plural (thus German). No other choices are attested. The motivation for these forms is suggested in Brown & Gilman's classic article on the usage of these pronouns (1960): the polite forms are used towards *alters* who are *powerful*, and from whom the speaker is socially *distant*. The *plural* form is an icon of power; the *third person* form, whereby the addressee is treated as absent, is an icon of distance.

It is noteworthy that one could as easily signal exceptional closeness by another kind of motivated "lie": while the distant addressee could be called by his own appropriate term of address, that is, 2sg., the intimate term of address, signaling exceptional closeness, could be *first person*. As far as I know this logically possible option is never exercised in any language. "Plain speech" is everywhere associated with low registers, embellishment and distortion with higher ones.

We may witness the same contrast between "four letter words" and their corresponding euphemisms in English. The terms of the lower register are invariably short: the euphemisms invariably longer. To say that the euphemisms are borrowed from a higher register begs the question why higher registers would be more prolix than lower ones. To the extent that the correspondence between form and extra-linguistic context is as predicted in (141), the form is motivated. Is it also iconic? Does the length of the message correspond to some other kind of *length*? Does the embellishment and distortion of the message correspond to some other kind of embellishment and distortion?

It seems to me that both length and euphemisms serve a common purpose of obfuscation of the message, to the point where (in theory) it is virtually unintelligible. The addressee is consequently protected from the contents of the message from a social inferior. In the same way, s/he is protected from other non-verbal emanations of the social inferior by physical distance.

Now, physical distance can be simply interpreted as an icon of social distance. But, as such an icon, it serves not only a referential, but also an instrumental, function. In maintaining a physical distance, two actors are not only signaling a lack of intimacy, but *preserving* it. The maintenance of physical distance is a kind of homeopathic magic, an activity which creates what it depicts. I would suggest that the obfuscation of the message is an example of the same kind of homeopathic magic: it is not only an icon of a social relationship, but a guarantor of it as well. The social relationship is the same as the one which is signaled physically by spatial distance and other gestures of respect and protection.

Gobbledygook is an icon, pure and simple, of non-linguistic formal behavior. Like formal behavior in general, it aims at artifice and convention in the avoidance of unpleasant truths, and is reserved for *alters* who "deserve" protection from them.

PART II
ECONOMY AND THE EROSION OF ICONICITY

In a diagram, and in a language, iconicity may be impaired by requirements of economy. In a diagram, and in a language, iconicity may be impaired by the use of diacritics (although the diacritics as a system may manifest some iconicity within the system of which they are a part), and the use of these diacritics is also, in the final analysis, motivated by requirements of economy. Finally, in a diagram, and in a language, iconicity may be impaired by the inherent limitations of the medium: for example mapping a conceptual space of three dimensions on to a medium of only two results in the familiar distortions of a map; similarly, mapping a conceptual space of indefinitely many dimensions on to the medium of language will result in far more extensive distortions. Ultimately this kind of limitation may also be said to be economically motivated, the simplicity and manipulability of a diagram (as opposed to the conceptions of which it tells) being one of its greatest values.

Chapter 3 enumerates some of the familiar kinds of distortion and opacity that are introduced by the drift from analysis to agglutination, and from agglutination to synthesis in languages. This is a well-trodden area of linguistics, cf. the classic discussions in Meillet 1958 (1912), Saussure 1969 (1916), Frei 1929, Havers 1931, Zipf 1935, or Meinhof 1936. It has been rediscovered by creolists (see the contributions in Hancock 1979) and students of other linguistic systems which have evolved rapidly from a relatively iconic to a somewhat more opaque structure, notably sign language (cf. Frishberg 1975, Klima and Bellugi 1979) and child language (cf. Slobin 1980, to appear). Although I may use some unfamiliar examples, my discussion of these kinds of changes will be entirely derivative and uncontroversial.

As stated most forcefully by Meillet, economically motivated abbreviations lead to allomorphy, allotaxy, redundancy, and opacity. Economy in languages, no less than in other diagrams, is opposed to iconicity, and contributes to its erosion.

Chapter 4 deals with a specific case of *competing motivations* for a single form in languages: gerundive expressions which are expressed by *-ing* clauses in English, and their analogs elsewhere. The essential motivation for the reduced form of these clauses, I shall argue, is economic: what is not expressed in these "small clauses" (Williams 1975) is that which is identical with what is expressed elsewhere. But the reduced form of gerundive clauses is also compatible with another, iconic, motivation: what is of reduced importance is given reduced expression. The "competition" between iconic and economic motivations for the same syntactic or morphological structures can be illustrated with other examples. The specific example that I discuss here should be seen as representing the same phenomenon of "association" already discussed in the closing pages of chapter 1.

Chapter 5 presents evidence for the contention that there is an inverse correlation between the lexicon (= the diacritics) and the grammar (= the diagrams) of a language: the greater the lexicon, the greater the opacity; the smaller the lexicon, the greater the transparency and iconicity of the linguistic (sub)system. The point is illustrated with particular reference to subsystems of a language with a specialized technical or arcane vocabulary, and artificial languages with reduced vocabularies.

Chapter 6 deals finally with cases of competing iconic motivations, which lead inevitably to apparent arbitrariness, and which in turn are an inevitable result of the limitations of the medium of spoken language.

Before proceeding, we should make it clear that we have used the word *economy* in two sharply distinct senses: paradigmatic and syntagmatic. Paradigmatic economy, discussed in chapter 1, economizes on the inventory of signs within a system. It underlies Bréal's principles of specialization and repartition, and allows us to account for the asymmetry between synonymy and homonymy in human languages. This kind of economy is more than compatible with iconicity, and is explicitly identified with the tendency to establish isomorphism between form and meaning, or *invariability*, by Frei (1929:33). Economizing on lexical inventory preserves isomorphism inasmuch as no two distinct forms will have the same communicative function. The same economy also contributes to motivation (as we shall see in chapter 5) inasmuch as the circumlocutions, periphrases, and definitions in languages of a relatively reduced vocabulary are invariably more perspicuous than the words they paraphrase in a lexically elaborated register.

Throughout the latter half of this book, however, we shall be discussing syntagmatic or discourse economy: the tendency to economize on the length or complexity of any utterance or message. This tendency towards brevity, again as recognized by Frei (1929), is directly opposed to transparency and invariability. There is a widely acknowledged trade-off between the length of a message, and the inventory of signs which are available for its expression: definitions are longer than the terms they define. Morse code with two symbols is less compact than standard English orthography with twenty-six, and so on. How pervasive and far-reaching is this trade-off, the next four chapters of this study can only begin to show.

3 Economic motivation

In this chapter, I will be contrasting pidgins and child languages (recently identified by some researchers as having "universal grammar") with the more familiar languages into which they ultimately develop. As is well known, the development is always in the direction of opacity, and its motivation is always (at least in part) economic.

3.1 The iconicity of "universal grammar"

Saussure (1969 (1916):183) proposed a possible typology of languages along the dimension of *motivation*, where motivation was exemplified by transparent compounds like the Latin *in-imicus* "not-friend", and its opposite, opacity, by the monolexemic French (or English) translations "ennemi" or "enemy", I will return (p. 166) to Saussure's reasons for mistakenly identifying the contrast *motivated/opaque* with the familiar distinction *agglutinating/isolating* in a while. For the moment, I want to draw attention to the self-evident fact that

(1)   Iconicity (or motivation) will be relatively high in pidgins.

since the users of a pidgin, by definition, will have no shared conventions of interpretation.

Irrespective of their lexical origins, pidgin languages manifest a number of shared properties which can in no way be construed as evidence either of a common origin, or of innate "hardwired" properties: see Koefoed 1979 for a convincing dismissal of both monogenesis (as argued by, among others, Keith Whinnom 1971) and innateness (as argued most recently by Bickerton 1981). Among these shared properties are

(2)   a. a sharp reduction of allomorphy,
        b. the loss of grammatical agreement,
        c. parity between morphological and semantic marking,
        d. a sharp reduction of the basic vocabulary.

Each of these may be considered, consistently with the definitions developed so far, as a step towards the heightening of iconicity. Let us examine each in turn.

a. Sharp reduction of allomorphy
Of all the properties of pidgins, this seems to have received the most attention. By allomorphy, I mean two things that are frequently treated as separate in traditional grammars: the existence of phonetically conditioned alternations, like the plural /s/ ~ /z/ in English, and the existence of morphological classes like declensions or conjugations. The first arises transparently as the consequence of sandhi, and a single "underlying" form may be posited for the alternating forms. The second, it would seem, does not.

Yet, allomorphy of both types can only arise in general as the consequence of agglutination and synthesis. And allomorphy of both types is equally avoided in analytic and isolating languages such as Chinese and Vietnamese.

Pidgin languages in general are, like Chinese and Vietnamese, strongly analytic languages in which, as Naro (1973:58) has correctly emphasized, "each separately intuited element of meaning [is associated with] at least one phonologically separate invariant stress-bearing form". Givón (1979a:23–4) also comments on the relative absence of bound morphemes in pidgins, and the absence of inflections, which entail the consequence that there will be a one-to-one correspondence between meaning and form in these languages, with no ambiguity or homophony or morphophonemic variations.

Perhaps the most widespread example of this kind of shift from the agglutinative to the analytic type is the representation of personal pronouns. In the target language, pronouns may have features of gender, number, and case, and may appear as bound morphemes. In pidgins generally, pronouns are always free-standing *words* (commonly derived from topicalized forms in the target languages), and manifest no inflectional categories.

New Guinea Pidgin, derived from English, reduces the impoverished inflectional system of English pronouns even further: the allomorphy *he/him*, *I/me*, etc. disappears, as the 3sg. becomes invariable *em*, the 1sg. invariable *mi*, the 1pl. invariable *yumi* (inclusive) or *mipela* (exclusive), the 3pl. invariable *ol*. Similar is the fate of the pronouns in Kenya Swahili from standard Swahili (Hinnebusch 1979:220–1, Heine 1979:94–5, Scotton

1979:115). Bound subject and object pronominal affixes on the verb give way to independent invariable pronouns in a rigid SVO order, where the order of constituents alone determines their grammatical function (see also Goodman 1964 for French creole; Naro 1973 for West African pidgin; Heine 1979:94 for Fanagalo (from Zulu)).

A concomitant change, to a fixed and invariable word order, may be interpreted, and named, a tendency towards the avoidance of *allotaxy*: different word orders for the expression of the same grammatical relationships. A number of natural languages have SVO word order when the O is a full noun, but SOV word order when the O is a pronoun. The fact that pidgins derive their pronouns in general from stressed topicalized pronouns in the target language means that pronouns thus exhibit the same word order as full noun phrases, and we encounter SVO consistently. Compare standard Swahili in (3) with Kenya Pidgin Swahili in (4).

(3)   Ni-ta-m-piga
        I-will-him-hit   (SOV word order)
        "I will hit him"
(4)   Mimi ta-piga yeye
        I   will-hit 3sg.   (SVO word order)
        "I will hit him"

Givón (1979a) has argued that SVO word order is the most common order for pidgins because it is the easiest to process (subject precedes object, a relationship which, as Greenberg (1966) has pointed out, is nearly universal, presumably because it is motivated, and subject is separated from object, thus reducing the possibility of confusion between the two even further). For our present purposes, it is enough to note that the word order is *invariable*, in the same way that the analytic structure makes the morphology of the pronouns invariable. The tendency in each case is to a greater isomorphism between form and meaning.

Noun class systems and the systems of verbal concord to which they frequently give rise are notoriously dysfunctional. So too are conjugation categories. Generally, there is very little semantic homogeneity to the members of a noun class system, and none at all to the members of a verbal conjugation. The phenomenon of grammatical agreement seems a clear case of the victory of the indexical aspect of language over its iconic aspect inasmuch as categories such as *number* and *case*, properly associated with nouns, are copied onto verbs and adjectives. Not surprisingly, there is a sharp reduction, in many cases a complete disappearance, of all of these features in pidgin languages.

Again, New Guinea Pidgin (hereafter, NG Pidgin) may offer a simple example: English has a rudimentary gender system (*he/she/it*) which disappears in NG Pidgin: the 3sg. pronoun, irrespective of natural or grammatical gender, is *em*. Swahili has 15 noun classes; Kenya Pidgin Swahili, only 6 (Heine, ibid.). Agreement in English is rudimentary: 3sg. *sits*/other persons and numbers *sit*; in NG Pidgin, this rudimentary agreement is abandoned (though it has been replaced, in the present language, by another kind of "agreement", the irregular distribution of the predicate marker *i*): *mi sindaun* "I sit down", *em i sindaun* "3sg. sits down". In pidgins generally, all agreement is lost. Compare standard Swahili (5)

(5)   Juma a-li-leta   vi-kombe vi-wili jana
        Juma 3sg.-past-bring pl.-cup   pl.-two yesterday

(in which the adjective agrees with the noun *cup* for number) with the Kenya Pidgin

(6)   Juma na-leta   kikombe mbili jana
        Juma aorist-bring cup   two   yesterday
        "Juma brought two cups yesterday"

in which the redundant expression of both noun class and plurality is eliminated in the invariant forms. That noun classes create great allomorphy is evident from a consideration of Swahili forms such as

(7)   baridi byi-ngi "very   cold"
        maji   me-ngi "much water"
        watu   we-ngi "many people"

in which the same morpheme of quantity *-ngi* occurs with a variety of personal prefixes which agree with different noun classes. This "synonymie inutile et dangéreuse" is eliminated in the Upcountry Pidgin of Nairobi and Kampala (Scotton 1979:116) in which the most common classifier *mi-* has been reinterpreted as part of a new, invariable, lexeme *mingi*, as in (8).

(8)   baridi mingi
        maji   mingi
        watu   mingi

Verbal paradigms are in general simply reduced to a single invariant form. In Fula, the verb shows variation in number: *wari* "3sg. came", *ngari* "3pl. came"; *laari* "3sg. saw", *ndaari* "3pl. saw". In the derivative Cameroun trade language, Bilkiire, a single verbal form is used throughout the paradigm: *wari* "came", *laari* "saw" (Noss 1979:176–7). There is a strong tendency to express those categories which are expressed by bound morphemes in the target language, either through invariable free-standing words, or not at all. Thus, the categories of tense and mood are frequently left completely unspecified or, if they are expressed at all, are rendered by invariable adverbs (cf. Koefoed 1979: 48–9). Gender (in the sense of natural gender) is either eliminated, or expressed by means of separate words like "man" and "woman": NG Pidgin *pikinini man* "male child, boy", *pikinini meri* "female child, girl". Number is expressed also (facultatively) by a separate word: NG Pidgin *man* "man", *ol man* "men"; Bilkiire substitutes for the singular and plural noun classifiers of Fula, the separate quantifiers *duudum* "much", and *duudi* "many", which again are invariable (Noss 1979:177).

The category of negation in Swahili is a typical example of one which is so basic that it must be expressed. The allomorphy of this morpheme is considerable in the standard language. Duran (1979) points out at least three different forms, given in (9).

(9)　　a. Si-mu-on-i
　　　　　I-him=neg.-see-neg.
　　　　　"I don't see him"
　　　　b. Si-ja-mu　　　　　on-a
　　　　　I-not=yet-him=neg see
　　　　　"I have not seen him yet"
　　　　c. U-si-je
　　　　　you-neg.-come=imp.
　　　　　"Don't come!"

In the Pidgin Swahili of West-Central Kenya, all kinds of negation are expressed by the single invariable word *hapana*:

(10)　　a. Mimi hapana one yeye
　　　　　1sg.　neg.　see 3sg.
　　　　b. Hapana kuja
　　　　　neg.　　come=imp.

Cf. Scotton (1979:117) for similar observations on Nairobi and Kampala varieties of Swahili.

b. Loss of grammatical agreement

Grammatical agreement is redundant: not only non-iconic, but meaningless.[1] Rather than have one meaning represent one form, we find one

---

[1] I argue here that the elimination of agreement marking is motivated in part by a tendency to maximize iconicity (inasmuch as agreement markers are both redundant and, as bound morphemes, subject to allomorphic variation). There is also a sense, noted by Sturtevant

meaning represented in several forms at once, signaled again and again. The result is a violation not only of motivation (since categories which are not truly associated with one part of speech are represented on it), but of isomorphism (since there is no one-to-one correspondence between a form and a meaning). Pidgins seem to strip themselves spontaneously of this kind of luxury. In a pidgin, every morph pays its way with a contribution to the total content of the message. For this reason, we find not only a loss of concord markers and agreement, but also a loss of purely grammatical categories and distinctions such as grammatical gender.

Copula verbs, which function basically only to mark tense, and to distinguish stative from non-stative predicates, are typically lost in both pidgins and child language. The copula in English is a morphological luxury for this otherwise austere, nearly analytical language, with an agreement system, at least for English, of unparalleled richness. In NG Pidgin, it is eliminated: *mi stap* "I stay" or "I am", vs. *mi hangri* "I am hungry". The difference between stative and active predicates is a function of their lexical meanings, and there is no need to indicate it redundantly. Another function of the copula, to indicate tense with adjectival or nominal predicates which cannot mark this category themselves, is also rendered unnecessary by the generally facultative and analytic mode of expression for the categories of tense, aspect, and mood. Relatively fine-grained categorial distinctions like that between adjectives and adverbs of manner also go by the board.

It may be said that pidgins offer only one means of packaging redundancy: massive and wholesale repetition of the entire message. Although it is extensively employed, repetition is still facultative and stylistic rather than obligatory (and grammatical).

c. Parity between morphological and semantic marking

Subject to the considerable limitations noted in 2.3.1, there is a rough parity between morphological and semantic marking. But there are languages in which this parity is even messier than usual. The Bantu languages in particular, in which singular and plural markings are frequently equipollent, offer a perfect example. In Zulu, for example, the semantic opposition

(1917:166, 175), among others, in which this kind of elimination is *economical*. That is, analytical languages are more economical in terms of the number of syllables required to communicate a given message, because they avoid redundant repetition. But, this kind of "economizing" is only possible if each morpheme is heard with total clarity. Frequent repetition results – by economy – in the diminution and decay of each morpheme, and this diminution, in its turn, results in a demand for redundancy.

singular/plural is rendered by a morphological contrast $x + root/y + root$ where x and y are of strictly comparable complexity: $um + sila$ "tail", vs. $imi + sila$ "tails". In the derivative trade language Fanagalo, this discrepancy between morphological and semantic marking has been "corrected": *msila* "tail", *zi-msila* "tails". The structure $sg. + root$ has been reinterpreted as a new root, to which a new, invariable plural prefix has been added (Heine 1979:93).

d. Reduction in vocabulary

As a direct consequence of their impoverished vocabulary, pidgin languages exhibit a high degree of motivation and transparency in compounding. For example, such semantically related but phonologically diverse words as agriculture, law, accounting, business, architecture, medicine, and the like are all rendered in NG Pidgin as compounds of *wok* "work": *wok gaden*, *wok dokta*, etc. (cf. Mühlhäusler et al. 1979:273).

Taboo languages with sharply restricted vocabularies but identical grammars to the everyday standard also furnish numerous examples. Such languages are known in Australia (cf. Dixon 1971, 1977; Haviland 1979), and demonstrate the same iconic compounding as we find in pidgins. There seems to be an inverse correlation between the lexical expansion of a language and the iconicity of its grammar, a correlation which was noted by Saussure in his *Cours* (1969:183), but, I believe, misinterpreted by him.

For Saussure, opacity was highest in a "lexical" language, motivation highest in a "grammatical" language. Saussure and I differ in our interpretation of the terms "lexical" and "grammatical". For me, "lexical" means "having a large stock of primary roots", while "grammatical" means having a relative small stock of such roots and making up the deficit in periphrastic constructions. Thus, most established languages are relatively "lexical", while pidgins, argots, trade languages, child language, and imperfectly known second languages are more "grammatical". For Saussure, "lexical" seems to have been synonymous with isolating/analytic: thus, Chinese is the lexical language par excellence. "Grammatical" was synonymous with agglutinative/synthetic: a particularly good example of a grammatical language was therefore Sanskrit.

My own impression is that Saussure confused here two independent properties of maximally iconic languages: their lexical impoverishment, and their isolating structure. Pidgins have both properties: lexical impoverishment leading to greater isomorphism. Established analytic languages like Chinese and Vietnamese, on the other hand, have only the property of *greater isomorphism*: there is no evidence that the basic vocabulary of these languages is either larger or smaller than that of other languages. But to the extent that analytic languages exhibit greater isomorphism, they are *more iconic*, less arbitrary, and therefore presumably *more grammatical*, than synthetic languages like Sanskrit. (This question is complicated, in any case, by the fact that *once a form is learned*, its iconicity or motivation may no longer be perceived by its users, and is thus irrelevant. Undoubtedly the absence of conscious motivation is one of the factors which permits sound change to obfuscate the morphology of most compounds.)

An often noted fact about the development of pidgins into creoles, and, ultimately, into "established" languages, is that all of these iconic features are eventually lost. Independent words become grammaticalized, and begin to exhibit allomorphy (cf., for example, Sankoff & Laberge 1974); reduced forms are reenforced by independent words, in effect creating agreement systems (cf. Meinhof 1936, Givón 1979); reduced forms become "crystallized" and obligatory, assuming inconsistent or "figurative" meanings (cf. Zipf 1935); and the lexical resources of the language expand, destroying the clumsy but motivated compounds and periphrastic expressions of the lexically impoverished pidgin.

Why should these changes occur? I wish to suggest (following Zipf 1935) that the common factor in all of these changes is primarily a tendency to economize effort. "High frequency", Zipf observes (1935:29) "is the cause of small magnitude". Bound morphemes (whence allomorphy and agreement systems) arise from frequently occurring collocations of independent words; and lexical expansion is motivated by the same desire to give reduced expression for common concepts.

A further covariation, between brevity and opacity, is easily demonstrated, as we shall see, in the so-called "technical" vocabulary or jargon of any specialized group. The fundamental principle was enunciated, once again, by Zipf:

The more articulated [or motivated; or iconic (JMH)] we find a given configuration, the less integrated do we suppose the configuration to be in the collective experience of the group; and conversely (ibid. 273).

The point was well demonstrated by Zipf in his extended comparison of the kin "terms" "mother" and "uncle's second wife's tenth child". The concept of "mother" is far from simple; and "the only reason we do not have an equally simple word for one's uncle's second wife's tenth child is because the concept does not possess a significantly high frequency of occurrence" (ibid. 235).

This is also attested by notorious clichés like the several dozen Eskimo words for "snow" (a locus classicus is Sturtevant 1917:104–5). We also have them in English: we talk, on the rare occasions where we have to, about "packing snow", "powder snow", "wet snow", and so on, maintaining compounding and motivation for concepts which are not terribly significant in our everyday lives. (In the same way, to Hmong speakers it must seem that English has several dozen words for different kinds of paper: maps, passports, contracts, and the like.) To groups whose members are constantly concerned about different kinds of snow (or paper), these terms are too prolix, and are replaced by abbreviations that are opaque but economical.

3.2 Reduction of reflexive and reciprocal forms

There is probably no language in the world in which "man", "woman", "see", or "run" are expressed by sesquipedalian words, for all the mystery and complexity they represent. The brevity of their expression is an economically motivated index of their familiarity. (In fact, insofar as there is an inverse correlation between the relative complexity of an expression and its familiarity, we may speak of a correspondence between a point on a "linguistic dimension" and one on a "non-linguistic dimension", and hence, of a kind of iconicity, even here.)

An example of this kind is furnished by the different means of expressing reflexive and reciprocal objects, both in English and in other languages.

(11)   a. I got myself a beer
        b. I got me a beer
        c. I got a beer
(12)   a. They touched each other
        b. They touched

As demonstrated in (11), a benefactive reflexive object of *get* (and of a small number of other verbs) may be rendered by an emphatic reflexive (as in (11a)), an ordinary personal pronoun (as in (11b)), or as zero (as in (11c)).

With most transitive verbs, the reflexive object (denoting variously the body, the image, or the behavior of the agent) can only be expressed by the emphatic reflexive pronoun:

(13)   Harry kicked *himself* (*Harry kicked ____; *Harry kicked *him*)

With a small group of verbs, among them *shave*, *bathe*, *wash*, and *dress*, the reflexive object is typically (although not necessarily) expressed by zero:

(14)   Harry shaved ∅ (himself/*him)

The semantic homogeneity of the *shave* class of verbs is readily apparent: without exception, verbs of this class denote actions that one usually performs *on oneself*. This includes not only verbs of grooming like *shave*, but also verbs denoting change of position, such as *sit down* or *stand up*. The correlation is not exact – there are verbs like *comb*, for example, which denote personal grooming, which require an expressed object – but by and large the coreferential object can be represented by zero in those cases where coreference is what is *predictable*.

The sentences of (12) are analogous. Notionally, reciprocal sentences like (12a) are equivalent to a conjunction, where the relationship of "touching" is symmetrical. As pointed out in section 2.1 above, symmetry may be either necessary or contingent. By and large, the reciprocal pronoun which specifically indicates symmetry may be rendered by zero in precisely those cases where symmetry is necessary or very likely. This is the case where the predicate is a verb like "touch", since whenever A touches B, B must also touch A by definition. Where symmetry is contingent or unexpected, as is the case for predicates like "love", reciprocity must be explicitly indicated by the full form of the reflexive/reciprocal expression *each other*.

Related examples of the same kind have puzzled grammarians for some time. Given the classical theory of reflexive pronouns assumed in the framework of Chomsky's *Aspects* (1965), sentences like (15–17)

(15)   He has a gun on him (*himself)
(16)   Max saw a snake near him (*himself)
(17)   I got me a beer

are deviant, particularly given the minimally contrasting (18–20).

(18)   He pointed the gun at himself (*him)
(19)   He drew attention to himself (*him)
(20)   I wrote myself (*me) a letter

Attempts to account for these differences in structural terms are beside the point, it seems to me. The non-emphatic pronoun is used in (15–17) because in these sentences coreference between pronoun and antecedent is *expected*; the emphatic form of the reflexive pronoun is used in (18–20) because here coreference between pronoun and antecedent is not expected. Note that in

(15–17), all reference to the coreferential object may be eliminated, as in (21–3).

(21)   He has a gun on ∅
(22)   Max saw a snake near*by* ∅
(23)   I got ∅ a beer

Let us label those predicates whose objects are necessarily or typically coreferential with their subjects, and those predicates which are necessarily or typically symmetrical, *introverted predicates*. Then those predicates whose objects are not necessarily or typically coreferential with their subjects, and those predicates which are not typically symmetrical, can be called *extroverted predicates*. We can then state the following general correlation:

(24)   Reciprocal and reflexive objects of introverted predicates are given reduced expression

By and large, this correlation is true in English, although there are exceptions like *comb* which may engender some skepticism. If we turn our attention to other languages, however, we find very often that the membership of the class of introverted predicates is much the same as in English, and that principle (24) also holds. Principle (24) is then an *economically* motivated principle.

We may begin with Latin, which has distinct forms of expression for the reflexive object (*se* in various cases) and the reciprocal object (*inter se*, *invicem*, or *mutuo*). Thus

(25)   a. Se videt
           "3sg. sees self"
        b. Mutuo (inter se) dabant
           "They were giving each other (something)"

Introverted reflexive verbs generally express reflexivity by means of the *deponent* inflection (schematically equivalent to Verb + passive suffix), and typically include verbs like *lavor* "bathe", *induor* "dress", *ornor* "decorate oneself", *campestror* "put on armor", *cingor* "put on belt", *alor* "eat" (= "feed oneself"; cf. *se atque alios alunt* "they feed (both) themselves and others", where the reflexive object is in focus and contrasted with another possible one), and dozens of others which Flobert (1975:384–5) divides into three broad classes: curative verbs *of toilet* (e.g. "wash"), *of dress* (e.g. "dress"), and *of nourishment* (e.g. "eat"). Introverted reciprocal verbs also express reciprocity by means of the same deponent inflection. This class includes most of the verbs defined as "symmetrical predicates", such as *conflictor* "fight", *maritor* "marry", *colligor* "gather" (Flobert, 386), *amplector* "embrace", *altercor* "struggle", *discordor* "differ with", *litigor* "dispute", *misceor* "assemble", *osculor* "kiss", *luctor* "wrestle", *proelior* "join in battle", *pugilor* "box", *rixor* "brawl", *copulor* "join with" (Baldi 1975:13).

Both Flobert and Baldi point out that with a large number of such introverted verbs, the full reciprocal or reflexive pronoun is optionally present (exactly as it is in English). Both moreover point out that for such introverted verbs, the fuller form of the reflexive or the reciprocal was often an almost indistinguishable variant of the reduced form. Thus, for example *mē tondeō* could alternate with *tondeor* "I shave".

What is most significant, however, is the fact that the deponent option of expressing reciprocity or reflexivity is available for pretty much the same class of verbs in Latin as the English verbs which express reciprocity or reflexivity by a zero object. In each language, reduced expression of the object ($\emptyset$ in English, the *-r* deponent suffix in Latin) is possible in those cases where the identity of the object is largely predictable. Fuller expression of the object (*each other* or (*him*)*self* in English, *mutuo* or *se* in Latin) is obligatory where the object is the object of an extroverted verb, and thus not predictable.

Similar contrasts exist in Russian between the full reflexive (*sebja*) and reciprocal (*drug drug-*) pronouns, which occur as the object complements of extroverted verbs, and the reflexive suffix *-sja*, which denotes the coreferential object complement of introverted verbs. Thus

(26) a. On vidit sebja
        "He sees himself"
     b. Davali drug drugu
        "They were giving to each other"

But introverted reflexive verbs take the *-sja* suffix, and include many of the same verbs of grooming as English and Latin: *brit'-sja* "shave", *odet'-sja* "get dressed", *myt'-sja* "wash", *razodet'-sja* "undress" are all reflexive derived intransitive verbs whose roots are transitive (cf. *brit' kogo-nibud'* "to shave someone"). In the same way introverted reciprocal verbs also take the *-sja* suffix: thus *vstretit'-sja* "meet", *ssorit'-sja* "quarrel", *soedin'at'-sja* "unite", and many others. Nor is this contrast limited to Indo-European languages. One can find the same contrast between full reciprocals (*egymás-*) and reflexives (*maga-*) and the reduced suffix *-kod~koz* in Hungarian:

(27) a. Látja magat
"3sg. sees oneself"
b. Adnak egymásnak
"They are giving to each other"

Introverted reflexives include *fésül-köd* "comb one's hair", *mosa-kod* "wash", *vet-köz* "undress", *törül-köz* "dry oneself with a towel"; introverted reciprocals, *talál-koz* "meet", *vesze-kad* "quarrel", *vere-ked* "fight" *házas-od* "get married".

Similar is the contrast between the full reciprocal (*biribiri-*) and the reduced reciprocal suffix *-Iş* in Turkish; and between the full reflexive (*kendi-*) and the reduced reflexive suffix *-In*.

A somewhat different, but fundamentally parallel pattern appears in Hua of New Guinea. In the languages discussed so far, unexpected coreference has been marked, while expected coreference has been unmarked or reduced. In Hua, as in these languages, expected coreference is unmarked (and expressed, as in English, by zero). But *unexpected non-coreference* between subject and object (as when an introverted verb like "wash" takes an object distinct from its subject) is marked by a special construction. Hua is an SOV language, and for extroverted verbs both subject and object are expressed, as in (28).

(28) Buroʔ Kamaniʔ ke
"Buro saw Kamani"

For introverted verbs, no object is expressed when the object is, as expected, identical with the subject. Thus:

(29) Buroʔ ekenimo bre
"Buro put on ornaments"

But where the personal object of such an introverted predicate, contrary to expectation, is distinct from the subject, then that object is expressed, but not simply as the object of the predicate *ekenimo bro-*. The analog of (28), in other words, is ungrammatical:

(30) *Buroʔ Kamaniʔ ekenimo bre
"Buro put ornaments on Kamani"

Rather, the introverted verb is conjoined with a transitivizing verb *to-* "put", which itself takes object prefix pronouns agreeing in person and number with the human object:

(31) Buroʔ Kamaniʔ ekenimo *brona te*
"Buro put ornaments on Kamani"

The different forms of the reflexive and also reciprocal pronouns depending on whether they are largely predictable or not is only a case of a much more general phenomenon. We observe exactly the same *kind* of alternation between the forms of "ordinary" and "disjunctive" pronouns in languages such as French. Ordinary or predictable pronouns are expressed either as clitics or affixes on the verb, while disjunctive or focussed pronouns share more of the properties of separate noun phrases. The differences are not always confined to purely phonological properties.

In French, clitic pronouns cannot take contrastive stress, cannot be conjoined with nouns (or, for that matter, with each other), occur in a fixed order, and often have reduced phonological form (e.g. *moi* contrasts with *me* "me"; on the other hand, *nous* is the same phonologically as a clitic and as a noun). Object disjunctive pronouns, like other object nouns, follow the verb, while object pronoun clitics precede it.

Although non-disjunctive subject pronouns occur in the same sentence-initial position as "real nouns", there is evidence that they are in fact bound morphemes or affixes (cf. Meinhof 1936:29, Kayne 1975:84–5) which cannot occur in the absence of the verb to which they are adjoined as prefixes. There remains only the observation that such anaphoric pronouns typically encode given information, and the contrasting behavior of clitics and disjunctive pronouns in French is parallel to the contrasting behavior of pronominal and affixal expressions of reciprocity and reflexivity in the other languages enumerated above.

For a superficially rather different, but, I think, ultimately related phenomenon, consider the following facts about Kannada, pointed out in Bhat (1978:44–5). In Kannada, the morphological expression of the reflexive and the reciprocal is distinct. The reflexive is expressed by a verbal suffix *-kon*, while the reciprocal is expressed by a separate word *ondannondu* "each other". In one class of semantically homogeneous verbs, however, the reflexive (bound) morpheme is used with reciprocal meaning: this is the class of introverted verbs, including such members as "meet", "fight", "embrace", and "collide". Thus the contrast between (32) and (33) is neutralized in introverted, or NP* reciprocals, as shown in (34):

(32) Naanu paarṭige nannannu aamantrisi-koṇ-ḍidde
      I   party=to me=acc.   invite-refl.-had
      "I had invited myself to the party"   (ibid. 23)
(33) Naayi mattu bekku ondannondu nooḍiduvu
      dog   and   cat   each=other saw
      "The dog and the cat saw each other"   (ibid. 44)

(34)   Kaaru mattu bassugaḷu dikkihoḍedu-koṇ-ḍuvu
          car   and   bus   dash=against-refl.-past
          "The car and the bus collided"   (ibid. 46)

Although there seems to be no contrast between predicted and unexpected reflexives, there is a contrast between predicted and unexpected reciprocals, and the predicted reciprocal in Kannada, as in English, Hungarian, and Turkish, is given reduced expression.

Zipf's fundamental insight, that the complexity (and, hence, the transparency) of a linguistic expression varies inversely with its frequency, has often been repeated in the literature. For some recent discussions, cf. Bolinger 1961:25–9, Fidelholtz 1975, Jespersen 1909:I:,#9.214, Manczak 1978, Osgood 1953:716–17. Further exemplification seems to me unnecessary.

What I wish to do now is to indicate how this well-documented tendency to express the familiar as concisely as possible and the reductions of form which it entails are responsible for the destruction of iconicity as pidgins become creolized. In section 3.3 I will discuss an example of how this process results in the creation of morphological classes; in section 3.4, several examples of the origin of agreement and redundancy; and in section 3.5, an example of the creation of an exotic and redundant grammatical category.

3.3 The rise of conjugations

Natural generative phonology, restating Grammont's *Traité de phonétique* (1965), has urged that all phonological rules are natural processes, motivated in the final analysis by Zipf's principle of least effort. Certainly in any grammar, a large number of the recognized rules are readily identified as rules of *assimilation* or of *syllable structure simplification*, and of the residue of different processes which seem to run counter to this tendency, a large number can be explained on physiological or aerodynamic grounds (cf. Ohala 1974, Stampe 1979). For example, in Hua, two functionally related natural processes seem to conspire to create the ideal syllable structure CV. Coalescence converts the clusters *glottal stop + consonant*, "a" into a single consonant "b", often homorganic with, and invariably of lower sonority than "a". (Thus the coalescence rules are at once rules of assimilation and syllable structure simplification.) A very general rule of epenthesis inserts a reduced vowel shwa between all remaining consonants that are contiguous. Running counter to this set of rules, however, and creating phonetic consonant clusters in Hua, are the related rules of preglottalization and prenasalization of voiced anterior stops /b,d/. Both processes are attested in a variety of languages (cf. Greenberg 1970, Stampe 1979) and are to be understood as ways of making the utterance of voiced stops easier: prenasalization because it allows the passage of air through the duration of at least part of the voicing, and preglottalization by creating a subglottalic pressure and thus a greater airflow to sustain voicing.

Let us grant the correctness of the assumption that all phonetic changes originate as natural processes. What harm do they do to iconicity? They convert analytic structures to agglutinating, and, ultimately, synthetic expressions. The result is extensive allomorphy. The phenomenon is too familiar to require extensive exemplification here: but it can be illustrated in unexpected ways.

The existence of different declensions or conjugations is a well-known burden on the language learner, and one that has no redeeming cognitive features (one may argue of course that such complications reenforce the solidarity of the "in group" that speaks the language correctly, and thus serve as the moral equivalent of a Masonic handshake or the old school tie). There is an iconic tendency to assign membership to noun classes on the basis of some semantic homogeneity (cf. Dixon 1968) and, to a lesser extent, perhaps, to do the same for verb conjugations as well (cf. Montgomery 1978). But generally speaking, conjugations simply have to be memorized, and represent a commonly occurring violation of the isomorphism condition (whereby one meaning is mapped onto a multiplicity of forms).

Given that conjugations do not exist in pidgins, but tend to develop in creolizing languages, the question arises: where do they come from? An examination of a single family of languages in New Guinea (the "Gorokan family", including Hua, Gimi, Fore, BenaBena, Gahuku, Siane, and Gende) suggests a general mechanism whereby conjugations may arise as the result of economically motivated sound changes.

Verbs in all the languages of this "Gorokan family" agree with their subjects for person and number, marking these by suffixes. Ideally the agreement suffixes should be constant and independent of the verb to which they are added. Gimi is one language which approaches this ideal of isomorphic invariance, with personal endings (see Table 7).

Furthest from this ideal are languages like Hua, Gahuku, and Gende, in

Table 7

	Singular	Dual	Plural
1	-ove	-ure	-une
2	-ane	-are	-ave
3	-ie	-are	-ave

which there are three separate conjugations. Complete (aorist) paradigms for these three conjugations in Hua are given in Table 8, exemplified by the verbs *hu-* "do, say", *do-* "eat, ingest", and *mi-* "give".

Table 8

	Singular			Dual			Plural		
	1	2	3	1	2	3	1	2	3
hu-	hue	hane	hie	huʔe	haʔe	haʔe	hune	hae	hae
do-	doe	dane	de	doʔe	daʔe	daʔe	done	dae	dae
mi-	mue	mine	mie	muʔe	miʔe	miʔe	mune	mie	mie

The personal endings have become fused synthetically with the root. All synchronic attempts to separate out a set of "recurrent partials" corresponding to an invariant set of personal endings are doomed.

Intermediate between Gimi and Hua is Fore, which seems to be in the process of acquiring four conjugations, although the differences among them are still more or less transparently the result of motivated phonetic sandhi processes. The basic endings are shown in Table 9.

Table 9

	Singular	Dual	Plural
1	-uwe	-use	-une
2	-ane	-ase	-awe
3	-ye		

Verb stems may end in the vowels /a/ (e.g. *na-* "eat"), /e/ (e.g. *mae-* "get"), /u/ (e.g. *tumu-* "descend") or /i/ (e.g. *i-* "ascend"). Representative paradigms of verbs in these four classes are given in Table 10. The different

Table 10

	na- "eat"	*mae-* "get"	*tumu-* "descend"	*i-* "ascend"
1	nauwe	maeyuwe	tumuwe	iyuwe
2	naane	maeyaane	tumene	iyene
3	naye	maeye	tumiye	iye
1	nause	maeyuse	tumuse	iyuse
2/3	naase	maeyase	tumese	iyese
1	naune	maeyune	tumune	iyune
2/3	naawe	maeyawe	tumuwe	iyewe

patterns of root+suffix combinations can be generated from the phonological rules (a–f).

(a) ∅ →y / e, i____V (glide insertion)
(b) a →e / iy____ (palatalization of /a/)
(c) u →i / ____ye (palatalization of /u/)
(d) uu→u (coalescence)
(e) ua→e (no longer phonetically motivated)
(f) a →aa / ey____ (unmotivated)

Rules (a–d) not only share a common result – the elimination of vowel chains – but are phonetically motivated. Rule (e) also eliminates the vowel chain /ua/, but is unmotivated phonetically. Rule (f), finally, is totally unmotivated in Fore at this point. Rules (e) and (f), whatever their original phonetic motivation may have been, are now morphologized. (I see as worth noting, however, that rule (e) is similar to (b) in that /a/ is converted to /e/ after a high vowel.)

In Gende, we are forced to recognize four conjugations depending on whether the final vowel of the stem is /e/ (e.g. *bre-* "hit"), /o/ (e.g. *to-* "split, say"), /a/ (e.g. *a-* "come") or /A/ (e.g. *kwA-* "see"). Representative paradigms are shown in Table 11.

Table 11

	bre-	*to-*	*a-*	*kwA-*
1	brue	toe	ue	kwae
2	breni	tani	ani	kwani
3	brie	tie	ae	kwaie
1	bruri	tori	uri	kwari
2/3	breri	tari	ari	kwari
1	bruni	toni	uni	kwani
2/3	bree	tae	ae	kwae

Assuming a consistent set of personal desinences similar to those of Gimi, i.e. 1sg. *-ue*, 2sg. *-ani*, 3sg. *-ie*, 1dl. *uri*, 2/3dl. *ari*, 1pl. *-uni*, 2/3pl. *-ae*, the existing forms *can* be derived by the six rules of vowel deletion given in (a-f).

(a) u $\rightarrow \emptyset /$ A,o___

(b) i $\rightarrow \emptyset /$ a___e

(c) a $\rightarrow \emptyset / \begin{cases} ___u \\ e___ \end{cases}$

(d) e $\rightarrow \emptyset /$ ___ +high

(e) o $\rightarrow \emptyset /$ ___a,i

(f) aa $\rightarrow$ a

and the absolute neutralization rule (g):

(g) A$\rightarrow$a

But other than generating the correct results these rules have little to recommend them. Given that the membership of the /A/ class is very limited, and that its verbs are often treated like /a/ verbs, this class may be treated as exceptional. The verbs of the other three classes may be more succinctly characterized by the three morphophonemic rules (a–c).

(a) [-round] $\rightarrow$ u/(1st person subject)

(b) [+round]$\rightarrow$a/(2nd person subject)

(c) [-low] $\rightarrow$ i /(3rd person subject)

The verb stems will be directly followed by a set of personal desinences which manifest an only threefold distinction: *-e* (1sg., 3sg., 2/3pl.), *-ri* (dl.), and *-ni* (2sg., 1pl.).

The steps whereby this morphologization of rules of crasis may have occurred are unknown. But the end result is a system that is very similar to that of Hua, where no purely phonetic description of the reduction of the root+suffix combination is even possible, and the three conjugations have to be taken as an irreducible given. What has happened is that the perspicuous, but phonologically unstable structure *root+suffix* (=CV\$V . . .) has yielded to the phonetically motivated synthetic structure of Hua (=CV\$C) in which root can no longer be segmented from suffix, and in which different vowels of the verb root determine different conjugations.

The mechanics of crasis in the different member languages of this family are complex but the end result to which all crasis reductions tend is the creation of a more stable phonological structure, and the simultaneous creation of a less perspicuous morphological structure. Rather than learn one set of verbal endings which s/he may add to any verbal stem, the Hua language learner has to learn three different sets of alternations, all (at least at this time) perfectly synonymous. It seems plausible that conjugation classes in other languages may also have originated as the result of such phonetically motivated reductions of a more perspicuous structure.

In his *Cours*, Saussure (1969/1916) pointed out that sound changes tend to diminish *transparency* (which I identify with motivation): thus, *in +imicus* becomes the opaque *ennemi*, and so forth. What can be as easily demonstrated is that sound changes, in creating such grammatical phenomena as conjugations, will also destroy *isomorphism*, the correlation of one meaning with one form.

Indeed, this same process may also be partially responsible for another kind of violation of isomorphism, the rise of the phenomenon of agreement. Agreement is a violation of isomorphism insofar as a single element of meaning is expressed repeatedly, that is, through a number of forms. It is at least plausible that agreement originates when the reduced forms of personal pronouns (now affixed to the verb) are no longer sufficiently distinct to identify the subject, which thereupon requires another formal exponent. That is, a possible line of development for agreement systems is:

Stage one: NP#V
Stage two: np + V   (motivated by economy)
Stage three: NP#np + V   (motivated by the need
                                       for maximal distinctness)

In traditional transformational terms, the agreement marker np + is synchronically "posterior to" the full NP whose features it is supposed to "copy" on to the verb. Diachronically, however, it is almost certain that the reduced affix *np +* is prior to the full NP (cf. in particular Meinhof 1936:58, Givón 1971, 1979:chapter 5).

Synchronic analyses of agreement have often been motivated by a completely tacit (iconic, and essentialist) assumption about "deep structures": that at this level of syntactic representation, grammatical features are associated only with those categories in which they are *inherent*. Thus, for example, person and number are inherent features of NP and occur in deep structures on NP alone: if they appear elsewhere in surface structure, it is only by virtue of copying rules.

There is purely synchronic evidence from a number of languages, however, that this essentialist position may be a mistaken one. While this evidence, to be presented in the following section, does not argue for the correctness of the Meinhof–Givón analysis of agreement markers, it is worth examination for another reason. It suggests an entirely different way in which violations of isomorphism may arise in natural languages.

3.4 Agreement, essentialism, and redundancy

A road forks, one branch going left, the other slightly to the right. A sign may indicate the fork in this way:

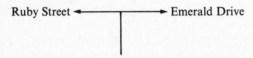

That is, the sign distorts and exaggerates the actual angle of the fork in the road. Its purpose, after all, is not to be accurate, but to be understood. Possibly language operates in the same way. This section explores one aspect of *redundancy* in natural languages, the redundancy created when one part of speech agrees with another with respect to certain features: these features are then marked more than once, and presumably are thus redundant at least some of the time.

The function of such redundancy, I would like to suggest, is similar to the function of exaggeration and redundancy in other kinds of signs. Iconicity is functional: to the extent that the sign is similar to the concept, it is easy to get the sense of it. But there is a point beyond which iconicity is dysfunctional. I have suggested earlier that isomorphism may be dysfunctional if too much detail is provided. To avoid missing the forest of fact for the trees of irrelevant observations, sign users work with signs that abstract and generalize on experience. There may also be a point at which motivation is dysfunctional. A category properly associated with one part of speech appears not (only) on that part of speech, but on others, and perhaps only on others. The main concern is that the category be expressed *somehow*.

In generative syntax, agreement phenomena are described through the use of an assumption that is spelled out and explicated only in the realm of generative phonology: that what is present in "deep structure" is only what is *distinctive*, while "surface structure" contains *redundant* features as well.

Jakobson, Fant, & Halle (1967:8,38), in one of the very few justifications for the distinctive/redundant distinction in phonology, argue that we can tell what is distinctive from what is redundant on the basis of the following two criteria:

(i) redundant features are unnecessary for linguistically significant discrimination;
(ii) hence, they appear less regularly than distinctive features, which are always present on the surface.

Redundant features are thus identified as such by virtue of the fact that they do not always appear.

Consider, however, the logical possibility that a given category may be implemented in either or both of two exponents, the precise implementation being a matter of indifference. A banal example of this is the expression of assent, which may be communicated by either a nod or a word, or both. Neither the nod nor the word is distinctive: each is redundant in the presence, distinctive in the absence, of the other.

A formal bias against the recognition of such intuitively natural relationships between expressions of a given category in morpho-syntax is reflected even in the nature of phrase structure (PS) rules. Such rules provide us with two devices for the "expansion" of a single term A having exponents B and C.

$$(35) \qquad A \rightarrow \begin{cases} B \\ C \end{cases}$$

In (35), the relationship between B and C is one of exclusive disjunction: A may be realized as either B or C but not both.

$$(36) \qquad A \rightarrow B \ C$$

In (36) A is realized as (possibly both) A and B. Whichever one is bracketed (if either one is) is redundant, while the one that is invariably present is the essential exponent of the category A. For example, the PS rule in (37)

$$(37) \qquad VP \rightarrow V \ (NP) \ (NP)$$

identifies the V as the essential component of the VP. The PS rule in (38)

$$(38) \qquad NP \rightarrow (Article) \ (Quantifier) \ (Adjective) \ N$$

identifies the N as the essential component of the NP.

The formalism provides no shorthand for the situation where A is realized as B, C, or BC: that is, for the situation where the relationship between B and C is one neither of exclusive disjunction (as in (35)), or conjunction (as in 36)), but inclusive disjunction.

A possible formalism for "capturing" such a relationship is

(39)   A→B v C (where v signals inclusive disjunction)

It is not immediately clear that such a formalism serves any useful function. In the examples above, it would be incorrect to assert that

(40)   VP→V v NP
(41)   NP→Adjective v N

for example. Or would it?

It is well known that vocative expressions in English can be exactly as described in (41), as illustrated in (42–4).

(42)   (Go), lovely rose (NP = Adjective Noun)
(43)   (Hello), dog   (NP = Noun)
(44)   (Hello), up there (NP = Adjective)

Expressions like (44) are usually analyzed as having a deleted head "one", so that their underlying structure conforms with that of (42). But the only reason this structure is posited is precisely to make the structure conform with that pattern, and consequently, for a rule like (38).

Given that the function of a vocative expression is to make it clear whom you are addressing, there is no need that this function be exercised by a noun. It may be exercised by a descriptive adjective or by a locative expression such as "over there"; cf. "Hi, there".

It seems to me that cases in natural languages which require something like rule (39) for their description are fairly widespread. The significance of these cases, and of the formalism which describes them, is that they deny the existence of a fundamental distinction between distinctive and redundant exponents of a category. What seems to operate in all the cases which I shall review below is that a category be expressed, and a distinction be made, *somewhere*: the exact location of this category, and the number of times it is expressed, seem to be a matter of indifference.

Case 1: anticipatory desinences in Hua

Non-final or medial verbs in Hua contain a final morpheme which indicates the person and the number of the subject of the following verb. (This is true only in the unmarked case where the subjects of the medial and final verb are distinct, and the person of the subject of the medial verb is unambiguously indicated by a preceding medial desinence.) Call this the anticipatory desinence.

The anticipatory desinence is marked in two ways: first, through a vocalic alternation which affects the final segment of the immediately preceding medial desinence; second, through a suffixed morph, a segmentable entity. There are seven persons in Hua, three in the singular, and two in the dual and the plural. (No distinction is made between second and third person in dual and plural.) The suffixed morphs of the anticipatory desinence are given in Table 12.

Table 12

	Singular	Dual	Plural
1	-da	-taʔa	-ta
2	-ka	-taʔa ~ tinaʔa	-ta ~ tina
3	-na		

One allomorph of the 2/3dl. is identical with the 1dl.; one allomorph of the 2/3pl. is identical with the 1pl.

The vocalic alternations associated with the anticipatory desinences are given in (45).

(45) $a \rightarrow i/\underline{\quad} +$ anticipatory morph
$$\begin{bmatrix} -1 \text{ person} \\ -\text{sg.} \end{bmatrix}$$

What is crucial in this example is that the distinction between first person and non-first person in the plural can be made in two ways. First, the 2/3 dl. or pl. anticipatory morph may be distinguished from the corresponding first person morph by addition of the infix *-in-*. Second, the 2/3 dl. or pl. anticipatory morph may cause ablaut of the preceding vowel by rule (45).

In a standard classical generative description, one of these means of person marking would be considered redundant, or both could be obligatory, or both could be optional. What we find in fact, however, is that the relationship between these two means of marking 2/3 in the non-singular is one of inclusive disjunction. For the medial form of the verb *hu-* "do, say", we find:

(46) a. hu-ga-t*in*a   (infix, no ablaut)
       b. hu-g*i*-ta   (ablaut, no infix)
       c. hu-g*i*-t*in*a   (infix and ablaut)
       "I did and 2/3 pl . . ."

The most frequently occurring form is (46b), but both (46a) and (46c) are produced and accepted. All that is required is that 2/3 be kept distinct from 1 person in the non-singular numbers. There are two ways of doing this, infixation and ablaut, and it seems that ablaut is preferred on a statistical basis. But both are possible, and neither is essential.

Case 2: the distinction between conditional clauses and relative clauses in Hua

The standard conditional protasis in Hua is marked by personal desinences on the verb which are identical with the personal desinences on relative clauses in this language. The morphological similarity between relative clauses and conditionals is not confined to Hua (cf. Hale 1976, McKay 1975, Haiman 1978), but in Hua, what is crucial is that the two categories are kept distinct in some way, for all their partial similarity. Conditional clauses, unlike relative clauses, are followed by a topic particle -*mo*. The distribution of this particle is our present concern. Almost everywhere it occurs (on all expressions capable of acting as the topics of the utterances in which they occur) this suffix is *optional*. Following relative clauses which act as conditional protases, however, it seems to be obligatory. This makes functional sense: the nominal character of topics is sufficiently indicated by other morphological appurtenances in most cases. But the nominal nature of the protasis is indicated in Hua only by the topic suffix -*mo*. Given the (language-specific) requirement that conditional protases be distinguished from adjectival relative clauses, the obligatory nature of the otherwise optional topic suffix seems to follow naturally.

On closer inspection, however, it seems that there are other means of indicating the nominal nature of the conditional protasis: among them is the suffixation of the restrictive quantifier -*goʔ* "only", a morpheme which (like case suffixes) cooccurs with nominal constituents alone. Where this suffix appears on the conditional protasis, the topic suffix -*mo* may follow it – but is no longer obligatory.

Thus we find the following three as possible conditional protases:

(47)   a. hisima-*mo*   (topic suffix, no restrictive quantifier)
        b. hisima-*goʔ*   (restrictive quantifier, no topic suffix)
        c. hisima-*goʔ-mo*   (topic suffix and restrictive quantifier)
           "(only) if 3sg. does it, . . ."

Either the quantifier or the topic marker is sufficient to mark the protasis as similar, in some way, to the adjectival relative clause. Neither is distinctive or redundant in implementing this distinction.

Case 3: conditional sentences in Salt-Yui

In a number of languages, *S1 S2* may be interpreted as a conditional sentence. Salt-Yui is apparently not such a language, and conditionals are morphologically distinguished from clauses in parataxis (cf. Irwin 1974). Conditional sentences are distinguished by the addition of the suffix *-ia* (which replaces personal desinences) to the verb of the protasis, or the verb of the apodosis, or both. In Irwin's formulation (1974:66),

(48)   Conditional sentence = + Circumstance $\pm$ ia + Consequence $\pm$ ia

$$\text{ia} \atop +$$

Given the clauses

     S1: hamen wai tam + gwo "the sky will be clear"
     S2: nimin sikinam + gwi   "it won't rain"

possible conditional sentences are

(49)   a.   hamen wai tam + *ia*, nimin sikinam + gwi   (*ia* on protasis)
       b.   hamen wai tam + gwo, nimin sikinam + *ia*   (*ia* on apodosis)
       c.   hamen wai tam + *ia*, nimin sikinam + *ia*

                            (*ia* on both protasis and apodosis)

The presence of the conditional marker *ia* is possible, but not essential, on either protasis or apodosis: what is essential, in Salt-Yui, is that the sentence be marked as a condition in *some* way.

Case 4: plural marking in Tagalog

On the face of it, Tagalog is very much like French, German, or Russian. Nouns are marked in singular or plural. Adjectival predicates will agree with their subjects in number, as illustrated in (50).

(50)   a.   Ma-Ø-ganda?   ang babae
          adj.-sg.-beautiful   the woman
          "The woman is beautiful"
     b.   Ma-ga-ganda?   ang mga babae
          adj.-pl.-beautiful the pl.   woman
          "The women are beautiful"

Plurality is indicated on nouns by the plural marker *mga*; on adjectives, by a reduplication of the first syllable of the adjectival root. (Schachter & Otanes (1972:229) claim that pluralization of adjectives is also possible with the *mga* pluralizer. In my own fieldwork with one native speaker, I did not find this possible, but the distinction between her dialect and that reported by Schachter & Otanes does not bear on what follows.)

One might hope to characterize these facts by means of an agreement transformation. In deep structure, plurality is indicated only on the subject of the sentence. Thus, the deep structure of (50b) might be something like (50c).

(50)   c. Ma-Ø-ganda? ang mga babae
           adj.-sg.-beautiful the pl. woman

An agreement transformation copies the feature *+plural* onto the predicate adjective. In favor of this analysis is the fact that (50c) happens to be a perfectly grammatical sentence, apparently synonymous with (50b). One could then say that the agreement transformation in Tagalog (unlike those of French, German, and Russian) is an optional one. Unfortunately, sentence (50d) also is grammatical:

(50)   d. Ma-ga-ganda? ang babae
           adj.-pl.-beautiful the woman

What is common to (50b,c,d) and distinguishes them equally from (50a), is that plurality is marked *somewhere* in the sentence: on subject in (50c), on the predicate in (50d), and on both subject and predicate in (50b). Assigning priority to any one of these forms and positing that form as the deep structure source for all plural marking in the surface representation of the sentence seems to be arbitrary.

The same fluidity of plural marking seems to obtain in noun phrases which consist of an article, adjective, and head noun. Once again, Tagalog seems at first blush to resemble familiar European languages in that attributive adjectives agree with their heads in number:

(51)   a. ang ma-Ø-gandang   babae
           the adj.-sg.-beautiful woman
           "beautiful woman"
        b. ang ma-*ga*-gandang *mga* babae
           the adj.-pl.-beautiful pl. woman
           "beautiful women"

Once again, however, we discover that the plural form has synonyms in which the plurality is expressed on just the attributive adjective, or just on the head noun:

(51)   c. ang ma-*ga*-gandang babae   (plurality on adjective only)
           the adj.-pl.-beautiful woman
        d. ang ma-Ø-gandang   *mga* babae   (plurality on noun head only)
           the adj.-sg.-beautiful *pl.* woman

The situation may be further complicated when a noun phrase consisting of an attributive adjective and a head acts as the subject of an adjectival predication. Plurality may then be expressed on the head noun, on the attributive adjective, and on the predicate adjective. While there is some dialect variation here, there are at least some speakers for whom any of (52a–g) are acceptable renditions of the sentence "the rich women are beautiful".

(52)

	Plurality marked on		
	Pred. Adj.	Attrib. Adj.	Noun
a. Ma+*ga*+*ganda?* *ang ma*+ *ya* +yamang *mga* babae	+	+	+
b. Ma+*ga*+ganda? ang ma+ *ya* +yamang babae	+	+	+
c. Ma+*ga*+ganda? ang ma+ +yamang *mga* babae	+	−	+
d. Ma+*ga*+ganda? ang ma+ +yamang babae	−	−	−
e. Ma+ +*ganda?* *ang ma*+ ya +yamang *mga* babae	−	+	+
f. Ma+ +*ganda?* ang ma+ *ya* +yamang babae	−	+	−
g. Ma+ +ganda? ang ma+ +yamang *mga* babae	−	−	+

All speakers apparently agree that the only utterance which cannot mean "the rich women are beautiful" is one in which plurality is not marked anywhere. As long as it is marked somewhere, the sentence is acceptable with plural meaning.

Case 5: verb–object number agreement in Waskia

In Waskia plurality on nouns is indicated by means of a postnominal determiner or article: *buruk* "pig", but *buruk nunga* "pigs". Plurality of the object of a transitive verb may also be indicated by means of an object suffix -*nd*- on the verb. Thus the contrast between (53a) and (53b).

(53)   a. Nu buruk kidi-am
                3sg. pig   cook-3sg.past
                "He cooked the pig"
    b. Nu buruk nunga kida-nd-am
                3sg. pig   pl.   cook-pl.-3sg.past
                "He cooked the pigs"

Once again, we find that plurality may be expressed either by the plural article *nunga*, or the plural object marker, or both. The last option is attested in (53b); the second in (53c).

(53)   c. Nu buruk kida-nd-am
                3sg. pig   cook-pl.-3sg.past
                "He cooked the pigs"

Essentially, plurality is a feature of the noun rather than of the verb of which it is the object. Thus, we might expect to find that plural marking on nouns is distinctive, while plural marking on verbs is redundant. The very acceptability of (53c) forces us to abandon this hypothesis, however. Moreover, as Ross & Paol (1978:166) point out, plurality is hardly ever marked on the object noun phrase. Apparently, there are in Waskia 17 different verb classes, all but one of these allowing plural object suffixes on the verb root. Only in this exceptional class of verbs, it seems, is plurality marked on the object: elsewhere, it is marked exclusively on the verb stem, as it is in (53c).

Once again, we are led to conclude that *where* a category is expressed, or how often, is to some extent a matter of indifference. In any case, a sentence like (53c) violates a kind of motivation: categories or attributes which in fact are associated with *things* should be associated in language with the signantia of those things, that is, with *nouns*. Typically, they are, and so nouns are at least partly defined in terms of the (universal) morphological categories which are expressed as affixes on them, such as number, case, etc., and verbs are also defined morphologically in terms of the "verbal" categories of aspect, tense, and mood. But there are violations of these generally well-established tendencies, of which agreement phenomena such as those attested above are representative examples.

Case 6: diminutives in Spanish
The Spanish diminutive suffix *-ito* (fem. *-ita*, etc.) connotes a "fundamentally favorable and often affectionate implication" (Gooch 1970:6) and typically occurs on nouns: *el niño* "the child", but *el niñito* "the (sweet/dear) child". Gooch, however, maintains that the distribution of this suffix is actually rather free, so that the following pairs of sentences are virtually synonymous:

(54)   a. El niño tiene dos años   can be rendered diminutive by:
         b. El niñ-ito tiene dos años
         c. El niño tiene dos añ-itos
           "The (sweet) child is two years old"

(55)   a. El pobre está muy cansado   can be rendered diminutive by:
         b. El pobre-cito está muy cansado
         c. El pobre está muy cansad-ito
           "The poor thing is very tired"

One can even put the diminutive on both words in the above sentences, in effect thereby sprinkling goodwill on every word that is morphologically equipped to accommodate a diminutive.

(54)   d. El niñ-ito tiene dos añ-itos
(55)   d. El pobre-cito está nuy cansad-ito

The only limitation on this apparently promiscuous proliferation of diminutives is a stylistic constraint in elegant Spanish which militates against repetition (Gooch 1970:16,17).

Against Gooch, Wierzbicka (1980:58–9) takes the viewpoint that the differences of form reflected in (54b–c), (55b–c) are reflected in differences of meaning, and, moreover, that these differences in meaning are motivated. To wit, the speaker of (54b) has good feelings about the *child*, while the speaker of (54c) has good feelings about the *age*.

Given the reality of isomorphism and motivation, this is certainly what we would expect. It seems to me, however, that this position cannot be maintained, given sentences such as (56).

(56)   El caudillo está muy cansad-ito
        "The leader (i.e. Franco) is very tired"

Such a sentence, in which the diminutive occurs only on the predicate adjective "tired" is acceptable only if the speaker feels warmly towards the *caudillo*. Otherwise, as we would expect, it sounds extremely sarcastic. This suggests that irrespective of the "landing site" of the diminutive morpheme, its scope is everything in the sentence (at least in sentence (56)). Wierzbicka cedes this point but adds that "even if the good feeling in question should always be taken as directed towards the [subject] the source of this good feeling is different" (1980:59). It seems to me that this is wishful thinking. That is what the different forms (54b,c) *ought* to mean, but it may be simply "to consider too curiously, to consider so". The expression of goodwill in Spanish, like the expression of plurality in Tagalog, has a number of possible realizations in the surface structure of the language. Where this category is expressed, or even how often, is not as important as the fact that it is expressed somewhere or other. In all of these cases we have diagrams that are in effect distorting or exaggerating reality in order to communicate this reality more clearly.

Case 7: the expression of possession in Hungarian
For a final example, we may hark back to an earlier example of the trade-off between morphology and syntax (cf. pp. 67–8). Possession in

Hungarian may be expressed by contiguity of possessor and possessum, dative case marking on possessor, or both. That *a kis lány* "the little girl" is the possessor of *(a)fésüje* "(the)comb=3sg.possessor" is indicated in (57a) by the syntactic contiguity of the possessor and possessum within one constituent.

(57)   a. A tolvaj ellopta [a kis   lány fésüjé-t]
              the thief stole   the little girl comb-her=acc.
              "The thief stole the little girl's comb"

It is indicated in (57b) by the addition of the dative suffix *-nak* on the possessor NP, which is separated from the possessum:

(57)   b. [A kis lány-*nak*] a   tolvaj ellopta [a   fésüjé-t]
              the little girl-*dat*. the thief stole   the comb-her=acc.
              "The thief stole the little girl's comb"

But it can also be (redundantly) indicated by both, as it is in (57c).

(57)   c. A tolvaj ellopta [a   kis   lány-*nak* a   fésüjé-t]
              the thief stole   the little girl-*dat*. the comb-her=acc.
              "The thief stole the little girl's comb"

   Where does redundancy "come from"? Or rather, how does it become grammaticalized, so that it is obligatorily built in to the grammatical code? A comparison of pidgins and fully evolved natural languages seems to suggest that the grammaticalization of redundancy is a part of the drift from analytic to synthetic structure.

   A suggestive parallel development occurs in ASL and perhaps in all sign languages. Since its (not too remote) inception as a set of relatively pantomimic gestures, ASL has developed into a much more stylized and conventionalized system in which iconicity has been suppressed in a number of ways. Many of these ways are familiar to us from our experience of similar changes in language, motivated by a principle of least effort. For example, Frishberg (in Klima & Bellugi 1979:77) notes

one tendency . . . to focus the lexical information in the hands and their movements rather than in movements of the face or body . . . another . . . toward assimilation of the formational components of multipart signs, resulting in a fluidity characteristic of unitary lexical items. All of these changes are in the direction of simplifying visual–manual forms.

But among these tendencies there is another, which is apparently motivated by the need to maximize the ease of perception. This is the tendency to develop symmetrical two-handed signs from originally one-handed signs:

examples are the signs for "angry", "journey", "hurry", "die", and "ambitious". Frishberg (ibid.) points out that such a tendency not only "facilitates articulation by allowing the signer to program both hands at once", it also "may increase the ease of perception by increasing the redundancy of the signal". It is interesting that at least in one documented historical case, the development from the iconic quasi-pidgin original gesture language of its inventor l'Epée to the conventionalized and opaque ASL of today does include a tendency towards the greater expression of redundancy. This is certainly parallel to the rise of agreement phenomena in agglutinating and synthetic languages as described in some detail by Meinhof (1936) and others. In general, grammaticalization, motivated by economy, obscures the signal, which must therefore be repeated to ensure comprehension. Hence, one kind, at least, of redundancy.

For another, rather more interesting, example of redundancy arising from the drift towards agglutination and synthesis, we consider in some detail the genesis of the "medial verb" category in a number of Papuan languages.

3.5 Redundant grammatical categories

The most striking and exotic grammatical feature of a large number of Papuan languages is undoubtedly the all-but-universal morphological distinction between sentence-internal (medial) and sentence-final verbs. Although this distinction has been familiar ever since the appearance of Pilhofer's classic grammar of Kâte in 1933, no attempt has ever been made, as far as I know, to identify the diachronic origins of this pervasive and remarkable distinction. It seems to have the status of a given.

It should be noted, however, that a feature such as the medial/final distinction is not only exotic but also quite redundant: it does no more, in a sense, than to recapitulate the information provided by the linear order of clauses themselves, and by their intonation and prosodic features such as pauses or their absence. The redundance of the grammatical category is clearly indicated by the absence of anything similar in most of the languages of the world.

Absence of relevant data makes it impossible to speak of the diachronic origins of the medial/final distinction in the over 500 languages where it is known or conjectured to exist. I believe that one can show, however, that where information is available, it is possible to show that the distinction arises by familiar processes from familiar structures. I will attempt such a demonstration by reference to the most extensively documented family of Papuan languages: the so-called "East-Central family" of the Eastern New Guinea Highlands Stock (Wurm 1975), which I will refer to as the Gorokan family.

Following is an enumeration of these languages, and the major sources of documentation on them: Gende (Brandson mss), Asaro (D. Strange 1973, G. Strange 1975), Gahuku (Deibler 1976), BenaBena (Young 1964, 1971), Kamano (Payne & Drew 1966), Kanite (McCarthy 1965, Gibson & McCarthy 1975), Move (Renck 1975, 1977), Hua (Haiman 1980), Gimi (McBride & McBride 1975, Haiman 1980), Siane (James ms, Haiman 1980), Fore (Scott 1973, 1978).

As recognized in a trailblazing study by Arthur Capell (Capell 1948–9), the Gorokan languages are closely related to the languages of Wurm's "Eastern family", which I will refer to as the Kainantu family of languages. Most of the information that is readily available on these languages (including Usarufa, Awa, Auyana, Kosena, Gadsup, Tairora, Binumarien, and Waffa), is anthologized in McKaughan 1973, to which I will make references. I should emphasize, however, that the information available on languages of this family is not sufficient to determine what the origins of the medial/final distinction may be there.

My hypothesis is that the medial verbal desinences in Gorokan languages arose by a process of fusion (agglutination and synthesis) of the final desinences and a following coordinate conjunction.

Wherever a structure $X \# Y$ becomes $X + Y$, the resulting structure is shorter and thus represents an economy of effort for the speaker. It is also less transparent, and thus represents a loss of iconicity. Where the two elements $X + Y$ become totally fused into a new category Z, this category may be strictly speaking redundant. I shall argue in this case that $X =$ final desinence, $Y =$ coordinate conjunction, and that the resulting $Z =$ medial desinence.

Two caveats: The formula above is proposed as the origin of different-subject (DS) medial verbs only. The reason for this is that in same-subject (SS) medials, X is typically null by coordination reduction (cf. Haiman 1983a), and the SS form is frequently a participial form.

Second, DS medials in Gorokan languages (and in many Kainantu languages as well) occur with two sets of verbal desinences, a medial desinence agreeing with the subject of the medial verb, and an anticipatory desinence agreeing with the subject of the following verb. I shall be concerned in these pages only with the origins of the medial desinence (M).

The anticipatory desinence (A), which typically occurs on both SS and DS medial verbs, almost certainly originates as a pronoun subject of the following clause, and cliticizes across the preceding clause boundary to become a suffix on the medial verb (cf. Haiman 1983a: in arguing for the origin of M here, I am claiming that in the Gorokan languages, at least, the same process of boundary-crossing cliticization occurred twice – the first time when (Final desinence # conjunction) became the medial desinence M; the second time, when (Medial desinence # pronoun) became (M + the anticipatory desinence A).

The bimorphemic origins of the medial desinences are more or less transparent, and recognized to be so, in Fore (Scott 1978:120), Kanite (McCarthy 1965), and BenaBena (Young 1971:55,57). In each of these languages, the grammarian has recognized in the medial desinence a personal desinence followed by a suffix of some kind: Fore *-ki-*, Kanite *-ke-*, BenaBena *-go*. I have argued elsewhere (Haiman ms) that this suffix can be reconstructed in each of the other Gorokan languages. Moreover, the fusion of desinence and this *-KV* suffix proceeded by means of four phonological rules, each of which is still productive in one or more of the Gorokan languages as spoken today. These four rules are given in (i–iv).

(i)   Modal vowel deletion $(V \rightarrow \emptyset / [\overline{\text{Mood}}] + C)$
(ii) Nasal cluster simplification $(C \rightarrow \emptyset / N\_\_\_)$
(iii) Nasal becomes glottal stop
(iv) Glottal coalescence $(? + C_1 \rightarrow C_2$, where C_2 may be identical with C_1, but is wherever possible homorganic with, and less sonorous than, $C_1)$

Presented in Table 13 are the medial desinences (for high back vowel stems in those languages which, like Hua, have conjugation classes, cf. section 3.3 above), followed by the proto-Gorokan forms which can be reconstructed by means of "undoing" rules (i–iv).

Given the four rules, the reconstructed forms of the medial verb in the Gorokan languages correspond exactly to the following formula:

Medial Verb = Verb + final desinence + KV

Where the derivation is transparent, as in BenaBena and Kanite, previous investigators (e.g. Young 1964, 1970 on BenaBena; McCarthy 1965 on Kanite) have described *-KV* as simply some kind of "transitional morpheme". But there is in fact reasonably good evidence (also summarized in Haiman ms) that *-KV* is cognate with the coordinating conjunction "and", not only in languages of the Gorokan family, but in several other Papuan languages from the Koiarian family of Southeastern Papua

Table 13: Medial desinences in Gorokan languages

		Hua	Kamano	Siane	Gimi	Gahuku	Gende	*Proto-Gorokan	
	1	uga	uge	o(ne)	oko	ugo	oxo	ue	KV
sg.	2	ana	ange	ange	ako	ako	aningo	ane	KV
	3	iga	ige	(a)i	iko	igo	ixo	ie	KV
dl.	1	uʔga	uge	oi	uko	usigo	orixo	O+	*dual marker* KV
	2/3	aʔga	aʔge	ai	ako	asigo	arixo	a +	*dual marker* KV
pl.	1	una	uʔge	onge	uko	uko	oningo	One	KV
	2/3	aga	age	a	ako	ago	axo	ae	KV

Note: in this table /ng/ represents a prenasalized /g/; the graph *x* in Gende represents a voiced velar fricative; in the reconstructed forms, /O/ represents a rounded back vowel of indeterminate height, /K/ a velar stop of unspecified voicing, and /V/ a vowel of indeterminate quality. The daughter languages have innovated in the expression of the category *dual*: glottal stop in Hua and Kamano, /i/ in Siane, /si/ in Gahuku, /r/ in Gimi, and /ri/ in Gende. It is an open question how many ancestral forms underlie the apparent diversity of the existing forms, cf. Haiman 1977, appendix A, for evidence that glottal stop and /r/ may be related, for example.

(Dutton 1975:306–7) to Chuave and Chimbu of the Central family of the Highlands (cf., for example, Thurman 1978).

The familiar mechanism of fusion, motivated in the last analysis by whatever factors contribute to the drift from analysis to synthesis, was responsible for the creation here of a redundant grammatical category.

The observation that Zipf's law is responsible for this kind of drift is of course a commonplace of historical linguistics. The drift from analytic to agglutinative and ultimately synthetic expression results "from the rapprochement which takes place between words that are habitually grouped together" (Meillet 1958:147).

3.6 Conclusions

Many of the examples discussed in this chapter are curiously reminiscent of the hierarchy of linguistic distance presented and discussed in chapter 2.2 and repeated here.

(88) a. X # A # B # Y
      b. X # A # Y
      c. X + A # Y
      d. X # Y
      e. X + Y
      f. Z

There is a well-known diachronic drift from (a) to (f) – the drift from analysis to synthesis being only a part of this general tendency – and it is well known also that, at least in part, the motivation for this drift will be *iconic*: speaking of the development from (d) to (e), Meinhof (1936:41) observes that fusion is motivated by the fact that "Stamm und Affix zusammengehörig empfunden werden, und verstärken ihrerseits das Bewusstsein der Worteinheit." (The stem and affix are felt to belong together and (the fusion) in turn reenforces the impression of the unity of the (resulting) word.) This motivation for reduction is also explicitly recognized by Zipf 1935:249–50, and by Meillet 1958 [1912], in his classic paper on the origin of grammatical affixes.

Nevertheless, the motivation for reduction is also partially *economic*: one gives less expression to that which is familiar or predictable.[2] And whatever the motivation for the reduction, whether iconic or economic, the outcome in all cases is a reduction of iconicity. "Reduction breeds opacity." The fact that either economy or iconicity may be responsible for the form of an expression is itself a factor which vitiates iconicity, inasmuch as competing motivations for a given form are effectively a kind of *homonymy*. In some cases, this homonymy may become confusing, as the example discussed in the next chapter will illustrate.

---

[2] Havers (1931:21–4) devotes several pages to discussion of the loss of a *pause* between constituents, a loss motivated, in his view, by frequent repetition of the form *A pause B*. Among the examples he discusses are the transition from question to conditional protasis (21), the transition from interrogative words *utrum*, *poteron*, *whether* to complementizers introducing indirect questions (22), the evolution of conjunctions from nouns or interrogative expressions (German *trotz* "in spite of" from *Trotz* "defiance"; French *car* "for" from *qua re* "why", 23–4). It should be noted that not only pause, but intonational and prosodic coloring may be lost by dint of frequent repetition. The latter accounts in part for the evolution of forms like *car* in French, *zašto* in Serbo-Croatian, etc.; and it accounts entirely for the evolution of interrogatives into exclamations (e.g. Do I know Harry!?). Havers conjectures that originally such exclamations were repetitions of questions addressed to the speaker "um die Verwunderung über die Frage auszudrucken" (25) (in order to express amazement at the question).

4 *Iconicity vs. economy:*
the case of clause incorporation

We have already seen in section 2.3.1, and in our discussion of the reflexive and reciprocal constructions in particular, how reduction and fusion may be motivated by either iconicity or economy. The resulting meanings of the reduced or fused reciprocal morpheme were relatively easy to distinguish. There are other cases in which competing motivations for reduction make it very difficult to distinguish between the meanings of a single form. The present chapter focusses on the ambiguous status of one such form, the gerundive clause in *-ing* represented by such examples as

(1)   *Leaving her children*, she fled for safety

In English generally, and in many other languages as well, such reduced clauses are near paraphrases for full coordinate clauses like the italicized portion of (2):

(2)   *She left her children* and fled for safety

The question to which this chapter (like a number of earlier studies) is directed is the following: are gerundive clauses like that of (1) coordinate with, or subordinate to, the following clause? To answer this question, we must assume that we know what is meant by terms like coordination and subordination. I think it will turn out that our notions of these terms are actually quite vague, and our criteria in some cases mutually inconsistent. But there is a sense which I will try to explicate in which gerundive clauses do partake of both coordinate and subordinate properties. And they do so, I contend, because their reduced form and other syntactic properties are compatible with an iconic and an economic motivation.

I undertake to demonstrate below that reduced clauses not only can paraphrase coordination-linked full clauses, but share the same range of meanings that full coordinated or paratactic clauses may have. This, in traditional accounts, constitutes their only claim to full coordinate clause status. For, morphologically and syntactically, reduced clauses are *incor-*

196

porated within, and thus function as parts of, the following clause. If we represent the clauses of sentences (1) and (2) as *S1 S2*, then the reduced clause in (1) is part of a structural configuration that we can diagram as

$$_{S2}[\ldots [S1] \ldots]_{S2}$$

And this configuration, which we can demonstrate with respect to a number of different criteria in different languages, is taken as defining S1 as subordinate to S2 in all traditional accounts.

Against this traditional account, I wish to argue that both reduction and incorporation may affect gerundive clauses, as they affect coordinate clauses, when such clauses are conceptually close to the clauses with which they are conjoined. In fact reduction of the gerundive clause marks all kinds of conceptual closeness with the "main clause": the reduced clause typically shares a subject, tense, and mood with the main clause, and frequently the two clauses together describe the same "event" or episode. That is, I contend that the reduction and incorporation of gerundive clauses are *economically* motivated because

(3)   Reduction because of *identity* (as in coordinate clauses) is economically motivated.

There is another possible *iconic* motivation for reduction, of course, in traditional accounts, namely that

(4)   Reduction iconically reflects *backgrounding* (as of subordinate clauses).

Because the structure in question is compatible with both motivations, the status of gerundive clauses is indeterminate.

While I do not wish to deny that gerundive clauses frequently do seem to be backgrounded, I will concentrate here on the evidence which favors the "Cinderella hypothesis", (3), and disfavors the traditional hypothesis, (4). First, there is evidence from a number of languages that backgrounded clauses are *not* reduced. Second, there is evidence that both reduction and incorporation are motivated, in many cases, quite unambiguously, by conceptual closeness rather than any notion of backgrounding. Having presented this evidence, I shall reiterate my basic claim, that the "syntactic indeterminacy" of reduced -*ing* clauses in English (and their analogs in many other languages) is due to the fact that they are compatible with both an economic and an iconic motivation.

But first, a look at the form and behavior of these clauses in some unrelated languages. The languages selected for exemplification here

(Turkish, Japanese, Hindi, Hungarian, Lenakel, and Hua) are sufficiently disparate that we may expect similar patterns in a fair number of other languages as well.

4.1 The (near) synonymy of sentences (1) and (2)

The claim I wish to defend here is that a full coordinate clause (like that in (2)) may be paraphrased by a reduced gerundive clause (like that in (1)). The fact that the two constructions share not only a "core" meaning, but the same "peripheral" meanings as well, argues that at some significant level the gerundive construction *is* a coordinate clause.

In Turkish, the two constructions are diagrammable as in (5a,b).

(5)   a. S1 + *Ip* S2
      b. S1   *ve* S2

In (5a), the suffix -*Ip* is an invariable (historically participial) ending that replaces the verbal suffixes of mood, tense, and person–number agreement. In general, the construction is possible only where S1 and S2 share a common subject, tense, and mood. In those cases only, constructions of the form (5a) and (5b) are described by Underhill (1976:379) as semantically equivalent, although he notes that the latter form is by far the more common. He also remarks, without discussion, that -*Ip* is a subordinating suffix (1976:377–8).

Given that *ve* "and" is the maximally unmarked conjunction, the semantic relationships between S1 and S2 are predictable largely from the linear order of the two clauses. So too are the semantic relationships between S1 and S2 with the gerund construction. Thus the equivalence of (6a) and (6b).

(6)   a. Mehmet gel-*di*-∅   *ve*   git-ti-∅
         Mehmet come-*past-3sg.* and go-past-3sg.
         "Mehmet came and went"
      b. Mehmet gel-*ip*   git-ti-∅
         Mehmet come-*Ip* go-past-3sg.
         "Mehmet came and went"

In Japanese the two constructions are:

(7)   a. s₁ [S O V + *tense/mood*] s₁ *si* [S2]
      b. s₁ [S O V + *te*] s₁   [S2]

The subject of S1 need not be identical with that of S2 in (7b). Nevertheless, "the gerund being timeless and moodless, it takes from the final predicate the tense or mood required for the translation" (Martin 1975:485). The range of meanings for (7a) is that allowed by the linear order of two clauses conjoined by *si* "and" and includes temporal order, causal succession, simple conjoining, and condition. The range of meanings for (7b) seems to be significantly greater, including (Martin 1975:479) those given in (8).

(8)   a. temporal sequence
           b. consequence
           c. manner or appearance: "-ing; -like"
           d. contrast: "and/but"
           e. concession: "yet, even so"
           f. condition: "ing"="if/when"
           g. instrument: "by . . . -ing"
           h. witness or exemplification: "and in proof thereof"
           i. simple conjoining: "and"

Both (8c) and (8e) are impossible for *S1 si S2*. Reading (8c) with *-te* is a consequence of the incorporation of S1 with *-te*, and I shall be returning to it in section 4.2; but the possibility of (8e) with *-te* is problematic, since a relationship of concession is not signaled by the linear order of clauses alone. To the extent that *S1-te S2* can mean "Although S1, S2", the morpheme *-te* must mean something more than *si* "and".

Martin shows, however (1975:497), that the extra meaning of concession is provided not by *-te* itself but by the additional focus marker *mo*, as illustrated in (9).

(9)   a. Ame ga   hut-te iku
              rain sub. fall-te go
              "If it rains, I'm going"
           b. Ame ge   hut-te *mo*   iku
              rain sub. fall-te *focus* go
              "Even if it rains, I'm going"

In Hindi the two contrasting constructions are (10a,b) (Davison 1981).

(10)   a. $_{S1}$[S O V + tense/mood/aspect]$_{S1}$ *aur phir* [S2]
          b. $_{S1}$[S O V + *kar*]$_{S1}$ [S2]

Davison identifies *-kar* "perfective" as close in meaning to *aur phir* "and then". She lists as possible interpretations of (10b) the following meanings:

(11)   a. and then
          b. on . . . ing
          c. V-ly
          d. even though/if

    e. instead of
    f. after
    g. because of
    h. if

All but (11c,d,e) may be said to follow as possible interpretations, given no more than that S1 and S2 occur in order, and that *-kar* is perfective. (11c), like (8c) in Japanese, is an index of incorporation, and discussion of it will resume in section 4.2; but (11d,e), like Japanese (8e), suggest that *-kar* contributes more to the sentence than an "unmarked conjunction" would. Once again, however, the additional semantic contribution is made by other additional words. *S1-kar S2* is not in itself concessive: *S1 -kar bhii S2*, where *bhii* means "also" (= "even") is concessive, as in (12).

(12)   Tum   ustaad hoo-kar bhii yah nahĩ̃ jaantee?
              you=fam. teacher be-kar   also this not   know=imperf.
              "You don't know this even though you are a teacher?"
                                        (Davison 1981:111)

In the same way, *S1-kar S2* cannot mean "Instead of S2, S2". S1 must contain in addition the morpheme *na* "not".

Davison's illuminating essay is devoted to showing the range of differences between (10a) and (10b), and we shall be returning to these below. For now, however, it should be noted that the list of possible interpretations of (10b), as given in (11), is compatible with the analysis of *-kar* as virtually synonymous with the "unmarked conjunction" *aur* "and".

In Hungarian, the two constructions are:

(13)   a. $_{S1}$[S O V + *tense/mood + person*]$_{S1}$ *(é)s* [S2]
         b. $_{S1}$[S O V + *vE*]$_{S1}$ [S2]

(13b) is possible only where S1 and S2 share a common subject and tense. When this condition is satisfied the two constructions are frequently found by native speakers to be interchangeable, as in (14) and (15).

(14)   Karomat felemel-*t-em* *és* éreztem az elem   ellenállását
              my=arm raise-past-1sg. and I=felt   the element resistance=its=acc.
              "I raised my arm and felt the resistance of the element"
(15)   Karomat felemel-*ve* éreztem az elem ellenállását
              "Raising my arm, I felt the resistance of the element"

Sentence (15) has a number of meanings which it shares with (14), crucially including simple coordination, temporal succession, and causal succession. Those meanings which it does *not* share with (14) include the expression of simultaneity and of manner adverbs. Both of these, to which we shall return in section 4.2, are indicative of the diminution of conceptual distance between S1 and S2 which is signaled in the incorporation of the one within the other.

In Hua, as in many other Papuan languages, there are no independent clausal conjunctions like "and". Moreover, there is hardly any possibility of paraphrase: when two conjoined clauses have a different subject and (possibly) a different tense or mood as well, then they are conjoined in a structure similar to (1); on the other hand, when they share the same subject, tense, and mood, then they *must* be conjoined in a structure like (2). (The alternative, *S1, S2*, while possible, marks a conceptual distance between S1 and S2 equivalent to putting them in separate paragraphs.) The two contrasting structures, then, are (16a,b).

(16) a. $_{S1}$[S O V + *tense* + *medial person* + *anticipated person*]$_{S1}$ [S2]
      b. $_{S1}$[S O V + *anticipated person*]$_{S1}$ [S2]

where (16a) is required where the subjects of S1 and S2 are distinct, and (16b) only is possible where the subjects, tense, and mood of S1 and S2 are identical: there, however, it is necessary, unless S1 and S2 are in effect different paragraphs. Thus the contrast between

(17) a. Mi-*su-ga*-na   dogie
          give-*fut.-1sg.med.*-3sg.ant. 3sg.=will=eat
          "I will give him/her (some) and s/he will eat"
      b. Mi-na   dogie
          give-3sg.ant. 3sg.=will=eat
          "H/she will give him/her some and eat"

The range of meanings of (16a) is exactly what we would predict, given the linear order of S1 and S2 without further information:

   (a) after
   (b) because
   (c) if
   (d) and

The range of meanings of (16b) is slightly more restricted inasmuch as the conditional reading is impossible without a special auxiliary -*to*- on the verb of S1 (Haiman 1980:150–3, 400–10, passim). The general ability of (16a) to occur as a conditional protasis is one aspect of a more general constraint on such clauses: that they must agree in mood with the clause to which they are conjoined. Reduced clauses (16b), like -*ing* clauses, also can function as manner adverbs, and indicate simultaneity, in contradistinction to the structures (16a). Both in the common meanings which they share and in the semantic ways they differ, the structures (16a) and (16b) are analogous to (1) and (2), although, unlike those, they are not interconvertible.

Examples up to now have been of languages in which the reduced (-*ing*) clause is the first of *S1 S2*. Lenakel is an example of a language of which the reduced clause is S2. This seems to correlate with the fact that Lenakel is an overwhelmingly prefixing language, as the following phrase structure representation of the Lenakel verb makes clear (Lynch 1978:42):

> V → ((intention)future) person tense (continuative) (interrogative)
> number STEM (suffixes)

The language is SVO; contrasting sentence types for *S1 S2* are (18a,b),

(18) a. S1 kani   s2 [S *full V*   O] s2
      b. S1 (kani ka) s2 [S *reduced V* O] s2

where *full V* is as given in the phrase structure rule above, and *reduced V* differs from this in the following respects:

> (a) intentional and future prefixes never occur
> (b) instead of a variable person prefix, an invariable "echo-subject" prefix *m-* occurs
> (c) tense, continuative, and interrogative prefixes may be deleted under identity with the corresponding prefixes in the verb of S1
> (d) number prefixes may not be deleted.

The maximally reduced verb of S2 in a construction like (18b) is therefore something like *m*+STEM (Lynch 1978:45). Examples are (19a,b).

(19) a. I-im-kin   nuw nenav   *kani t-n-ak*-kin   nuw nivin tolauk
         1exc.past-eat yam yesterday *and fut.-2-cont.*-eat yam some tomorrow
         "I ate yams yesterday, and you will eat some tomorrow"
      b. I-im-kin nuw nenav (*kani ka*) *m*-vin i-imwa
         (as (19a))   and that echo-go loc.-house
         "I ate yams yesterday, and went home"   (Lynch 1978:114)

Lynch (1978) treats (18b) as the form of *S1 S2* whenever they share a common subject, tense, and mood. There is thus no possibility of having minimal contrast pairs like (1) and (2) in Lenakel: reduction is the obligatory signal of identity of subjects, but is only possible when S1 and S2 are in the same tense.

That the range of meanings of (18a) and (18b) are the same with respect to the nature of the interclausal relationships expressed is indicated by the fact that reduction is impossible in sentences where the conjunction between S1 and S2 is other than *kani* "and":

(20)   R-is-mis-aan,   merou *r-n*-akimw   am
         3sg.-neg.-die-neg. but   *3sg.-perf.*-run=away just
         "He didn't die, but just ran away"   (Lynch, 52)
         (*r-is-mis-aan merou *m*-n-akimw am)

Having established that analogs to the forms (1) and (2) are nearly
synonymous in each of the languages under discussion, both being similar
to the totally unmarked structures *S1 S2*, we now turn our attention to
some of the ways in which these constructions differ.

4.2 Peculiarities of *-ing* type clauses

Reduction: all *-ing* clauses are reduced. Typically, they do not mark those
grammatical categories with respect to which they agree with the full
clause. The direction of reduction (S1 is reduced where the categories are
expressed as suffixes, S2 where they are prefixes) suggests that S1 and S2 are
coordinate structures, and that coordination reduction is responsible for
reduction (cf. Ross 1970).

Incorporation: all *-ing* clauses are incorporated into, and function as
immediate constituents of, the clause with which they are conjoined. Where
reduction suggests that *-ing* clauses are coordinate with the full clauses,
incorporation of course suggests that they are subordinate to these clauses.
Not all the languages in question provide the same evidence for incorporation, but in all of them, *-ing* clauses are characterized by one or more of the
following properties:

(A)   Reduced clauses are within the scope of negation expressed as a category
        in the full clause.

Thus Hindi (Davison 1981:113)

(21)   Woo doostõõ-see mil-*kar*   nahĩĩ ayaa
         3sg. friend-with meet-*kar* not   come=perf.
         "He came without meeting his friends"

(To ensure that S1 does not fall within the scope of a negation on S2, the
particle *bhii* "also, even" must separate the clauses, cf. (12) above.)
So too, Turkish (Lewis 1967: chapter 11):

(22)   Zengo-yu gör-*üp* kork-ma-mak imkânsı z-dı
         Zengo-acc. see-*Ip* fear-neg.-inf impossible-was
         "It was impossible not to see and fear Zengo"

To ensure that S1 does not fall within the scope of a negation on S2, the particle *dA* "also, and" must separate clauses:

(23)   Zengo-yu gör-*üp* de kork-ma-mak imkânsızdı
       "It was impossible to see Zengo, and not fear him"

There is one other circumstance under which S1 does not fall within the scope of a negation on S2, and that is where (as in indirect polar questions) the negative is the only category with respect to which S1 and S2 may differ:

(24)   Orhan-ı   sev-*ip* sev-me-diğ-i-ni   bil-m-iyor
       Orhan-acc. love-*Ip* love-neg.-nom.-3sg.-acc. know-neg.-prog.-3sg.
       "She does not know whether she loves Orhan or not"(Lewis 1967:178)

So also Hua:

(25)   Sokohu-ka   ʔaʔ-ha-ne
       good-2sg.ant. neg.-do-2sg.final
       "You didn't do it well"

To preserve S1 from being within the scope of negation on S2, another verb form must be used for S1, or the two clauses may be separated by the conjunction *ito* "but, and", as shown in (26–7).

(26)   Fumo p-mi-maʔ-borava   ʔaʔ-de-e
       pork them-give-3sg.med.-but neg.-eat-3sg.final
       "He gave them pork but ate none"
(27)   Fumo p-mi-ro-na   ito ʔaʔ-de-e
       pork them-give-perf.-3sg.ant. but neg.-eat-3sg.final
       "He gave them pork but ate none"

It is notable that (27) even with *ito* is not quite acceptable unless the verb of S1 occurs with the perfective auxiliary *ro-*, which is usually employed to indicate that S1 and S2 are separate episodes with an intervening time lapse. Thus the peculiarity of (28) which is identical with (27) but for the absence of this perfective auxiliary.

(28)   ?Fumo p-mi-na ito ʔaʔ-de-e

   The possibility of negation penetrating into the reduced clause contrasts with the impossibility of such penetration into a full coordinate clause, in English as well as in any of the languages exemplified above.

(B)   Reduced clauses are within the scope of interrogation expressed as a
       grammatical category in the full clause.

Thus Hindi (Davison 1981:108):

(29)   Tum   Teelefoon kar-kee aaoogii?
            you=fam. telephone do-kar come=2=fut.=fam.=fem.
            "Are you going to make this call before you come?"
            Literally: "Are you going to come, having made this call?"

To keep S1 out of the scope of interrogation on S2, S2 must be separated from S1 by the clause-initial polar question particle *kyaa*.
Thus, Turkish:

(30)   Oku-yup gel-di   mi?
            read-Ip come-past=3sg. int.
            "Did s/he read it before coming?"
            Literally: "Did s/he come having read it?"

So also Hua:

(31)   P-mi-na   de-ve?
            them-give-3sg.ant. eat-3sg.=int.
            "Did he give it to them and eat?"
            Literally: "Giving it to them, did he eat?"

To protect S1 from being in the scope of negation or interrogation on S2, the same verb form – a conditional desinence – may be used in S1, as for example in (32).

(32)   P-mi-mamo   de-ve?
            them-give-cond.=3sg. eat-int.=3sg.
            "Given that he gave it to them, did he eat?"

So also in Hungarian, especially in those cases where S1 signals a concomitant activity:

(33)   Énekel-ve$_{S1}$][$_{S2}$jöttek-e   haza?
            sing   vE   they=came-int. home
            "Did they come home singing?"

The answer "nem" (= "no") would mean that they were not singing rather than that they did not come home.
So also, apparently, Lenakel (Lynch 1978:98):

(34)   T-i-ak-etu-ol$_{S1}$]   [$_{S2}$m-ign-in   iik?
            fut.-1exc.-conc.-int.-do echo-fear-trans. you
            "How could I be frightened of you?"
            Literally: "How could I do and I fear you?"

So too in Japanese (Martin 1975:486), although "the general pattern is for the negative not to carry back through the earlier gerunds . . . where the negative does carry through, the phrase is often a rather tight idiom". But the very fact that such tight idioms are possible with *S1-te S2* constructions is evidence for the incorporation of S1 into S2, at least as a possibility of this structure. There are three possible interpretations for (35).

(35)   Kare ni   at-te $_{S1}$]$[_{S2}$sore o   tutaenakatta kara . . .   (ibid. citing
         he   dat. meet-te   that obj. not=tell=past   Mikami 1963:36–7)

On the first (and, according to Mikami, the most common), negation is confined to S2: "I met him, and I didn't tell him that". On the second, negation is confined to S1: "I didn't tell him that face to face". On the third, negation is in both S1 and S2: "I didn't meet him and I didn't tell him". In none of these languages does negation in either S1 or S2 "carry into" the other clause when both are full clauses conjoined by "and".

(C)   Word order facts indicate that reduced clauses function as constituents of
        the full sentence with which they occur.

The facts are of two different kinds. In Hua, Japanese, and Hindi, we find that the reduced S1 may be surrounded by material from S2. In Hungarian, the behavior of separable verbal prefixes and the grammaticalization of preverbal focus position within a given clause force us to identify reduced clauses as elements of the clause with which they occur.

In Hindi, Davison (1981:107) points out that *S1+kar*, unlike *S1 ∥ aur phir*, allows elements of S2 to appear to the left of it, thus establishing the structure $_{S1}$[. . . [$_{S2}$] . . .]$_{S1}$. For example, the acceptability of both (36a) and (36b) contrasts with the difference in acceptability between (37a) and (37b).

(36)   a. Akeelee baiTh+kar *caay* pii   thii
           alone sit   kar *tea* drink be
        b. *Caay* akeelee baiTh+kar pii   thii
           tea alone sit   kar drink be
           "He sat alone drinking tea."
(37)   a. Akeelee baiTh+aa   aur *caay* pii   thii
           alone sit   perf. and *tea* drink be
        b.*caay akeelee baiTh+ aa   aur pii   thii
           tea alone sit   perf. and drink be
           "He sat alone and drank tea"

Davison (1981) proposes that the ungrammaticality of (37b) is because it violates Ross' (1967) coordinate structure constraint. The contrasting acceptability of (36b), of course, then suggests that S1 in this sentence is not coordinate with S2, but in some other relationship to it. Davison argues that this relationship must be one of subordination. We might say, more neutrally, that the relationship is that diagrammed on p. 197, that of incorporation.

Similar facts obtain in Hua, although I have only textual evidence rather than judgments of grammaticality to go on. Briefly, there are no cases where an element of S2 can occur before S1, if S1 and S2 are regarded as conjoined clauses. On the other hand there are many cases where material from S2 may precede S1, if S1 is an adverb (usually an adverb of manner) modifying S2. Thus, contrasting with the ungrammaticality (or at least, the non-occurrence) of sentences like (38) is the frequent occurrence of sentences like (39).

(38)　　*Eva?*　zumo risanada　　　　　kmigue
　　　　　money work you=will=do=and=I I=will=give=you
　　　　　"You will work and I will give you money"

(39)　　*Fumo* brgefita　　　　　dae
　　　　　pork　they=were=quick=and they=ate
　　　　　"They ate the pork quickly"

The word order criterion in Hua forces us to distinguish between incorporation and subordination. Incorporated S1 may be preceded by elements of S2, as in sentence (39) above. Subordinated S1 (such as, for example, conditional protasis clauses) may not be, as witness the non-occurrence of sentences like (40).

(40)　　*Eva?*　zumo risapamo kmigue
　　　　　money work if=you=do I=will=give=you
　　　　　"If you work, I will give you money"

In Japanese, Martin (1975:511) observes that in those sentences where S2 acts as an auxiliary "the gerund cannot be separated from the following auxiliary by adjunct phrases; all sentence adjuncts [i.e. elements of S2] must PRECEDE the gerund [i.e. S1]". This would mean that where S2 is an auxiliary, the word order $_{S2}[\ldots [S1] \ldots]_{S2}$ is *obligatory*.

The data in Hungarian are somewhat more complex and the criterion for incorporation more language-specific, but the bottom line is the same. Reduced S1 function as constituents within S2. Here is the evidence.

A number of verbs occur with a separable prefix which, like separable prefixes in German or post-verb particles in English, seems to mark aspect or direction. Usually, this prefix cannot occur anywhere but before the verb. Note the contrast between (41a) and (41b).

(41)   a. Meg-álltam
            perf.-I=stopped
         b.*Álltam   meg
            I=stopped   perf.
            "I stopped"

The position immediately preceding the verb stem is reserved for items in focus (in positive assertions in the perfective aspect). This allows the two possibilities

(a) ... X prefix + Verb ...
(b) ... X Verb # prefix ...

where "X" is not in focus in the (a) schema, but "X" is in focus in the (b) schema. Note the semantic contrast between (42a) in which *akkor* is not in focus and (42b) in which it is.

(42)   a. Akkor meg-álltam
            then   perf.-I=stopped
            "I stopped then"
         b. Akkor álltam   meg
            then I=stopped perf.
            "It was then that I stopped"

Now consider sentences in which a sentence like (41) functions as an S2 following another element S1. Where this S1 is a full clause conjoined with S2 by a conjoining word *és* "and", then S1, however surprising or focussed, cannot act as the focus which triggers verb-prefix inversion in S2. Contrast the acceptability of (43a) with the unacceptability of (43b).

(43)   a. Meghökkentem és   meg-álltam
            I=was=shocked and perf.-I=stopped
            "I was shocked and stopped"
         b.*Meghökkentem és   álltam   meg
            I=was=shocked and I=stopped perf.
            "I was shocked and stopped"

On the other hand, where S1 occur as the gerundive clause, both word orders occur. The semantic contrast is exactly parallel to that between the sentences of (42).

(44)   a. Meghökken-ve meg-álltam
            shocked-ve   perf.-I=stopped
            "I was shocked and stopped"
         b. Meghökken-ve álltam meg
            "It was in amazement that I stopped"

This suggests that *S1 + ve* is a constituent of S2 in exactly the same way that an adverb like *akkor* is a constituent of the sentence in (42).

It may be appropriate to note here that in Germanic languages which observe the verb-second constraint, similar behavior is attested. Reduced S1 function as elements of S2 and force the finite verb of S2 to follow them directly. Full S1 do not function as elements of S2, and allow the subject of S2 to follow them. Thus the contrast between (45a)

(45)   a. Er atmete tief und (er) blieb   stumm
            he breathed deep and (he) remained silent

in which the finite verb of S2, *blieb*, may follow its subject and still be able to satisfy the verb-second constraint, and (45b),

(45)   b. Tief atme-nd blieb   er stumm
            deep breath-ing remained he silent

in which subject–verb inversion in S2 is necessary to keep the verb in second position. The impossibility of (46a) demonstrates that *S1 und* cannot function as the first constituent of S2. On the other hand, the ungrammaticality of (46b) shows that *S1 + nd* must function as the first constituent of S2.

(46)   a.*Er atmete tief und blieb er stumm
        b.*Tief atmend er blieb stumm

The word order criterion is different from that which allows us to identify clause-constituency in Hungarian; but the criterion yields the same results.

4.3 On the conceptual closeness of *-ing* clauses and full clauses

In all the languages under discussion here with the exception of Japanese, reduced clauses must have the same subject as the full clauses with which they are conjoined. In all these languages, with no exceptions, the reduced clauses have the same tense as the full clauses with which they are conjoined.

The category of mood is a little more complicated by virtue of the fact that it includes two mutually independent dimensions. The dimension of assertion vs. interrogation has been described in 2.2. It cannot be said that S1 and S2 agree in mood. However, it is generally true, as discussed in the last section, that S1 may be within the scope of interrogation that is marked only on S2. The dimension of modality includes indicative, subjunctive, and imperative. Along this dimension, S1 and S2 agree entirely.

In addition to these kinds of conceptual closeness, which are relatively uncontroversial, we should also note the following:

4.3.1 S1 + *ing* S2 constructions frequently mark a single event

While constructions of the form *S1 and S2* frequently denote two events with a time interval between them, constructions of the form *S1 + ing S2* have as one of their characteristic meanings the simultaneity of S1 and S2, with the result that the two are often perceived as aspects of a single episode rather than two separate events. Thus the use of *S1 + te* in Japanese to express instrumentality, (8e); and the apparently universal use of reduced clauses to express adverbs of manner.

Thus, Davison (105) points out that the Hindi sentence in (47) is ambiguous.

(47)　　Us-nee　sooc-kar　kaam　kiyaa
　　　　3sg.-erg. think-kar work　do=perf.

On one reading, in which it is nearly synonymous with *S1 aur phir S2*, it describes two episodes: "Having thought, s/he did the work". But on another reading, which is peculiar to this construction, S1 acts as an adverb of manner modifying the verb of S2: "S/he did the work *carefully*". Note that on this latter reading, the conceptual closeness between two clauses is so great that a two-clause interpretation is impossible.

In Japanese, Martin (1975: 491) lists "many single-gerund statements of manner...: *waratte* 'laughingly', *isoi-de* 'rushing=hastily', *yorokon-de* 'rejoicing=gladly', *iradat-te* 'impatiently'... " and many others.

In Hungarian, *Verb + vE* functions as an adverb of manner in sentences like (33), as well as in (48a) whose meaning contrasts with that of (48b).

(48)　　a. Nyög-ve　ülő　helyzetbe　　emelkedtem
　　　　　　groan-vE sitting position=into I=raised=myself
　　　　　　"Groaning, I raised myself into a sitting position"
　　　　b. Nyög-t-em　es　ülő　helyzetbe　　emelkedtem
　　　　　　groan-past-1sg. and sitting position=into I=raised=myself
　　　　　　"I groaned and raised myself into a sitting position"

In Hua, all adverbs of manner are reduced clauses whose verb consists of the stem followed by the anticipatory desinence. One example was given in (25) above. Another is given in (49).

(49)　　Brgefu-na　　rmie
　　　　quick-3sg.ant 3sg.=went=down
　　　　"He went down *quickly*"

Other verbs which may act as manner adverbs are *zapuahuna* "vigorously" (from *zapua hu-* "exert oneself"), *amanamahuna* "easily" (from *amanama hu-* "be easy"), *kona* "carefully" (from *ko-* "look, see"), *hazohuna* "correctly" (from *hazo hu-* "do properly") and so on.

Systematic data on adverbs of manner in Lenakel are not available, but the following are suggestive facts:

(a) directional adverbs of motion are syntactically *m + verb stem* forms as in (50).

(50)   I-im-aliuok   m-vin   apwa Lenakel
lexc.-past-walk echo-go loc.   Lenakel
"I walked to Lenakel"

(Lynch 1978:75)

(b) the interrogative adverb "how" seems to be the compound verb *etu-ol* "how do", acting as S1, while the "main verb" occurs as an echo verb in S2. Thus, sentence (34) above.

(c) *S1mS2* seems to be the standard means of indicating simultaneity, as in (51).

(51)   R-im-am-arik   l-auanu m-am-ataw-ol
3sg.-past-cont.-stay in-village echo-cont.-what-do
"What did he do while he was staying in the village?" (Lynch 1978:99)

(d) Lynch derives *m-*, the echo-subject marker, from a morpheme meaning "and" (cf. Lynch 1983). In present-day Lenakel, the clause conjunction "and" is *kani*, and the nominal coordinating conjunction is *mine*, so there is no similarity between them. However, it is highly significant that "when two conjoined NPs are thought of as being almost inseparable . . . *mine* usually contracts to *m*" (Lynch 1978:101–2). This alternation not only validates Lynch's later (1983) etymological conjecture about the origin of *m-* through phonological identity, it is compatible with the observation that *S1 m S2* are conceptually closer than *S1 kani S2*.

The greater conceptual closeness of clauses of the form *S1-ing S2* has not gone unrecognized. Thus, in Hindi, Davison (1981:120) notes that there is a tendency for *S1-kar S2* constructions to indicate what is conceptualized as a single episode, while *S1 aur phir S2* marks a transition from one episode to another, as illustrated in (52).

(52) a. Mantrii-nee vinay-see   sir jhukaayaa *aur* dhiree-see   jawaab diyaa
minister-erg. humility-with head incline=perf. *and* slowly-rather answer give=perf.
"The minister inclined his head modestly and slowly gave his answer"
b. Mantrii-nee vinay-see sir jhukaa-*kar* dhiree-see jawaab diyaa
"The minister, inclining his head modestly, slowly gave his answer"

In Japanese, Martin (1975:975) points out that *S1 si S2* "differs from the gerund in that there is no necessary logical or temporal connection between the two sentences linked with si . . .", which may therefore be elements of an enumeration rather than parts of a single conceptual unity:

(53)   Kyuuzitu da si tenki da si Yamada ga kuru daroo
        "It's a holiday, the weather is nice, and Yamada will come, I think"
                                                      (Martin 1975:976)

4.3.2 Auxiliarization or serialization

The extreme of conceptual fusion between verbs is represented where one loses its status as a verb and becomes an "auxiliary" to the other. Intuitively, we might expect that the verb which is reduced is the one which becomes an auxiliary, insofar as there is some sense in which "auxiliaries" are less important or less central to the meaning of a sentence than are "main verbs". In fact, this expectation is disappointed, and auxiliarization does not in general correspond to degree of reduction. We find that in many verb-final languages (e.g. Japanese, Turkish, Hua) it is the (final) auxiliary in the verb complex which has all the *morphological* trappings of a verb while the semantically main verb (and all auxiliaries but the last) consist of the bare verb stem.

What is significant is that often the structure *S1-ing S2* has only one-clause translations, in which either S1 or S2 is acting as an auxiliary rather than as a separate verb. The lexicalization of the meaning of the reduced construction is (by definition) idiosyncratic, but the common denominator is that a bi-clausal translation is in every case impossible, a fact which attests to the total incorporation of one clause within the other.

In Hua, the construction *V1-anticipatory desinence V2* has a number of possible meanings for which no two-clause paraphrase is possible. Some of these are:

(a) compound verbs: *ri-* "take", "hold" +*o-* "come" means "bring". Compare (54a) with (54b).

(54)   a. Ri-na   e-e
           take-3sg.ant. come-3sg.=final
           "He brought it"
        b. Ri-ro-na   e-e
           take-perf.-3sg.ant. come-3sg.=final
           "He took and he came" (where the perfective auxiliary *ro-* indicates a
           time interval between S1 and S2)

(b) where V2 is *iro-* "leave", it acts as an auxiliary expressing "freedom of action" (Haiman 1980:357). Thus compare (55a) with (55b).

(55)   a. Do-ka   iro-o!
           eat-2sg.ant. leave-imp.sg.
           "Eat away!"
        b. Do-ro-ka   iro-o!
           eat-perf.-2sg.ant. leave-imp.sg.
           "Eat and then leave some!" (where again, the perfective auxiliary *ro*-
on V1 ensures a two-clause interpretation by indicating a time interval between S1
and S2)

    (c) where V2 is *to*-, it acts as a transitivizing auxiliary (cf. Haiman
1980:355–7, Haiman 1982a). Compare (56a) with (56b).

(56)   a. Zuʔ ki-na   d-te-e
           house build-3sg.ant. me-put-3sg.final
           "He built me a house"
        b. Zuʔ ki-ro-na   d-te-e
           house build-perf.-3sg.ant. me-put-3sg.final
           "He built a house and put me (down?)"

It is difficult to interpret (56b) because it seems that *to*- has almost lost its
meaning as a separate verb "put".
    (d) where V1 is *kaso*- "exceed, surpass", it functions as a comparative
auxiliary, as in (57).

(57)   D-gaso-na   zaʔzafi-e
        me-surpass-3sg.ant. tall-3sg.final
        "He is taller than me"

The canonical structure of the $V + Aux$ complex in Hua differs from that of
the serial construction exemplified throughout this chapter:

        Serial construction: V1 + ant. (prefixes) V2
        Auxiliary construction: V1 + ∅ + ∅ + V2

That is, in a canonical auxiliary construction the main verb is stripped of all
suffixes and the auxiliary of all prefixes: V1 and V2 are contiguous. There is
sporadic evidence that a serial construction may sometimes be reduced to
the point where only its stress pattern differentiates it from an auxiliary
construction.
    Where the V2 is *to*-, the transitivizing auxiliary, and this verb happens to
have a non-prefixing form (i.e. the negative prefix *ʔaʔ*- is lacking, and the
object of the verb is 3sg. ∅-), then V1 may optionally lose its anticipatory
desinential suffix as well. I have not found any difference in meaning
between the standard (58a) and the sporadically occurring (58b), which is
morphologically parallel with constructions such as (59).

(58)   a. Vo-na   Ø-te-e
            lie-3sg.ant. 3sg.-put-3sg.final
            "He laid him down" (or: "He knocked him over")
         b. Vo-Ø Ø-te-e
(59)   Vo-re-e
            lie-perf.-3sg.final
            "He lay down/slept"

Where V2 is *bai-* "be, stay" there is again only a minimal difference between
the standard serial construction, exemplified by (60a) and the auxiliary
construction in the progressive aspect, exemplified by (60b).

(60)   a. Mi-na   bai-e
            give-3sg.ant. stay-3sg.final
            "Giving s/he stayed"
         b. Mi-bai-e
            give-prog.-3sg.final
            "S/he is/was giving"

In my fieldnotes and texts, I have a number of other, sporadic cases of V1
reduction, where the serial form *V1 + anticipatory desinence* is replaced by
the bare verb stem.

In Japanese as well, the construction *S1 + te S2* has a number of
meanings for which no bi-clausal paraphrase is possible. Martin
(1975:510–51) describes in detail some of the ways in which the verb of S2 is
auxiliarized, and I will repeat only a small number of his examples here,
noting first that about "half of all occurrences of the verb gerund are with
an auxiliary"(512).

(a) In many cases, the combination *V1 + te V2* has been phonologically
lexicalized, losing the stress pattern characteristic of a *gerund # verb*
combination. The status of *mot-te kúru* "holding, comes" and *mot-te iku*
"holding, goes" as "new tonic verbs" meaning, respectively, "bring" and
"take" seems to be universally agreed upon (513).

(b) The combination *V1 + te iru* is ambiguous. On one reading, it is a
coordinate construction:

(61)   Inaka e it-te nagaku soko ni   i-ta
            country go-te long   time there stay-past
            "I went to the country and stayed there a long time"   (Martin 517)

But where no nominal arguments intervene between V1 and V2, *iru* may be
an aspectual auxiliary with repetitive, continuative, or resultative meanings. Martin (517) points out that on the repetitive reading *V1 + te iru* is

almost entirely synonymous with the simple imperfect in -*ru* (with which *iru* is cognate?), as illustrated in (62).

(62)   a. Tosyo-kan de hon   o   yom-*(r)u*
         library   at book obj. read-*imperf.*
         b. Tosyo-kan de hon   o   yom-*te iru* (/yonde iru/)
         library   at book obj. read-*te stay*
         "(I) regularly read/will read books at the library"

(c) The combination *V1 + te aru* (*aru* = "exists") is used to form "a kind of roundabout passive that permits one to take the object of the transitive verb and turn it into the subject" (Martin 524).

(d) The combination *V1 + te simau* (*simau* = "puts away") is ambiguous between a bi-clausal reading, as in (63)

(63)   Huyumono o zenbu arat-te   sore-ra o simat-ta
         winter clothes   wash-te   put=away-past
         "I washed the winter clothes and put them away"   (Martin 533)

and (again, when no adjuncts intervene) an auxiliary reading meaning "finish", "do completely", or "finally do": "I finished washing all the winter clothes".

(e) The combination *V1 + te miru* (*miru* = "look") is also ambiguous between a single clause and bi-clausal reading. For example, the sentence (64) cited by Martin (541) can mean either "I took the book and looked at it" (two clauses) or "I tried reading the book (e.g. to see what the result would be)". On the latter reading, *miru* functions as a conative auxiliary.

(64)   Hon o   tot-te mi-masita
         book obj. take-te look-past

In each case of ambiguity cited here, the spoken language distinguishes (iconically) between a two-clause and a one-clause reading by the pause or absence of pause between S1 and S2. Not surprisingly, *S1 pause S2* indicates two clauses, while *S1 S2* in these (only lexically) ambiguous constructions indicates that the verb of S2 is acting as an auxiliary to the verb in S1.

In all of these cases, then, incorporation marks conceptual closeness. There is no evidence in Japanese that reduction indicates background-ing – indeed, quite the reverse seems to be true, since the reduced verb is the "main verb" in a Verb + Auxiliary construction.

4.4 On some properties of "subordinate" clauses

The notion of subordination is so familiar to us from our school days that (with rare exceptions; cf. Matthews 1981: chapters 9–10) hardly anyone bothers to justify the label in their own descriptive and analytical work. Thus, there is almost unanimous, if inarticulate, agreement that *-ing* clauses and their analogs in other languages are indeed subordinate.

To the extent that this opinion is supported by argument at all, we may find, or ourselves construct, the following rationalizations:

(a) *-ing* clauses are dependent (and dependent = subordinate)

(b) *-ing* clauses are reduced (and reduced = subordinate)

(c) *-ing* clauses are not coordinate with full clauses, since material may be removed from the full clause without violation of the coordinate structure constraint

(d) *-ing* clauses have the syntactic properties listed in section 4.2, all of which demonstrate that they are incorporated into, rather than conjoined with, the full clause on which they depend (and incorporated = subordinate)

(e) *-ing* clauses may either precede or follow the full clauses on which they depend without thereby implying a different order of events. They are not tense-iconic (and tense-iconic = coordinate)

(f) *-ing* clauses mark backgrounded activity (and backgrounded = subordinate)

Possibly there are other reasons one might consider, but the list above more than exhausts any catalog of criteria for subordination that anyone to my knowledge has yet proposed. Not all of these reasons are equally cogent, and I will begin my discussion by disposing of the weakest first.

(a) Dependence does not equal subordination
The argument that dependent clauses are subordinate is presumably based on the unacceptability of sentence fragments like

(65)   a.* because/if/after/when/although the fish stunk up the house

All of the constructions of (65a) are subordinate clauses and they cannot stand alone. Therefore, if a clause cannot stand alone, it must be subordinate. This argument is effectively eliminated by sentence fragments like (65b).

(65)   b.* The fish stunk up the house and

-*ing* clauses cannot stand alone: but whether they exhibit this property by virtue of their similarity to (65a) or (65b) is entirely open.[1]

(b) Reduction does not equal subordination

The reduction of -*ing* clauses is also characteristic of clauses which have undergone coordinate reduction. The evidence furnished by Lenakel, in particular, suggests very strongly that deletion under identity in -*ing* clauses is governed by coordination reduction or gapping: gapping goes forwards if the identical elements are prefixes on the verb, and backwards if they are suffixes.

There is in fact very good evidence that subordinate clauses are (at least partially) characterized by their *failure* to undergo reduction of the kind described in section 4.1: subordinate clauses mark subject, tense, and mood on the verb whether this is identical with that of the main verb or not. I established a set of criteria for distinguishing between coordinate and subordinate dependent clauses in Hua (Haiman 1976a; 1980:391–430), arguing that the distinctive property of subordinate clauses in general was their semantic independence of the clauses in which they were embedded: a subordinate S1 was not possible within the scope of either negation or interrogation on a matrix S2; a subordinate clause did not have to be in the same tense or the same mood as the matrix sentence, its tense being open, and its mood invariably assertive (the latter property being equivalent to the presuppositional or given nature of many subordinate clause types); a subordinate clause was not tense-iconic with the matrix clause, i.e. the sequence of events did not necessarily correspond to the sequence of clauses; and whether or not the subject of the subordinate clause was identical with that of the principal clause in which it was embedded was not marked by any switch-reference device. Subordinate clauses so defined *never* undergo the reduction characteristic of Hua -*ing* clauses exemplified in (17b) (repeated below) and always mark tense, mood, and subject. Thus the contrast between (66) and (17b).

(66)   Mi-*gi-ma*-na   do gi-e   (S1 is subordinate)
       give-*fut.*-3sg.med.-3sg.ant. eat fut.-3sg.final
       "He will give her some and s/he will eat"

---

[1] For an amazingly prescient refutation of the identity of dependent and subordinate clauses cf. Paul (1880/1968:148). He argued that the mere fact that clauses are conjoined in discourse ipso facto makes them dependent on each other. He concluded that there could be no purely paratactic relationship between clauses, at least in the sense that neither determined the other, and that the only possible conception of parataxis was that in which dependence between clauses was mutual.

(The pronouns *he* and *she* are used as a convenient shorthand device for indicating coreference or the lack of it. The ambiguity of (66) indicates that the subordinate verb *migimana* fails to mark switch-reference.)

(17)   b. Mi-$\emptyset$-$\emptyset$-na   do-gi-e   (S1 is coordinate)
            give   3sg.ant. eat-fut.-3sg.final
            "He will give her some and eat"

(In (17b), it will be recalled, the suffixes of tense and person in S1 are zeroed under identity with those of S2.) Recent work in other Papuan languages such as Chuave (Thurman 1978), Usan (Reesink ms), Fore (Scott 1978), Tauya (MacDonald, to appear), Gimi (Haiman 1980:527), Siane (Haiman 1980:542), and Gende (Brandson mss) demonstrates the existence of the same set of distinctions between coordinate and subordinate dependent clauses. To the extent that the syntactic and semantic criteria adduced for subordinate clauses are valid, the reduction of *-ing* clauses is characteristic of *coordinate* clauses and these alone.

(c) Conceptual closeness, not backgrounding, motivates incorporation
In section 4.2 I presented some of the syntactic properties of reduced clauses which would seem to justify the following diagrammatic representation:

    s2[... [S1] ...]s2

In section 4.3 I argued that the reduction of these clauses was motivated by their conceptual closeness with the following (or, in the case of Lenakel, the preceding) clause. I now wish to demonstrate that the *incorporation* of the gerundive clause is also motivated by conceptual closeness: that is, not only the size of S1, but its "subordinate" rôle as a part of S2 is motivated by its conceptual closeness to S2. In many cases, it seems that incorporation is dependent on reduction, but there are other cases where there is no reduction involved and yet incorporation is accomplished.

The clearest evidence in support of this contention is provided by Japanese, as discussed by Kuno (1973:chapter 13). I will recapitulate his admirable account of the relevant facts here, dissenting only from his conclusions.

Kuno's discussion of *S1+te S2* constructions explicitly equates his "subordination" of S1 with the following syntactic criteria: S1 is more subordinate to the extent that

> (a) S1 is within the scope of the interrogative particle *ka* on S2 (1973:201);

(b) S1 is within the scope of negation marked on the verb of S2 (204);
(c) S1 is within the scope of a modal auxiliary on the verb of S2 (205);
(d) S1 may be surrounded by morphological material from S2 (206).

In structures of the forms *S1 + te S2*, S1 need not have the same subject as S2. But, "When V1-te . . . V2 appears with two different subjects, V1 ceases to be subordinate to V2" (207). What Kuno means, of course, is that S1 whose subject is different from that of S2 no longer exhibits any of the properties of "subordination" (a–d). For example, where S1 and S2 have different subjects, S1 cannot be surrounded by morphological material from S2. Thus contrast (67) in which S1 precedes S2, with the unacceptable (68).

(67)   [John ga   uwagi o   nui-de$_{S1}$]   Mary wa   hangaa ni kaketa
        John sub. jacket obj. take=off-te Mary topic hanger on hang=past
        "When John took off his jacket, Mary hung it on the hanger"
(68)   *Mary wa   [John ga   uwagi o   nui-de$_{S1}$]   hangaa ni kaketa
        Mary topic John sub. jacket obj. take=off-te hanger on hang=past
        "Mary, when John took off his jacket, hung it on the hanger"

That is, with respect to property (d) S1 is not "subordinate" to S2 where it does not share a subject with S2. In the same way, S1 is not subordinate to S2 with respect to the other properties Kuno enumerates, where S1 and S2 do not share a common subject (209).

There is no plausible definition of subordination whereby a clause is more subordinate by virtue of sharing a subject than it would be if it did not share a subject, with a following clause. Kuno has been describing not "subordination" with his criteria (a–d), but a property of incorporation. And to say that "incorporation" increases where clauses share a common subject is to adopt the familiar and iconic logic of the Venn diagram. Not only are the indices of "subordination" as enumerated by Kuno quite implausible: some of them are in fact the very opposite of what traditionally characterize "subordination" in traditional (but perhaps no less wrong-headed) accounts.

For example, the fact that reduced S1 may lie within the scope of negation or interrogation of modality is certainly an index of incorporation. But on what conceivable grounds is it an index of subordination? Consider the behavior of manner adverbials in English (and recall that all reduced S in the languages we are discussing can function as manner adverbials). As is well known, in many sentences, these are precisely the constituents which are denied or questioned, compare (69a,b).

(69)   a. You didn't do it carefully
        b. Did you do it carefully?

There are familiar analyses (e.g. Carden 1976) wherein this kind of behavior was used to identify such adverbs as higher (not lower) verbs. The criterial principle invoked by Carden was that only the highest verb within the complement of a negative operator was negated by this operator. The behavior of such manner adverbs certainly contrasts with that of relatively uncontroversial subordinate clauses such as those introduced by *when*, etc., as in (70).

(70)   a. When I saw you last, you weren't so pretty
        b. When I saw you last, were you already in high school?

Neither negation nor interrogation of S2 includes the verb of S1 in its scope. In fact, Karttunen's (1971) typology of "plugs, holes, and filters" demonstrates that there is no necessary isomorphism between inclusion within the scope of interrogation and negation on the one hand, and subordination on the other.

Scope inclusion, on the other hand, is a partial index of incorporation inasmuch as what is *not* incorporated within an S cannot possibly be questioned or denied within that S. But incorporation certainly is not the same as subordination with respect to this criterion.

I turn now to a group of languages, typified by Latin, in which it becomes necessary to talk about *degrees of incorporation*. (For an early attempt to formalize this notion, cf. Williams 1975.) For our purposes, it is enough to say that an element is more tightly incorporated into a clause when it functions as part of the *nucleus* of that clause than when it functions as part of the *periphery*. The nucleus is the verb and its arguments; the periphery, optional elements of the clause that are not governed by the verb.

By this criterion, ablative absolute clauses in Latin (like genitive absolutes in Greek, or dative absolutes in Balto-Slavic) are peripheral elements. What is essential about such a construction is not whether it is ablative, genitive, dative, or (as in English) nominative, but the fact that it is *absolute*: that is, the case is not governed by the verb. Consider now the standard (schoolboy Latin) minimal contrast pair cited by Kühner (1879) and given in (71).

(71)   a. *Aristide   patriā   pulsō,*   Persae
           Aristides=abl. from=his=country expelled=abl. the=Persians
           Graecōs aggressī sunt
           the=Greeks attacked

"When Aristides was expelled from his country, the Persians attacked the Greeks"

b. Aristides *patriā* *pulsus,* Lacedaemonium fugit
Aristides=nom. from=his=country expelled=nom. to Lacedemon fled
"When Aristides was expelled from his country, he fled to Lacedemon"

Standard wisdom dictates that the ablative absolute construction must be used where the subjects of the two clauses are *distinct* (as in (71a)), the conjunct participle where the subjects of the two clauses are identical (as in (71b)). While this is a bit of an oversimplification (cf. Morani 1973, Haiman 1983a), the following statement is probably valid: the ablative absolute construction is used when the subjects of the two clauses in question are distinct, and in some cases where they are identical; the conjunct participle construction is used only where the subjects of the two clauses are identical.

It is interesting to note in this connection Hale & Buck's (1903:220) characterization of the ablative absolute construction as a neutral one that *emphasizes a loose connection* between itself and the matrix clause. They illustrate the peculiar looseness of this connection with ablative absolute constructions used as concessives:

(72) Id paucīs defendentibus, expugnāre non potuit
it few=abl. defending=abl. to=drive=out not 3sg.=was=able
"Although few defended it, he was unable to drive them out"

It is clear that what marks ablative absolute constructions semantically is some kind of conceptual distance between themselves and the main clause. And this is reflected in their lower degrees of incorporation, compared with conjunct participles. Compare the phrase structure representation of the italicized clauses in (71) above. In classical transformational grammar both would be described as transformed versions of (the deep structure underlying) the sentence *Aristides patria pulsus est* "Aristides was expelled from his country". The ablative absolute construction of (a) is peripheral to (and optional relative to) the main clause:

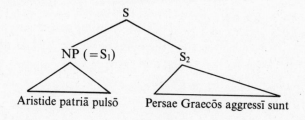

The conjunct participial construction on the other hand occurs as a relative clause on the subject of (and thus, a nuclear element of) the matrix sentence:

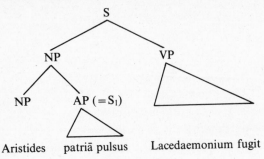

We may confidently assert that *Aristides* in this construction originates as the subject of S2 rather than as part of S1, because its case is determined by its relationship to the verb of S2 rather than to the verb of S1. In (71b), where the NP in question is the subject of both S1 and of S2, its origin seems ambiguous, but this ambiguity is cleared up in cases like (73) where S1 is presumably the same as in the example of (71).

(73)   Aristid-em   patriā   puls-um   vidērunt
       Aristides-acc. from=country expelled-acc. they=saw
       "They saw Aristides expelled from his country"

Aristides occurs in the accusative case here only by virtue of being the direct object of the verb "see". The minimal hypothesis consistent with the form of this sentence is that *Aristidem* originates as the object of S2, and the subject of S1 has undergone deletion.

As in Japanese, there is no sense here in which the degree of incorporation need be associated with anything like a traditional notion of "subordination". There *is* clearly a sense, however, in which the degree of incorporation is related to conceptual closeness.

To hammer this point home, I want to make a brief digression now to a subject that may seem totally unrelated: the distinction between direct and indirect speech. There are a number of well-known differences between the two, differences which call into question the superficial viewpoint that indirect speech can be derived from direct speech by the simple expedient of changing a couple of pronouns and the tense of the verb. Consider, for example, the difference between (74a) and (74b).

(74)   a. Max said "Aha!"
       b.*Max said that aha

The usually optional complementizer *that*, which marks a complement clause as an indirect quotation, renders (74b) ungrammatical. The reason, I maintain, is that the complementizer is an *incorporative* device: it functions as a nominalizer, and marks the following material as playing a rôle (in this case, that of a direct object complement) in the matrix sentence. While indirect quotations can be incorporated in this way, direct quotations in general cannot be. Witness the contrast between the unacceptable (74b) and the perfectly uncontroversial (75).

(75)   John said that he was inspired

The difference beween *aha* and the string *he was inspired* is the theme of my brief discussion now. I maintain that the first cannot be made into an indirect quotation and that is the reason for all the differences between them.

Munro (1982) surveys some of the other ways in which direct quotations fail to act as the direct object complements of the verbs of saying which effect them. She argues very convincingly that there is a difference in *syntactic transitivity* between clauses with direct and indirect speech object complements. With respect to a number of different criteria, the difference between them is diagrammable as follows:

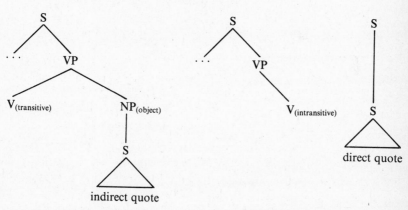

This contrast immediately accounts for the difference between (74a) and (74b): the direct quote "Aha!" *is not a part* of the matrix sentence. Therefore it cannot be made a part of it by the use of an incorporative device like the *that* complementizer. It is also possible to account for such facts as the widespread tendency to supply a lexically *intransitive* verb as the verb of saying when the object is a direct quote, as in (76a).

(76)   a. John went "Aha!"

Note that this locution (colloquial in English, but common in other languages) is impossible where the quotation is indirect, as in (76b).

(76)   b.*John went that he was inspired

From a purely semantic point of view, Munro's schema for direct speech complements seems rather odd. If transitivity is a semantically based notion at all, then presumably "effective verbs" like "make" – which create, and do not merely affect their complements – are highly transitive. All verbs of saying are then as transitive as it is possible to be. The direct quote which cannot function as the object of the verb of saying is the very product of the act of saying itself. Nevertheless, this visible, or rather audible, product of the verb of speaking may not be treated as its object: it cannot appear with a nominalizer like *that*; it cannot take a case marker; and so forth.

The reason for the facts pointed out by Munro was recently highlighted by James McCawley (1968a), who pointed out that a direct quotation is not necessarily an object of the same type as the matrix sentence in which it cannot be embedded. It need not be in the same language:

(77)   a. John said "arma virumque canō"

Nor does it even need to be language at all:

(77)   b. John said (imitation of camel belching)

Direct quotations, in other words, are *mentioned* sounds: although they may be human language, and are usually perfectly grammatical, in principle the only constraints imposed on the content of a direct quotation are the limitations of the organs of speech themselves. Indirect speech in effect has "tamed" these sounds and converted them into objects which are *used* in a linguistic system to refer to the world at large. An iconic index of this conversion is their embeddability into sentences which are linguistic objects of use as well.

That there is a profound difference between *use* and *mention* is familiar in traditional semantics, and often exemplified by such pairs as (78a,b) (adapted from Quine 1961:139–40).

(78)   a. Cicero/Tully was a famous Roman
        b. Cicero's/*Tully's name has three syllables in it

In (78a), where the names are *used* to refer to an individual, they are interchangeable. In (78b), where the names are *mentioned* as objects in their own right, they are no longer interchangeable.

I wish to suggest that there is a further systematic difference between sounds as objects and sounds as functioning units in a linguistic system:

(79)   The devices of incorporation (among them nominalization, case marking, and the like) cannot assimilate sounds as objects (mentioned sounds) into a matrix of sounds used as linguistic entities.

It is the conceptual distance – a difference in type – between use and mention, which I maintain accounts for the non-incorporation of direct speech complements into "object status" in many languages.

It is worth noting that with speech as with conjoined clauses, it is possible to talk of *degrees* of incorporation, and thus, of gradations in the use–mention distinction. In English, there are at least two indices which distinguish direct from indirect questions, for example. The first is that of word order, and the second is that of relative tense.

(80)   a. John asked "When is she going to get here?"
       b. John asked when she was going to get here

In (80a), we find inverted word order and the present tense, both characteristic of the question as uttered. In (80b), we find non-inversion, and the verb has the same tense as that of the matrix clause. Theoretically, the two properties might be independent of each other, so we might expect to find other sentences in which there is no inversion, but also no tense assimilation:

(80)   c.*John asked when she is going to get here

or tense assimilation but inversion also:

(80)   d.*John asked when was she going to get here

The fact that (80c,d) are unacceptable does not mean that these semi-incorporated quotations are always impossible. As Banfield (1973) has observed, preposed "semi-indirect" quotes like that of (80d) are perfectly acceptable with many verbs of saying (out loud or mentally):

(80)   e. When was she going to get there, John wondered

With respect to their preposability, these semi-incorporated questions pattern with direct quotations and contrast with indirect quotations. Compare the acceptability of (81a) and (81b).

(81)   a. "When is she going to get here?" John wondered   (direct quote)
        b.*When she was going to get here, John wondered   (indirect quote

The present significance of this pattern depends on our interpretation of the property of preposability. I shall argue that the kind of preposability which is exemplified by (80e) and (81a) is impossible for object complements. Direct object complements may be preposed in English where the verb is strongly focussed, as in (82).

(82)   That he is a scapegrace I grant you; but saving your reverence, that he is a whoremaster I utterly deny

This is clearly not the force of (80e) and (81a), in which the verb of saying is uttered almost as an afterthought. I maintain, then, that preposability of the sort exemplified in (80e) and (81a) is an index of *non-incorporation*, while the non-preposability of the indirect quotation complement in (81b), like the non-preposability of object nominals in general, is an index of *incorporation*. This leads us to set up, tentatively, a hierarchy of degrees of incorporation of quotation complements in English (see Table 14).

Table 14

	Unincorporated	Partially incorporated	Fully incorporated
inversion	+	+	−
tense-assimilation	−	+	+
	"MENTIONED"	?	"USED"

English is not the only language in which there are independent indices of incorporation. In German, direct quotations occur with verb-second order (at least of the main clause in the quotation), and whatever mood the utterance is in is maintained. Indirect quotations occur with a complementizer *dass*, verb-final order, and the subjunctive mood, as in (83b). Conversely a speaker retaining the word order and the indicative of a direct quotation may frequently wish to indicate that s/he subscribes to the truth of the reported assertion, as in (83a).

(83)   a. Er behauptet "Gott ist eine Frau!" (He says "God is a woman!")
        b. Er behauptet dass Gott eine Frau sei (He says that God is a woman)

In addition to these maximally distinct types, there exists a third, illustrated in (83c): verb-second order is maintained, there is no complementizer *dass*, but the mood of the reported assertion is given in the subjunctive.

Table 15

	Relatively unincorporated	Partially incorporated	Fully incorporated
verb-final, complementizer	−	−	+
subjunctive reported assertion	−	+	+

(83)   c. Er behauptet, Gott sei eine Frau (He says, God is a woman)[2]

Preposability in German, as in English, shows semi-incorporated quotations like that of (83c) pattern with direct quotations like that of (83a):

(84)   a. "Gott ist eine Frau" behauptet der Lehrer
         b. Gott sei eine Frau, behauptet der Lehrer
         c.*Dass Gott eine Frau sei behauptet der Lehrer

(On the other hand, with respect to the verb-second criterion mentioned above, both direct and semi-incorporated quotes are fully incorporated in that they force the matrix verb, as the second constituent of its clause, to follow them directly.) We may then tentatively establish a hierarchy in German (see Table 15) parallel in some respects to that we have set up for English quotation clauses.

It would be interesting to explore further the relative incorporation of intermediate structures like those of (83c) and (84b): unfortunately, the one clearcut index of incorporation in German (whether or not the preposed chunk "counts" as a constituent of the matrix sentence can be read from whether or not it forces the finite verb to immediately follow) does not distinguish types, treating both the direct quotation of (84a) and the semi-indirect quotation of (84b) as fully incorporated.

In tracing the incorporation of serial clauses, we have been looking at one kind of conceptual closeness: most typically, whether or not two clauses share a common subject. In briefly discussing the incorporation of

[2] Paul (1880/1968:146–7) draws attention to a *fourth* possibility with main clause word order, indicative mood, and only the pronominal deixis indicating a deviation from direct quotation: *Er meint, er kann dich betruegen* "He thinks he can fool you", as opposed to *Er meint, er koenne dich betruegen*. The closer the complement of the verb *meint* is to a direct quote, the greater the certainty of the speaker that he knows the actual thoughts and intentions that he is reporting, and thus, the greater his confidence in "playing the rôle" of the person whose thoughts he reports.

speech acts into matrix sentences, we have been looking at a more fundamental kind of conceptual closeness: whether the embedding and the embedded material are linguistic signs or objects in their own right.

It seems that neither subordination nor transitivity are the appropriate categories in terms of which these contrasts should be dealt with. Generalizations can be made, and contrasts explained, however, in terms of incorporation and the major conceptual motivation which gives rise to it, that of closeness or similarity.

The conceptual "subordination" of gerunds or of indirect speech is very questionable. It derives, in the case of gerunds, from the perception that what is reduced in structure is of "lesser importance"; but the perception that indirect quotations represent backgrounded material is totally unsupported.

With this, I conclude my digression on indirect and direct speech, and this section. I hope to have demonstrated that clause incorporation, a property which is often confused with, or simply misnamed, "subordination", is primarily an index of conceptual closeness between clauses. The more they share, the easier it is to incorporate one within the other.

4.5 On some "genuine" subordinate properties of reduced clauses

In 4.4, I described some "bogus" properties of reduced clauses: properties associated with the traditional term "subordination" which are motivated by conceptual closeness rather than by backgrounding.

It is now time to turn to some genuinely subordinate behavior of such reduced clauses which suggests that they really are backgrounded.

The most striking property of gerund or participial clauses which distinguishes them from full coordinate clauses is their freedom from tense iconicity, or their relatively free preposability. Note that *S1 and S2* does not mean the same as *S2 and S1*: the order of clauses mirrors the order of events. On the other hand, *S1 + ing S2* is very close in meaning to *S2 S1 + ing*. In most cases S1 and S2 describe simultaneous activities. In the few cases where they describe serial activities, the activity of *S1 + ing* is understood to precede that of S2, irrespective of their order. I have already argued, in the earlier chapter on symmetry, that free preposability is an index of backgrounding, or liberation from the "time line" on which all foregrounded events occur. Hopper (1979) and Traugott (to appear) both point out the fact that there are many languages in which the same words are both subordinators and markers of simultaneity, among them, of course, English with -*ing*.

But the fact that *S1* + *ing* constructions so typically express *simultaneity*, in turn, may be no more than a consequence of the fact that they signal conceptual closeness in general. Thus, the backgrounding of such clauses may be also finally motivated by nothing more than what motivates incorporation. This conclusion is strengthened by two observations.

First, there are a number of languages, among them Hindi (Davison 1981) and Turkish (Lewis 1967:179), in which the -*ing* morpheme derives etymologically from a past perfective participial ending: the meaning of simultaneity which it now enjoys in these languages is not its etymological birthright. Rather, it seems to have acquired this meaning by virtue of the fact that – through its function as an invariable marker on reduced verbs – it expresses conceptual closeness in general.

Second, the reduced clause is not always the one that is backgrounded. It is in English, Hindi, Hungarian, and Hua. It is not in Japanese, wherein the "full" verb serves as an auxiliary to the reduced verb. This kind of variety is compatible with the premise that all that is signaled directly by the construction *S1* + *ing S2* is the close connection of the events described in these two clauses. It is incompatible with the premise that the reduced clause is necessarily the one that is backgrounded or conceptually subordinate to the other.

4.6 Conclusion

I have argued here that many of the properties of -*ing* clauses, including their morphological reduction, their incorporation, and their freedom from tense iconicity, are motivated, directly or indirectly, by their conceptual closeness with the clauses with which they occur. Conceptual backgrounding is perhaps irrelevant to their present form and functions. Nevertheless, they are interpreted very often as backgrounded because their reduced form is compatible with this etiologically irrelevant motivation.

Reduced clauses are ambiguous between a coordinate and a subordinate reading. In this, they resemble the cases of ambiguity which offered evidence for distinct deep structures in classical generative grammar. Unlike these cases, however, we attribute their ambiguity *to their superficial form itself*.

5 *The case of lexical elaboration*

In creolizing, pidgin languages undergo two major changes; they develop morphology, as they undergo the drift from analysis to synthesis, and they develop an extensive vocabulary. In chapter 3, we discussed the first of these changes, and showed how the drift was part of a more general tendency to reduction, motivated by economic considerations: we also were able to see, in a number of cases, how this tendency resulted in a loss of iconicity.

In this chapter, I wish to consider the second major kind of creolizing change, and establish the following points:

> (a) increase in vocabulary size covaries with decrease in iconicity,
> (b) increase in vocabulary size is itself motivated by considerations of economy.

In section 5.1, I will try to establish at least the plausibility of the first claim, by considering a restricted set of lexically impoverished registers and comparing their grammars with those of the lexically elaborated languages on which they are parasitic. In section 5.2 I will try to demonstrate the correctness of the second claim, (b), by examining the development of a lexically elaborated jargon – "Nukespeak" – which, like any other jargon, is totally opaque to the uninitiated.

5.1 The inverse correlation between vocabulary size and iconicity

Peter Mühlhäusler, in his valuable discussion (1974), speculates that the degree of motivation in a language "is greater where the lexicon of the users of the language is small" – as it is in pidgins – and cites evidence from New Guinea Pidgin and the African pidgin Fanagalo in support of this speculation (1974:98).

Two of the kinds of example that he discusses can be very extensively documented from pidgins around the world. First, he points out that the

230

semantic relationship between *antonyms* is morphologically opaque in many languages: cf. the contrast between English *good* and *bad*, etc. In pidgins, with their relatively impoverished vocabulary, the relationship is often explicit: cf. the New Guinea Pidgin *gutpela* and *no + gut(pela)*, or Fanagalo *vuma* "agree" and *hayi vuma* "refuse".

Second, the semantic relationship between male and female individuals of the same type is often semantically opaque in many languages (cf. English *boy* and *girl*), while in the impoverished pidgins, this relationship is often transparently rendered by compounding of another sort (cf. New Guinea Pidgin *pikinini man* "boy", *pikinini meri* "girl").

In general, the claim that impoverished registers force speakers to substitute for complex concepts other periphrastic expressions which are more or less crude *definitions* of these concepts is strikingly borne out in the restricted registers of taboo languages reported in Australia by Hale (1973), Dixon (1971), and Haviland (1979a).

These taboo registers are generally euphemistic registers used for communication with avoided alters. Although their basic grammar (and grammatical inflections) are identical with the everyday vernacular language, their vocabularies are either partially (cf. Haviland 1979a) or totally (cf. Dixon 1971) disjoint from those of the vernacular. Moreover, their vocabularies, relative to those of the vernacular, are highly *reduced*, by a factor of four or even six to one. These taboo registers therefore provide a unique control situation wherein we can compare linguistic systems which differ ONLY in the size of their total vocabulary, and in no other significant way.

The heightened iconicity of these registers is noted particularly by Dixon (1971), who provides considerable documentation of the different modes of expression in Dyalnguy (restricted, taboo) and Guwal (everyday) registers of Dyirbal. Whereas in Guwal, transitive and intransitive pairs are morphologically unlike (e.g. *yanu* "go" and *mundan* "lead"), in Dyalnguy, the two concepts are rendered by *bawal + bin* "go + intransitive verbalizer" and *bawal + mban* "go + transitive verbalizer" (cf. Dixon 1971:447). While "there are a number of verbs (in Guwal) that have almost the same semantic content but differ only in transitivity . . . the members of such pairs are non-cognate. In almost all these cases there is a single transitive verb in Dyalnguy; the reflexive form of this verb is given as the intransitive member."

In general, the restricted register makes all kinds of taxonomic relationships more transparent than they are in the everyday vernacular.

While in the everyday language, there are three words meaning approximately "go up" (*waynydyin* "motion uphill"; *bilinyu* "climb a tree"; *bumiranyu* "climb a tree with a length of vine") with no morphological similarity reflecting their semantic common denominator, in the Dyalnguy register, each is rendered by the same word *dayubin* which may be modified to indicate the exact kind of upward motion intended (448).

Dixon argues that Dyalnguy correspondents of Guwal words are effectively definitions (450), necessitated, at least in part, by the fact that monolexemic expressions are available only for the "nuclear" concepts in the language. Dixon provides a partial enumeration of the kinds of definition which exist in Dyalnguy on pp. 458–61. Not only is the definition in each case more transparent (and thus more iconic) than the complex concept in a single lexeme, frequently there is iconicity in the means of definition that are employed: this is particularly the case where the Dyalnguy rendition of a complex Guwal expression necessitates the use of paralinguistic information of some kind. For example, *gundumman* "bring together" is the homophonous Dyalnguy expression for both *bugaman* "chase" and *dyulman* "squeeze". The second meaning is distinguished from the first only by means of a "squeezing mime, made by grasping the hands together" (460).

Essentially similar observations are made in Haviland 1979, 1979a about the taboo register of Guugu-Yimidhirr, and in Hale 1973 about the secret Damin register of Lardil (e.g. 442: antonyms in Damin, as in the pidgins discussed earlier, are formed by prefixing the positive word with the negative *kuri*: *tjitju* "small"; *kuri tjitju* "big", etc.). These data, I believe, are sufficient to suggest the correctness of Mühlhäusler's hypothesis that there is an inverse correlation between motivation and the size of the lexicon.

The converse of this is the familiar observation that in areas of lexical elaboration (which reflect familiarity with the semantic area involved) taxonomies are few: e.g. "the Arabs have a hundred words for different camels, but not a single word for camels in general", etc. The Dyirbal speakers have half a dozen different words for "telling", and no single word (in Guwal, at least) which covers the entire semantic area of this one English concept. The mistaken inference (cf. Sturtevant 1917:104–6) that the speakers of the language are thus unable to "generalize" is belied, in this instance at least, by the evidence of the taboo register, in which all these related meanings are brought under a single head.

The observation that, in general, lexical elaboration does reflect familiarity recalls Zipf's Law, of course. It suggests that the opacity which characterizes lexically elaborated registers is itself motivated by economic considerations: in particular, by the need to give concise, non-periphrastic expression to what is most frequently talked about. This tendency can be exemplified not only in the development of pidgins as they creolize (and borrow ever more heavily from the lexical resources of the "target" language) but in the development of a rich vocabulary in almost any area of specialization. I will now turn to the development of such an "anti-pidgin" register.

5.2 Vocabulary as abbreviation: the case of Nukespeak

The average English speaker of today may still recognize the transparent origins of new words like MIRV and SIOP, but in the future, if there is one, and if they enter common use, they may become indistinguishable from ordinary words like *radar* (radio detection and ranging) which are no longer perceived as abbreviations at all. Like any other technical vocabulary, Nukespeak is laden with words and expressions that are opaque to the outsider. What makes this jargon one of particular interest, however, is the fact that it is demonstrably only forty years old, and we can document within this extremely short span many of the tendencies which we find, or conjecture that we should find, in all languages.

Before embarking on a very sketchy survey of Nukespeak, we should counter the plausible objection that a major motivation for opacity in this register is the perceived need for euphemisms to replace direct reference to tabooed subjects. While terms like "countervalue capability" are certainly euphemisms for "bombs directed against human beings (rather than military targets)", it is impossible to claim that SIOP is a euphemism for "Single Integrated Operational Plan", itself already a euphemism for "plan for total nuclear war". There is in fact a tendency in the latter case to *lose* the euphemism by abbreviation, since the abbreviation, being opaque, is associated not with the full form but rather directly with the reality it names.

A particularly rich example is offered by the familiar-enough term *first strike*, defined in the newsletter of the Coalition for a New Military and Foreign Policy (February 1984:6) as "any capability to locate and destroy enemy nuclear warheads before they can be used". The term itself is not a euphemism. Indeed, as the same article points out, it is regularly replaced by a number of euphemisms, among them counterforce, countervailing strategy, hard-target kill potential, counter-silo capability, escalation dominance, damage limitation, or strategic force modernization. Nor is the term in any evident sense an abbreviation, and it is certainly not an acronym. Nevertheless, the term has become opaque in that it does not mean exactly what the compound elements of which it is made would indicate. As the newsletter puts it, "You don't need a first-strike ability in order to strike first. (All you need are nuclear weapons and fear.)". Striking first preemptively, as distinct from having a first strike capability, is known as *splendid first strike* (Barasch 1983:73). Once compounds lose their compositionality to this degree, they may legitimately be called opaque.

Nukespeak is mainly characterized by acronyms like SALT, START, ICBM, SLBM, ABM, CEP, INF, and TNF, but they are not the only manifestations of opacity by abbreviation. Some acronyms bear a fortuitous resemblance to real words, a fact which renders them more impenetrable than other obvious abbreviations: *Kneecap*, otherwise known as the US President's getaway plane in the event of a full-scale war, derives from *N*ational *E*mergency *A*irborne *C*ommand *P*ost; MAD, our rapidly obsolescing strategy of deterrence, from *M*utual *A*ssured *D*estruction; *Sink-Sack*, a faintly disreputable term for the *C*ommander-*in-C*hief of the *S*trategic *A*ir *C*ommand, from his periphrastic title.

Some terms, like GEO, are abbreviations by truncation (from geosynchronous orbit: as in "defensive systems are either based on earth, in its atmosphere, or in GEO"). Others, like ASAT, by a combination of truncation and acronymy (from anti-satellite capabilities and activities: as in "the new US ASAT constitutes an order of magnitude improvement over the existing Soviet ASAT").

On the cutting edge of nuclear technology are processes like LIS or *l*aser *i*sotope *s*eparation, an acronym formed from another acronym: LASER derives from *l*ight *a*mplification by *s*timulated *e*mission of *r*adiation, but this is now so much ancient history that a recent article on LIS (Palmer & Bolef 1984) which provided a glossary of acronyms (1984:29) failed to note that *laser* was itself originally such a word.

Abbreviation by truncation and acronyms is not peculiar to Nukespeak: postrevolutionary Russian is studded with acronyms like *sovnarkhom* (*sov*iet *na*rodnykh *kom*isarov "council of people's commissars"), *kolkhoz* (*kol*lectivnoe *khoz*jaistvo "collective farm"), *gosbank* (*gos*udarstvennyj *bank* "state bank") and *GUM* (*g*osudarstvennyj *u*niversal'nyj *m*agazin "state universal store"), and the like.

Nor is abbreviation confined in Nukespeak to these rather transparent and hence comparatively uninteresting, methods. Far more pervasive, and far less striking, is the use of various abbreviatory metaphors. Most newspaper readers are accustomed to seeing vertical underground missile launch tubes referred to as *silos*. Although this bucolic image seems to be an isolated one, there are a surprising number of sexual metaphors in Nukespeak. Missiles are *mated* with their warheads before they are *erected*; they are neither fired, shot, nor launched, but *released*; if all at once, *spasmodically* – to the point where some observers (Kaplan 1982, Caldicott 1984) see the arms race as motivated by "missile envy".

While it is tempting to find evidence of sexual disorders at the root of the arms race or militarism in general, we have no need of this hypothesis: or, to put the matter differently, if we find sexual obsessions underlying the arms race, we find them underlying the terminology of plumbing, electricity, and general contracting as well, to mention only a few areas of specialized activity and vocabulary.

What seems to be at work in Nukespeak, as in every other specialized jargon, is the tendency to use short and familiar words with specialized meanings which are opaque to outsiders who are familiar with only their standard meanings.

The development of a rich vocabulary in the technical area within the purview of modern Nukespeak is in itself just one example among many of the working of a universal law: well-trodden areas of semantic space will acquire a specialized vocabulary characterized by opacity and brevity. As always, the opacity will result from the brevity, and the latter will be motivated, in the last analysis, by economy: economy of effort in production; economy of time spent in communication; and economy of time spent in labeling and processing the familiar.

The only thing that distinguishes the development of Nukespeak from the other examples of economy discussed in chapter 3, above, is that economic considerations are seen to underlie the creation of a *lexicon*. A case can be made, it seems to me, for considering the lexicon as the linguistic analog of *diacritics*: like the diacritic labels in a diagram, individual words are signs whose meaning derives not from their internal diagrammatic structure, but from convention; and, as they multiply, they tend to destroy the iconicity of the structure within which they appear.

From a social perspective, Australian taboo languages and professional jargons like Nukespeak may seem totally parallel: both are special codes comprehensible only to the initiated. Yet from a structural standpoint, they are totally opposed. The "secret words" of Damin, for example, correspond to very simple concepts, for which the everyday equivalents are common words. The vocabulary is characterized by its smallness, and complex concepts tend to be expressed by transparent and motivated compounds. The secret words of Nukespeak, on the other hand, correspond to extremely complex and unfamiliar concepts, for which the everyday equivalents are themselves complex periphrastic expressions. The vocabulary is relatively large in the area of maximum concern, and morphologically simple forms express unfamiliar ideas in a maximally brief but opaque manner.

6 *Limitations of the medium: competing motivations*

One limitation of a terrestrial map is that three dimensions must be expressed in a medium which has only two. Another limitation is that a map usually carries information which is not thought about in terms of dimensions at all – rainfall, the difference between rivers and highways, the distinctions between towns, cities, and capitals, and so on. The second limitation may be more serious than the first.

One of the built-in limitations of human speech is its linearity. A natural consequence of this property is that relations of asymmetry are readily and almost universally modeled iconically, but that relations of symmetry, it would seem, are not. As we have seen in section 2.1, there is no great difficulty in expressing conceptual symmetry iconically by means of a few additional diacritics: just as there is no great difficulty in representing three dimensions on a sheet of paper.

Another consequence of linearity is much more serious. It is the fact that the linear arrangement of morphemes and words is virtually the ONLY means for representing every conceivable semantic and pragmatic relationship. Given this extreme economy of means, it may often happen that there are competing motivations, all perfectly iconic, for a single order of elements. Conversely, any order of elements may be compatible with SOME motivation. Which is to say, that the concept of motivation is meaningless.

In this chapter, I will attempt to rescue the concept of motivation from this charge of meaninglessness, by considering a case of competition among three motivations whose validity has been discussed in the previous literature on functionalism.

(1)   What is old information comes first, what is new information comes later, in an utterance.

Although principle (1) is quite familiar, we have not as yet cited a classical source. To rectify this omission, we need only quote Behaghel, who lists it right after his principle of conceptual closeness (cited on page

237

106 above): "A second powerful tendency demands that the more important comes after the less important ... old concepts precede new ones" (Behaghel 1932:4). We have spent some time on (1) in our discussion of linearity and conditional constructions in chapter 1: the reason protasis precedes apodosis, and the reason that paratactic *S1S2* constructions are so widely interpreted as conditional sentences, is because (1) is true, as is its corollary, that what comes first is ipso facto old information. The fundamental truth of (1) is also what may be held to account for the overwhelming predominance of languages in which the subject precedes the object in basic word order.

(2)   Ideas that are closely connected tend to be placed together.

Jespersen (1949:56) refers to this familiar principle as that of cohesion. I have credited Behaghel with the initial expression of this principle, although Scaglione (1972:248) maintains that it dates back to Condillac. We have illustrated the power of this as an interpretive principle in section 2.2. Given minimally contrasting forms in which the linguistic distance between elements is different, greater linguistic distance reflects greater conceptual distance.

Countervailing these two principles, however, is another that we have not yet discussed, which is named by Jespersen the principle of actuality:

(3)   What is at the moment uppermost in the speaker's mind tends to be first
       expressed.   (Jespersen 1949:54)

Principle (3), it seems to me, could be cited as the motivation for *wh*-movement in languages like English, and for the tendency to put focussed elements in sentence-initial position in general.

But it is plain that (3) clashes not only with (1), but also with (2). Inasmuch as focus is both "new information" and "what is uppermost in the speaker's mind", principle (1) assigns focus to the last element in an utterance: principle (3), to the first. In fact, it seems that almost every possible position in a sentence can be grammaticalized in some language as the locus of focus. We can claim to have "predicted" this kind of variation by pointing out the existence of mutually contradictory motivations like (1) and (3), but there's really not much point. It seems much simpler and more honest to say that the position of focussed elements is a purely arbitrary, language-internal matter.

If one is still dogged enough to support a functional explanation for such facts, there are two legitimate ways to proceed: first, one may attempt to show that languages are *consistent* with respect to these motivations – that is to say, if a language puts question words in sentence-initial position, then it will always be consistent with principle (3), and never with principle (1). Second, one could attempt to show that variation occurs only in those cases where competing motivations can plausibly be ascribed, but that where there are no competing motivations, there is near unanimity in the way that languages will behave.

In what follows, I shall take the second approach. (I have been forced to reject the first because even a cursory examination of a small number of languages demonstrates that languages are *not* consistent: probably one can find evidence in every language of the effects of all three principles (1–3).) My approach is to contrast *wh*-movement in relative clauses with *wh*-movement in content questions.

In spite of the near similarity of these rules in English (and their even greater similarity in other languages like Irish), I defend the hypothesis that these rules are very different in their motivation.

(4)   *Wh*-movement in questions is motivated by principle (3): question words are fronted because they are in focus. In languages where focus position is not sentence-initial, *wh*-words will not be fronted.

Since principle (3) is opposed to both (1) and (2), I predict that there will be many languages in which there is no rule analogous to *wh*-movement in English. On the other hand,

(5)   *Wh*-movement in relative clauses is motivated by (2): relative pronouns are attracted to the head NP because they are referentially identical with it.

Since principle (2) in relative clauses is not opposed to either (1) or (3), I predict that there will be no languages in which relative pronouns are not attracted to the head NP.

I shall argue that both predictions are fulfilled; and that this fact provides some evidence for the reality of (competing) functional motivations, at least in this case. There is first, however, an important object to attend to: if (5) is true, what stops all anaphoric pronouns from being attracted to their antecedents? Coreference is coreference, and if the pull of conceptual closeness moves relative pronouns to the heads of their clauses, then the same pull should move all anaphoric pronouns to their antecedents. Although this objection appears quite devastating, I shall argue that the answer to it provides further support for the hypothesis of competing motivations.

In his typology of relative clause types, Comrie (1980:140–3) distinguishes among four major strategies for the treatment of the relative-clause-internal NP which is coreferential with the head:

(6)   a. no reduction: the head NP instead vanishes (e.g. in Bambara, Diegueño);
         b. total reduction (e.g. Turkish, Hua);
         c. retention as an anaphoric pronoun (e.g. Arabic, Persian);
         d. retention as a relative pronoun (e.g. English, Hungarian).

Of these four types, (6a) and (6b) are of no concern to us, but the contrast between (6c) and (6d) is important. Comrie notes in passing that in languages of type (6c), the sentence-internal pronoun is *not* attracted to the head, while in languages of type (6d), it is so attracted.[1] I think that this observation is basically correct: in my own investigation, I have encountered only one language, Ute, of type (6c) where the pronoun is moved towards the head (Givón 1980a:185),[2] and only one language of type (6d), Luganda, in which the relative pronoun is moved away from the head (Duranti 1977:128 notes that the possibility of this kind of movement is available in Haya also).

The question now arises, why should this correlation exist? Why should a morphological distinction between relative pronouns and anaphoric pronouns have anything to do with whether or not these pronouns are dislocated in the relative clauses where they appear? I suspect that there is in fact a causal connection between these facts, a connection that is immediately apparent when we compare parallel structures in languages of type (6c) and (6d).

(7)   a. *Hebrew (a language of type (6c): sample sentence from Keenan 1972)*
         Ha-isha   she   Yon natan la   ha-sefer
         the-woman comp. John gave   her the-book
         "The woman John gave the book to"
         b. *English (a language of type (6d))*
         the woman John gave the book to who(m)

[1] Types (6c) and (6d) are not in fact mutually exclusive. There are several languages, among them Arabic (Reckendorf 1895:614), Hausa (Taylor 1959:37–8), Fulani (Taylor 1953:28), and Haya (Duranti 1977:124), in which relative clauses of the type "the man who(m) I saw him" are common. It is nevertheless striking that even in those languages the two kinds of pronoun behave as Comrie predicts: anaphoric pronouns "stay put", and relative pronouns gravitate towards the head of the clause, exactly as in the (stigmatized) English model above.

[2] Taylor (1953:34) suggests that Fulani may be another language in which the relative pronoun is indistinguishable from the anaphoric pronoun, but it seems to me that this is not entirely true. Unlike the anaphoric pronoun, the relative pronoun does not inflect for case (although it does mark gender), and there are thus in Fulani possible sentences like the Swahili sentence (17) below, in which both kinds of pronouns occur.

The relative clause in (7a) is identical with a grammatical utterance in Hebrew: anaphoric pronouns are identical with unbound pronouns, which can occur wherever full noun phrases do. The relative clause in languages like Hebrew is able to maintain its unmarked word order because there is a full sentence with which the relative clause is absolutely identical.

The relative clause in (7b), however, is not parallel to a "model" assertive clause, and there is therefore no analogical pressure to maintain the relative pronoun in its grammatical slot. The principle of attraction in this case is unopposed.

There is, of course, another explanation for the difference between (7a) and (7b). "Relative pronouns are complementizers; like interrogative pronouns, they are attracted to clause-initial position, because that is the position of the complementizer." This explanation, first ventured, I believe, by Bresnan (1972), and since then currently accepted in the generative literature, suffers from a number of defects, in my opinion:

(8)   a. It provides no explanation for the fact that relative pronouns are "complementizers" and anaphoric pronouns are not.

        b. It predicts that relative pronouns, or complementizers *in general*, will always be adjacent to the head NP. There are languages, however, in which the complementizer appears at the opposite end of the relative clause from its head, among them Arapesh (Fortune 1942:56–7), Ute (Givón 1980a:187), and Kanuri (Lukas 1937:31).

        c. It implies that a complementizer morpheme and a relative pronoun (or interrogative pronoun) are mutually exclusive. Yet there are languages which have both, like Swahili (Perrott 1957:54), and Georgian (Vogt 1971:43).

        d. It makes no structural distinction between relative and interrogative pronouns. Both are "complementizers". Such an identification, as is usual in generative grammar, completely ignores semantic or functional definitions of parts of speech in favor of purely structural properties. In this case, the structural property which defines complementizers is the fact that they precede, are in construction with, and are dominated by a node of the same sort as, the clauses which they introduce. From a functional perspective, a complementizer is anything which marks the clause in (or with) which it appears as a subordinate clause, and it is simply false to identify interrogative pronouns as complementizers. And even from a cross-linguistic structural perspective, this identification is mistaken, as I will now try to demonstrate.

In English, interrogative and relative pronouns are undoubtedly very similar. Minor differences forced Ross (1967) to the reluctant conclusion that the two rules of *wh*-movement were not identical, and the differences in

most of the Indo-European languages, with the exception of Armenian,[3]
are just as small. There are also an impressive number of non-Indo-Euro-
pean languages which manifest the same near-identity of syntactic
behavior, among them Arabic (Reckendorf 1895:74), Hausa (Taylor
1959:37–9), and Ute (Givón 1980a:185, 220ff), to mention only a few.
Nevertheless, this pattern is by no means universal. I contend that the
interrogative pronoun invariably is treated as a focussed constituent in all
languages. If a language grammaticalizes focus by a specific position in the
clause, then interrogative pronouns will be attracted into this position.
Focus position is subject to a great deal of cross-linguistic variation: some
languages do not grammaticalize the position at all; others identify focus
position as sentence-initial; others, as immediately preverbal; others, as
immediately postverbal; and I maintain that the reason for this cross-
linguistic variation is the existence of the competition between principles
(1) and (3). I contend further that the relative pronoun is invariably
attracted to the head NP, and that this is the result of the unopposed
pressure of principle (2).

A paradigm example of a language which treats focus and relative
pronoun position differently is Hungarian. A relatively free word order
language with a rich nominal case morphology, Hungarian allows every
possible permutation of the major constituents S, V, and O (in the
comparatively few sentences where all of these actually appear as full NP
and V). Each of the following is then a perfectly grammatical sentence,
although they differ in focus assignment in ways that we shall discuss in a
moment:

(9)   a. *SOV* Pista csak vizet iszik
              Steve only water drinks
              "Steve only drinks water"
         b. *SVO* Pista ivott egy pohár vizet
              Steve drank a   glass water
              "Steve drank a glass of water"
         c. *VSO* Elolvasta Pista   az egész ujságot
              perf.=read Stephen the whole newspaper
              "Stephen read the whole newspaper"
         d. *VOS* Megvizsgálta a   lovat a   baromorvos
              perf.=examined the horse the veterinarian
              "The vet examined the horse"

---

[3] For information about Arabic, my thanks to Joseph Greenberg. For tips on Georgian,
Armenian, Finnish, and Indonesian, I am indebted to Bernard Comrie.

e. *OSV* A lovat a grof hozta haza
  the horse the count brought home
  "The count brought the horse home"
f. *OVS* A lovat haza hozta a grof
  the horse home brought the count
  "The count brought the horse home"

Like almost all languages in which word order is not used to identify case rôles, Hungarian makes use of different word orders to signal differences in emphasis, contrastiveness, focus, and theme.

There is a strong general tendency in the modern language for the preverbal slot to be occupied by *some* constituent (Behrens 1982: 115–16) except in marked constructions which signal imperfective aspect, the imperative mood, or focussing of the verb. In the unmarked case, the preverbal slot is the subject. Now, the central rule of Hungarian word order is that in all cases but the unmarked case, the slot immediately preceding the verb stem is the focus position.

For example, in (9a) above, "water" is the focus of the sentence; in (9b), with the unmarked order "a glass of water" is not in focus. That is, (9a) could be given in answer to the question "What does Stephen drink?", but (9b) could not be the answer to the question "What did Stephen drink?". There is a similar contrast between (9e) and (9f): only (9e) is possible in response to the question "Who brought the horse home?", while (9f) answers the question "Where did the count bring the horse?". Sentences (9c) and (9d) seem to be verb-initial and thus should be interpreted as having verbal focus. Although the verb precedes both subject and object in these sentences, it is itself preceded by a separable prefix (*el-* in (9c), and *meg-* in (9d)), which carries the focus. The function of these separable prefixes is twofold: they may indicate the direction in which an action is carried out, or they may signal perfective aspect. In both (9c) and (9d), the prefixes signal perfectivity alone. In both sentences, therefore, the focus is on the completion of the action described by the verb. It is instructive to compare (9c) and (9d) with the minimally contrasting (9g) and (9h):

(9)   g. Pista olvasta el az egész ujságot
  Stephen read perf. the whole newspaper
  "It was Stephen who read the whole newspaper"
     h. A lovat vizsgálta meg a baromorvos
  the horse examined perf. the veterinarian
  "It was the horse that the vet examined"

Not surprisingly, question words in Hungarian occur obligatorily in the focus – immediately preverbal – position, as in (10).

(10)   a. Mit iszik Pista?
           what drinks Stephen
           "What does Stephen drink?"
        b. Ki itta meg a . pálinkámat?
           who drank perf. the my=brandy
           "Who drank my brandy?"
        c. A lovat ki hozta haza?
           the horse who brought home
           "Who brought the horse home?"
        d. A lovat hová vitte a grof?
           the horse where took the count
           "Where did the count take the horse?"

Given the overwhelming predominance of one-argument or no-argument sentences in natural discourse (Behrens 1982:161 found that in a colloquial but literary text, fewer than 10% of all principal clauses had both S and O arguments as actual NP or pronouns), immediately preverbal position tends to look like sentence-initial position. That is why the testimony of sentences like (10c) and (10d) is so important: it demonstrates that even though preverbal and sentence-initial position often coincide, the operative principle for *wh*-question placement – at least in this stage of the development of Hungarian – is to put the question word in immediately preverbal position.

The behavior of relative pronouns, on the other hand, is very similar to the behavior of relative pronouns in English, and the rule is that they are attracted to the head NP. As in English, relative pronouns are virtually identical with the corresponding interrogative pronouns: they consist of the definite article followed by the interrogative pronoun. Thus *a+ki* "who (rel.)", *a+mi* "which (rel.)", *a+hová* "whither (rel.)", *a+honnan* "whence (rel.)", and so forth.

Relative clauses in Hungarian follow the head NP, and relative pronouns occur clause-initially. Note how, in the following examples, the relative pronoun (unlike the interrogative pronoun which it so closely resembles) need not occur immediately before the verb:

(11)   a. az ujság *amit* Pista végig olvasott
           the newspaper *which* Stephen to=the=end read

   b. a pálinkámat, *amit* azok a csirkefogók elloptak
     the my=brandy *which* those the scoundrels perf.=stole
     "my brandy, which those scoundrels stole"
   c. a grof *akit* a baromorvos megmentett
     the count whom the veterinarian perf.=saved

In Hungarian, then, there is a superficial similarity between question word and interrogative pronoun placement. This similarity is a consequence of the preferred argument structure of Hungarian in which preverbal order is very frequently the same thing as clause-initial order. In time, it may well come about that the two are treated as the same by abduction, but for now, at least, a distinction exists which is of the sort predicted by our hypotheses (4) and (5). In other languages, the contrast is more apparent from the very beginning. One of these languages is Swahili. As English may be taken to represent the majority of Indo-European languages with respect to the behavior of question words and relative pronouns, so Swahili may stand for the majority of the Bantu languages.

    Swahili is an SVO language in which interrogative words are treated like adverbs in general. While, like them, they *may* be shifted to sentence-initial position, there is no need for them to do so (Perrott 1957:95,140):

(12)   a. A-li-fika   *lini*?
           3sg.-past-arrive when
           "When did s/he arrive?"
       b. Ni-m-jibu   *namna gani*?
           1sg.-3sg.-answer *how*
           "How am I to answer him/her?"
       c. *kwa nini* chakula ki-me-chelewa?
           why   food   3sg.-perf.-late
           "Why is the food late?"

Apparently, this situation is relatively general in Bantu (cf. Welmers 1973:438). Relative pronouns in Swahili follow the head. The sentence-internal token of the relativized noun occurs as a distinctive and variable pronoun affix on the verb. If this verb occurs with tense and polarity prefixes, the relative pronoun occurs as a following prefix; if tense and polarity prefixes are absent, the relative pronoun occurs as a verbal suffix (Perrott 1957:58–60):

(13)   a. *Tense prefix present: relative pronoun occurs as a following prefix*
       Ni-me-ijibu   barua i-li-*yo*-kuja   jana
       1sg.-perf.-answer letter 3sg.-past-*rel*.-arrive yesterday
       "I have answered the letter which came yesterday"

b. *Polarity prefix present: relative pronoun occurs as a following prefix*
Wa-tu   wa-si-*o*-kuja   jana   wa-end-e   kwa Bwana
3pl.-man 3pl.-neg.-*rel*.-come yesterday 3pl.-go-subj. to   master
"The men who didn't come yesterday should go to the master"

c. *No tense or polarity prefix: relative pronoun is a suffix on the verb*
m-toto   a-soma-*ye*
3sg.-child 3sg.-read-*rel*.
"a child who reads"

So far, it would seem that the operating principle of relative pronoun placement is perversely contradictory to our hypothesis. Not only does it seem that the relative pronoun is not allowed to get *too close* to the head (being moved into suffix position when there are not enough prefixes between the head and it); Swahili is also a language in which both anaphoric pronouns and relative pronouns coexist within the relative clause, and the relative pronoun follows the anaphoric pronoun within the verbal complex, and is thus further from the head than the anaphoric pronoun with which it is coreferential. But in all these cases, the relative pronoun does occur at least as an affix on the verb, which *is* the word adjacent to the head.

So far, however, there is nothing remarkable about this: in all the cases we have cited, the relative pronoun has been the subject of its clause. Given that the canonical order of constituents in Swahili, as noted, is SVO, there is, as yet, no evidence of any movement towards the head. Schematically, the abstract structure (14) is represented as either (a) or (b)

(14) NP_i (NP_i V O)
           (a) . . . np_i + V O
           (b) . . . V + np_i O

and what movement there has been, of the bound affix np_i, has been *away* from the preceding head.

Matters are different when we consider relativization of a *non-subject* noun, for example, the object. We might expect, on the model of (14), to find that the abstract structure (15) is represented as either (a) or (b).

(15) NP_i (S V NP_i)
           (a) . . . S np_i + V
           (b) . . . S V + np_i

where the decision between prefixation and suffixation would depend, as before, on the presence of other verbal affixes. Yet neither (15a) nor (15b) occurs. Instead, the canonical order of constituents is distorted, and the subject noun in the relative clause is *postposed*, creating an order in which "the verb following the head may not be separated from the head by a nominal subject" (Ashton 1947:113). Perrott (1957:61) is quite explicit about the functional motivation for subject postposing: it occurs "in order that the relative may be put near the word to which it relates". Thus the formal contrast between (16a) and (16b).

(16)   a. m-toto   a-li-*ye*-soma   kitabu
               3sg.-child 3sg.-past-*rel.*-read book
               "the child who read the book"
      b. kitabu a-li-*cho*-ki-soma   m-toto
               book 3sg.-past-*rel.*-3sg.obj.-read 3sg.-child
               "the book which the child read"

In (16a), the order of constituents is V O in the relative clause, while in (16b), it is V S. In both, the relative clause verb (and, with it, the relative pronoun) is adjacent to the head. Thus also the ambiguity of structures like (17).

(17)   wa-toto   wa-wa-penda-*o* wazee   wao
          3pl.-child 3pl.-3pl.-love-*rel.*-parents 3pl.poss.
          a. "children who love their parents"   (V O order in relative clause)
    OR b. "children whom their parents love"   (V S order in relative clause)

The functional motivation for subject postposing is highlighted by a contrasting and more recent relative clause structure in Swahili, in which the relative pronoun affix is attracted to an invariable clause-initial complementizer *amba*. Although the relative pronoun is still bound, it is not affixed to the verb but to a word which is sentence-initial already. Consequently, whether or not the order of words within the relative clause is V S or V O is going to make no difference to the closeness of relative pronoun and head. *Consequently*, given the Perrott hypothesis that subject postposition takes place *in order to* keep the relative pronoun next to the head, no postposition of the subject need occur. And none does. Observe the following (from Perrott 1957:64):

(18)   U-si-seme   maneno amba-*yo* hujayapima   vema
          you-not-use=imp. words   comp.-*rel.* you=haven't=weighed carefully
          "Don't use words you haven't weighed carefully"
(19)   kitabu amba-*cho* m-toto   a-li-ki-soma
          book comp.-*rel.*3sg.-child 3sg.-past-3sg.-read
          "the book which the child read"
(20)   wa-toto amba-*yo* wazee wao   wa-wa-penda
          3pl.-child comp.-*rel.* parents 3pl.poss 3pl.3pl.-love
          "children whom their parents love"
(21)   wa-toto amba-yo wa-wa-penda wazee wao
          3pl.-child comp.-rel. 3pl.-3pl.-love parents 3pl.=poss.
          "children who love their parents"

In none of the relative clauses in (18–21) is the normal SVO order transformed by subject postposing.

Duranti describes a parallel process in the Grassfields Bantu language Haya. In Haya, the relative pronoun is a bound prefix on the verb when it represents a subject – but a free standing, and fronted, word when it represents a noun with any other case rôle in the clause. The result of this variation is that the relative pronoun is always the morpheme which introduces the relative clause (Duranti 1977:119), as illustrated in (22–4).

(22)   *Relative pronoun = subject of relative clause*
        abáán? *á*-ba-a-gend?   ómu-kyaalo
        children *rel.*-3pl.-tense-go to-village
        "the children who have gone to the village"
(23)   *Relative pronoun = object of relative clause*
        omwáán? *ówó* n-a-bóna
        child   *rel.* I-tense-see
        "the child that I have seen"
(24)   *Relative pronoun = object of a preposition in the relative clause*
        eŋkony? *éyó* n-a-it?   éŋkóko ná-yo
        stick   *rel.* I-tense-kill chicken with-it
        "the stick with which I have killed the chicken"

Rather disconcertingly, Haya has an optional rule whereby the free relative pronoun may shift *rightwards* over the nominal subject and appear immediately before the verb. Duranti observes that this rule, while optional in Haya, is *obligatory* in Luganda, in which language

a full subject NP intervenes always between the head noun and the relative pronoun. This seems consistent with the general tendency in Bantu to mark on (or next to) the verb as much grammatical information as possible (Duranti 1977:128).

Incidentally, Luganda is the only language in my survey which regularly violates the otherwise unanimously followed principle of relative pronoun attraction. Whether or not the rightward shift of the relative pronoun is compatible with the Bantu tendency to mark all information on the verb, as Duranti conjectures, we must assume that the situation in Luganda is unstable, and that if the relative pronoun becomes agglutinated to the verb, subject postposing will soon follow.

Grammars of other Bantu languages repeat similar observations: subject postposing is the rule in relative clauses in Shona (Fortune 1955:184–5), Kihung'an (Takizala 1972) and Dzamba (Bokamba 1971). On the basis of these and similar findings, Givón has proposed a universal principle of pronoun attraction in Bantu languages:

whenever the relative pronoun is free – and thus can be positioned directly adjacent to the head noun – the rule of subject postposing does not apply obligatorily. However, when the (object) relative pronoun is bound to the verb, subject postposing applies obligatorily (Givón 1972:192).

It is worth pointing out, before we leave the Bantu languages, that there are some in which the contrast between relative pronoun movement and interrogative pronoun movement is more extreme than the general pattern exemplified by Swahili (leftward movement for relative pronouns, no movement for interrogative pronouns). In Aghem, relative pronouns are moved leftwards (Hyman 1979:62), while interrogative pronouns are moved to the focus position, grammaticalized in Aghem as the position immediately after the verb (Watters 1979:145). Since Aghem is an SVO language, this means that where the focussed element is the subject, it moves *rightwards*, as in (25).

(25)   À   mɔ   zí   *ndúghɔ̀bé-ɔ́*
        dummy past eat *who*   fufu
        "Who ate the fufu?"

Like Swahili, Fulani (an unrelated language of the Niger-Congo family), is basically SVO, and, in general, interrogative words are left in the same position as their non-focussed counterparts (Taylor 1953:27). Relative clauses follow the head NP and the relative pronoun, as in Swahili, is attracted to the head invariably (ibid. 28).

In Kalenjin, a Nilo-Saharan language of Kenya, the basic word order is VSOX. Focus position (as in Aghem) is the immediately postverbal position, and interrogative words are moved there (Creider 1978:188). Note that the canonical word order is changed in sentences where the interrogated element is anything but the subject:

(26)   Yáe nê: Kípe:t
        do what Kibet
        "What does Kibet do?"

Relative clauses follow the head NP and the relative pronoun is attracted to clause-initial position. So strong is this attraction in Kalenjin, apparently, that even violations of Ross' (1967) coordinate structure constraint are tolerated, as in (27).

(27)   ʔke:ré ci:tá   ne   pêntí: ak   la:kwɛ:ɲi Kâ:psá:pit
        I=see person who   are=going and his=son   Kapsabet
        "I see the person who and his son are going to Kapsabet"

(The point is emphasized by Creider, 1978:183–4.)

In Georgian, a Kartvelian language, relative pronouns regularly shift to the head of the relative clause (Vogt 1971:49–51), although one relative pronoun can be reduced and cliticized, and, as a clitic, may shift to second position within the clause, that is, away from the head (ibid. 51). Focus position is invariably the immediately preverbal position (as in Hungarian), and interrogative pronouns are invariably put into this position (ibid. 224).

Summing up: although there are many languages in which relative pronouns and interrogative pronouns undergo the same "movement rules" there are many in which they do not. The point which concerns us here is not the indubitable similarities, both morphological and syntactic, that exist between relative and interrogative pronouns, but a difference between them. Specifically, we find that while relative pronouns almost invariably gravitate to the head of the clause in which they occur, interrogative pronouns undergo a variety of different treatments. Such a difference poses an interesting problem for any theory of grammar – and a rather massive one for any theory that maintains that both are "complementizers", and structurally indistinguishable.

I contend that an explanation for this curious difference between relative and interrogative pronouns is offered by the theory of competing motivations. Once again, where there are competing motivations, and only there, we will expect cross-linguistic variation in the grammaticalization of such things as "focus position". Where there are no competing motivations, we predict that there will be unanimity across languages, as there is in the grammaticalization of "relative pronoun position". And with this demonstration, we take the respectability of a theory of competing motivations to be established. Often wrong in fact, perhaps wrong even in this particular instance, but defensible in principle.

A recent example of the same analytic approach is DuBois (to appear). He argues that both nominative/accusative and ergative case morphology are motivated by competing pressures:

S and A (= subjects) are united by their tendency to code human referents, which are usually topical. Thus, a discourse pressure to mark topic/agent motivates accusative morphology, while a discourse pressure to mark new information motivates ergative morphology. These two pressures compete to overlay a secondary function on the existing A/S/O base. So long as topicality and newness are not marked directly by independent morphology but are marked indirectly in the paradigm that marks person–number–role, only one auxiliary function can be marked: subjects or absolutives.

This explanation can be shown to be other than ad hoc by a consideration of the phenomenon of split ergativity. It can be shown that accusative morphology occurs in ergative languages in precisely the places where the pressure to mark a new/old contrast fails to operate (i.e. where reference is to participants in the speech act itself) so the pressure to mark topicality is unopposed.

The notion of tension or competition between functional motivations is nothing new of course. What is new is only the contempt in which this idea is currently held. Another possible defense of the idea, which I will do barely more than to mention here, is the following. It may be claimed that two tendencies are conflicting in one structure, with a range of possible results attested in a number of languages. It may then be demonstrated, on independent grounds, that another structure is related to the first. If it is now found that the range of variation in the second structure corresponds to the range of variation in the first, then it seems to me that this fact supports two conclusions: first, that the two structures really are related; and second, that the two tendencies really do exist.

The two structures of which this may be said are the prototypical coordinate sentence *S1 (and) S2* and the prototypical conditional sentence *If S1, S2*, both of which have been already discussed earlier.

In a study of conditional markers and conditional constructions in Romance, Martin Harris (to appear) makes the following important observations:

Interestingly, there appear to be two conflicting pressures operating at one and the same time: on the one hand, to maximize the degree of temporal/modal harmony between protasis and apodosis (particularly in non-real conditional sentences), thus reinforcing the truism that the reality of the two components in such sentences is (in general) identical; and on the other hand to avoid the repetition of tense and mood when one marking – in Romance, the apodosis – will suffice.

The first pressure is exemplified by the tendency (already noted in section 2.1) to form what Harris has called "double conditionals" in the counterfactual mood. These are conditional structures in which the protasis and apodosis have the same verbal marking and are often totally indistinguishable. Harris notes that even in languages like French and Italian, where such double conditionals are frowned on by normativists, they consistently recur in actual speech. The tendency is fully grammaticalized in many languages like Latin, Hungarian, Latvian, Russian, Gende, Guugu-Yimidhirr, Ngiyambaa, and Hausa.

The second pressure is exemplified by the mild tendency towards "demodalization" in one or another conjunct of the conditional sentence – according to Comrie (to appear) most frequently the protasis.

Both of these tendencies, that which creates symmetry, and that which destroys it for essentially economic reasons, are equally well attested in coordinate constructions. The tendency towards symmetry is most perspicuous in the peculiar behavior of the Coordinate Structure Constraint of Ross (1967), whose true significance was identified in Schachter's insightful article (1977): why is it that "movement" of a relative or interrogative pronoun out of *one* conjunct is ungrammatical, as in (28), while the same "movement" "across the board" is grammatical, as in (29).

(28)   *Who did Max saw Harry and Sam speak to ____?
(29)   Who did Max see ____ and Harry speak to ____?

Schachter argued, in my opinion absolutely correctly, that the constraint was not at all a constraint on movement per se, but on surface *asymmetry*. Coordinate constructions must be *symmetrical*. Recent work by Gazdar, as we have already noted, has formalized this insight and made it impossible, within generalized phrase structure grammar, to generate any asymmetrical coordinations at all.

On the other hand, the tendency towards asymmetry is attested by the general properties of constructions which were once viewed as arising from "coordination reduction". In most cases the abstraction and non-repetition of an element which occurs in all the members of a conjoined set does not create asymmetry, so long as "regrouping" occurs. The bracketed portion of $(AB)x$ is no less symmetrical than $AxBx$, and the bracketed portion of $x(AB)$ is no less symmetrical than $xAxB$. Asymmetry arises where either "regrouping" does not occur, although possible (as in ABx), or where it is impossible because the abstracted common element is central rather than peripheral (as occurs in gapping). It is worth noting that gapping, of all kinds of coordination reduction, is the least widely attested in the world's languages: a fact which can be explained in functional terms as an indirect consequence of Behaghel's "Streben nach Parallelismus" (striving for parallelism) in coordinate constructions. Nevertheless, the tendency to abstract and avoid repetition of a common element not only creates asymmetrical constructions of the form $A \ x \ B \ and \ C \ \emptyset \ D$, but structures like $AxB \ \emptyset$. Very possibly the coordinate structure analog of "conditional demodalization" is the use in a variety of languages of such structures as the "historical present" and the "injunctive mood" which Kiparsky argued in a classic article (1968) arise as a result of coordination reduction.

The existence of the same *kinds* of variation in related structures can be plausibly attributed to the existence of the same pressures. In fact, once we accept the existence of such structural pressures and motivations as the tendency to balance and the tendency to abstraction of a common element, we can even propose some (nearly) universal relationships among these and some of the other rules we have been discussing. Granted, at this stage the interrelationship among these tendencies merely recapitulates what we already know to be true in the languages we have studied, and it remains to be seen whether the same interrelationship holds in other languages. So the following is ventured as a set of statistical predictions:

(A) Perturbations of word order, even in so-called "free word order languages" like Hungarian or Russian, signal differences in meaning. (Principle (A) is derivable from the isomorphism hypothesis that difference in form must reflect some difference in communicative intent.)

(B) Where relative pronouns are distinct from anaphoric pronouns, they will be attracted to the head noun phrase. (Principle (B) derives from the principle of conceptual closeness of which referential identity is the most extreme example.)

(C) Interrogative pronouns will be moved into "focus position", whatever this position may happen to be in a given language.

(D) The abstraction of common elements from conjuncts (coordination reduction in the broadest sense, encompassing both gapping and right node raising) is an iconic signal of the unity of these conjuncts. (Principle (D) also derives from the principle of conceptual closeness.)

(E) The symmetry of conjuncts is to be maintained.

In some clearly predictable cases, these tendencies will conflict, and there is no telling, on purely structural grounds, which tendency will "win out" in any language, or in any stage of the development of a single language. There seem to be some hierarchical relations among these tendencies, however, which are universal.

For example: principle (E) is violated, at least in part, by structures thought to result from gapping (e.g. "I like coffee, and Mary, ____ tea"). One could imagine structures that satisfy both (D) and (E), such as *"I ____ coffee, and Mary ____ tea, like" in which a common element has been extracted from the *center* of two conjuncts. As far as I am aware there is no SVO language which allows such structures: the reason being, presumably, that the resulting ungrammatical sentence has superficial SOV word order, which is prohibited (perhaps only in part) by principle (A).

Principle (D) apparently outweighs principle (E) inasmuch as gapping is possible. Yet I should reiterate that of all kinds of coordination reduction (abstraction of a common element from the left, right, or center of a set of conjoined elements), gapping is the least frequent; and also, that it is the only one which entails a violation of principle (E).

The interaction of principles (E) and (D) will account for the correlation noted by Ross (1970) and Tai (1969), that where the common member of a set of conjoined elements is a *left* branch, the *leftmost* one remains, and vice versa. Thus, we encounter the sentences in (30) rather than the (logically) equally possible sentences in (31).

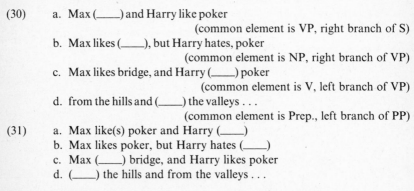

(30)   a. Max (_____) and Harry like poker
                        (common element is VP, right branch of S)
       b. Max likes (_____), but Harry hates, poker
                        (common element is NP, right branch of VP)
       c. Max likes bridge, and Harry (_____) poker
                        (common element is V, left branch of VP)
       d. from the hills and (_____) the valleys . . .
                        (common element is Prep., left branch of PP)
(31)   a. Max like(s) poker and Harry (_____)
       b. Max likes poker, but Harry hates (_____)
       c. Max (_____) bridge, and Harry likes poker
       d. (_____) the hills and from the valleys . . .

The examples of (30) maintain symmetry between conjuncts – a symmetry which is admittedly flawed in (30c), but still indicated by rhythm, and an impeccable symmetry in all other cases. No such symmetry is maintained between the conjuncts of (31).

Other principles we have not considered conflict with these as well. For example, the phonologically motivated tendency to assign cliticized constituents to sentence-second position countervails principle (B) in Basque, and possibly in Luganda as well. And none of these principles is absolute.

I think it is this property of functional explanations which makes them so intolerable to the theoretical "absolutist". The absolutist, like the physicist, seeks immutable absolutes, the linguistic analogs of Planck's constant, or of Maxwell's equations. Such absolute laws allow the physicist to make predictions about the future course of a well-defined physical system. The linguistic absolutist seeks to do likewise. So, he rejects functionalism out of hand, because competing motivations don't allow us to predict what changes will occur.

Ergo, so the absolutist theoretician would argue, a theory of competing motivations is unfalsifiable, and hence scientifically worthless. My own view is that our lack of predictive power in our theories – at least now – is entirely appropriate, and well accords with our factual inability to predict what changes a language may undergo. Perhaps this state of affairs will change, and perhaps it will not. But in the meantime, most absolute predictions that have been made encounter considerable embarrassment.

To take one example: one frequently encounters locutions such as the following, not only in the spoken, but also the written language:

(32)   Now we'll be able to see what each other is up to

Their currently substandard status is undeniable, as is that of such structures as "Between you and I", or "as far as the graduate requirements in the anthropology department". But with repeated usage, sentences like (32) may become totally acceptable, and thus, grammatical, at least on the basis of any sane definition of the term "grammatical". The trouble with such sentences as (32), as Chomsky has genially admitted (pc) is that "they violate every principle I can think of". Now, how does one proceed if these principles are, as Chomsky has argued, universal and innate? In principle, of course, there are a number of strategies one may adopt. I will begin with the most outlandish which I include only for the sake of completeness.

(A) The innate principles have changed. People who utter sentences like (32) are, in the strictest biological sense, mutants.
(B) The sentence is simply ungrammatical, and will continue to be so. That is, it will never catch on.
(C) Our understanding of the universal principles is false. We'll have to revise them to accommodate the possibility of sentences like (32).

Nobody has ever entertained the plausibility of (A), which we may therefore disregard. The explicit conscious strategy adopted by Chomsky and his students is of course the last, although a frequently repeated position is that counterexamples count for nothing unless they are explained by another (equally absolutist) theory. In the absence of such a theory, they can safely be ignored or, better still, dismissed as errors in performance. Let us assume, contrary to fact, that the absolutists intend their grammatical theories to be compatible with actual linguistic behavior rather than with a Platonic conception of "grammar"; let us assume, moreover, that they continue to revise their theories and principles until they find exceptionless universals to which all languages of all times adhere.[4] Can they be successful in this enterprise?

---

[4] In the light of von der Gabelentz' observation that "every innovation is originally a mistake" (cited in Havers 1931:54), this is equivalent to the claim that certain mistakes are impossible. My own impression is that the only mistakes which are impossible are those

I think not. There are two ways in which such an enterprise may fail. The first is as Newton's Laws of Motion fail: they are a good approximation to reality except at speeds approaching that of light. The theory of relativity, whereof Newton's laws can be seen as limiting instances, offers a better approximation. In time, no doubt, another theory which incorporates the theory of relativity as a limiting instance will offer a still better approximation. And so on. Let us call this kind of failure the failure of approximation.

The other kind of failure is never even considered. The rules fail not because they are not the right rules, but because there are *no* right rules. There are strong tendencies. There are statistical near-universals. But there are no absolute rules whatsoever, only tendencies which not only admit exceptions, but are opposed by other equally motivated tendencies. Which tendencies are paramount in any corner of a language may depend as much on social factors as on structural factors.

To return to sentence (32). Whether this sentence becomes perfectly grammatical or not may depend only on structural factors (such as the tendency to avoid center embedding and thus do away with discontinuous constituents like *each . . . other*), but on whether the form is popular or not.

Traditional sociolinguistic evaluations of popularity have focussed almost entirely on the factor of *prestige*, a vague but still overly restrictive impetus for innovation. A form may gain currency not only because it was used by model individuals or groups, but also because it may happen to tickle one's sense of humor. I have a quite unprovable (but overwhelming) hunch that sentences like (32) quite recently appealed to the ludic sense of their creators, much like the false analogy which added *snuck* (*sneak*, past tense) to the American vocabulary. Once the joke grows stale, as all things must, the once-comical form survives as dead metaphors do. Nobody snickers at *snuck* any more, but this does not stop everyone from using it.

As for sentence (32) and others like it, who can tell what the future will bring?[5]

which involve too great a deviation from the existing norm; but as the norm changes by accretions, the impossibilities of yesterday become increasingly likely tomorrow.

[5] Modesty forbade me to answer this question in the body of the text. I am confident, however, that I can predict exactly one innovation that will occur in English in the year 2074 – long after we are all dead. The symbol of the University of Manitoba, where I teach, is the bison; the university football team is called "The Bisons"; our logo on stationery and public relations materials is also a bison. The University was founded in 1874 and recently celebrated its centennial with the traditional hoopla. The second centennial will be advertised (by people who never read these lines) as the *Bisontennial*, and I am willing to stake my reputation as a linguist on this prediction.

Conclusion: some remarks on physics and grammar

People in other fields of endeavour, hankering to turn their disciplines into exact sciences, beset by what has since been called 'physics envy', set about converting whatever they knew into numbers and thence into equations with predictive pretensions. We have it with us still, in economics, sociology, psychology, history, even, I fear, in English-literature criticism and linguistics, and it frequently works, when it works at all, with indifferent success.

Lewis Thomas, Humanities and science, p. 145 in his
Late night thoughts in listening to Mahler's Ninth Symphony.

"If you really want to learn what's happening in languages, don't look at sentences like 'The farmer kills the duckling': the interesting stuff happens out at the margins, when you deal with long and incredibly complicated sentences." These words were spoken, as it happens, by John Ross in a lecture given at MIT about fifteen years ago. But the conception of grammar which they express is common to every formal theory of grammar of the last quarter century or so. What is implicit in these words is that the rules of grammar are well defined, consistent, absolute, and totally unconscious. It is only in the framework of such a set of assumptions that it makes sense to investigate the properties of sentences that are so "long and incredibly complicated" that no one outside a linguistic institute could conceivably recognize, let alone employ them.

The perspective adopted throughout this book has been the opposite. I have focussed on rules which are not only crude and simple, but amount to no more than tendencies which are forever in competition with each other. Surprising as it may seem, the choice between these perspectives (unlike so many other "issues in linguistics") is not an empirical, but an aesthetic one, because the basic question is not whether this theory or that accounts better for the "data". Rather, the question is, which data does the theory *try* to account for?

Following a tradition which derives from classical normativism via the Saussurean distinction between *langue* and *parole*, formal theories of

257

grammar make a sharp distinction between grammatical and ungrammatical utterances, a distinction orthogonal to the distinction between actually occurring and non-occurring utterances. The object of inquiry within this tradition, as Chomsky in particular has often stressed, is not "the language" (about whose very existence he has expressed some skepticism, cf. Chomsky 1981) but "the grammar": a system of rules, and the innate capacity for constructing such a set of rules on the basis of fragmentary data *from the language*. Since the linguist (like the language learner) can only infer the grammar from the actual data, it may seem that there is in principle no significant difference between the notions *grammatical* (compatible with the grammar) and *actual* (occurring in the data). A glance through the pages of any theoretically oriented work, however, will quickly dispel this illusion. Utterances are marked ungrammatical if they are incompatible with a tightly constrained theory, and acceptable if they are compatible with it. (To the native speaker of the language, committed to no theory, they all may look and sound like hash.) There is really nothing new, essentially, to this state of affairs. As Brugmann (cited in Havers 1931:1) trenchantly noted long ago "the old original sin of all grammatical science is that language is taken not as it is, but seen as the grammarian would like to have it".

Justification for (cf. Chomsky 1957) and attacks on (cf. Labov 1972) this methodology are sufficiently familiar that we need not repeat them here. In contrasting this framework of assumptions with my own, I would like to add only a few words on what Thomas has called "physics envy" (in the epigraph to this chapter), and on the status of anomaly.

Many of the triumphs of the hard sciences reduce to this: apparent anomalies are seen to be the natural result of underlying regularities. To take the most famous example, the irregular motion of the planets was an anomaly in the geocentric theory of the ancient astronomers, but it is no longer an anomaly in the heliocentric theory. The task of the sciences is to discover the minimal set of universal absolute principles from which all phenomena, including the apparent anomalies, can be deduced. The analogy with structural and generative linguistics is obvious: "pattern congruity" in phonemic analysis, like the "gap in paradigm" arguments in classical transformational grammar, appeal to the idea of underlying symmetry, as opposed to superficial (i.e. phonetic or morphological) irregularity. The competence/performance distinction is a powerful additional tool in the quest for underlying regularity. Apparently anomalous utterances that are compatible with a given theory are satisfactorily explained; similar sentences which are not compatible don't count.

The problems with this methodology in linguistics are of course well known. One of the most consistent, striking, and useful results from the study of "long and incredibly complicated sentences" is how our judgments tend to dislimn once we are out "at the margins". Far from being automatic and unconscious, our grammaticality judgments are the outcome of often complex chains of reasoning, affected by our theoretical persuasions, our imagination in devising plausible contexts for the utterances in question, and our differing personal commitment to either consistency or credibility.

Following another tradition in linguistics, no less respectable than formalism or structuralism, are the functional theories of grammar which tend to recognize no significant distinction between grammatical utterances and those which actually occur. The "object of inquiry" within this tradition is typically the facts of language themselves, and the chief insight, that all change originates as a violation of preexisting "rules". The focus of this kind of investigation is on the nature of these mistakes, and the factors which motivate them constantly, throughout the evolution of all languages. There is in fact a "grammar" to be inferred from linguistic data: but the "grammar of mistakes" (cf. Frei 1929) is no less significant than the grammar of "correct speech". Perhaps it is even more significant, since it attests directly to the dynamic forces which cause language change, while the grammar of correct speech at any time may be no more than an agglomeration of fossils. The formalist, committed to Meillet's dictum that *tout se tient*, looks for a system in this agglomeration; the functionalist–anarchist sees no reason to do so. To the functionalist, anomalies and inconsistencies are to be expected because he recognizes the existence of competing motivations, in particular, iconic and economic motivations. At any stage of any natural language, there will be areas in the grammar where originally iconically motivated structures have become grammaticalized, and there will be others where they have not. Given that "grammars code best what speakers do most" we should expect to find maximal coding (that is, economy and opacity) in well-trodden areas of semantic space, and minimal coding (that is, iconicity and transparency) at the peripheries.

(Given this reasonable expectation, we may even be able to point out some not entirely trivial correlations between language and culture. For example, it is a commonplace that structures which are common to "standard average European" languages, such as the comparative (with measure of difference phrases, as in "She's *twice as* smart as you are", "That one's *six inches* longer"), are absent in most "local languages", and can be expressed only by means of relatively clumsy and transparent periphrastic constructions. Surely it is legitimate to speculate that the

codification of comparison reflects a culture of individualism and competitiveness, and the absence of such codification a relatively egalitarian
culture. The ethnographic evidence certainly is consistent with such a
hypothesis.)

An essential attribute of human language, according to this view, is that
it is always changing in response to competing pressures, both within and
outside of the grammatical system itself.

There are two fundamental reasons, I believe, why this perspective may
seem distasteful to proponents of some variety of structuralism or
formalism. In the first place, it denies the axiomatic assumption, common
to most schools of linguistics since Saussure, that a language is a totally
autonomous system which can be understood in isolation from the world in
which it is employed. Second, in calling upon perceptual and cognitive
strategies such as the isomorphism and the motivation hypotheses, and on
hoary and partially discredited behavioral principles such as the principle
of least effort, all of which are relatively accessible to conscious observation, it seems to challenge the unchallengeable position that human
linguistic capacities are innate. As principled objections (as opposed to
visceral reactions) to a functionalist theory of linguistic structure, neither of
these is very cogent.

The idea of the autonomy of a linguistic system is a useful research
strategy: as Givon (1979:24) suggests, it is analogous to studying any
biological organism or phenomenon in vitro. Having established some of
the variable properties under conditions of controlled experiment, the
biologist then proceeds to study the same phenomenon, insofar as he is
able, in vivo. In elevating the principle of autonomy beyond this point, in
dismissing linguistic behavior in vivo as phenomena of "parole" or
"performance", the theoretical linguist is motivated, if not by physics envy,
then at least by the conviction that abstraction "away from the welter of
facts" is empirically justifiable. The danger of succumbing to "Brugmann's
temptation" and abstracting away only from the welter of facts that don't
fit the theory, while creating and welcoming an empirically indistinguishable welter of facts which do, is only one of the problems with this
approach. The other major problem lies in a fundamental difference
between the laws of physics and the laws of language. The law of gravity is
not modified by use: no matter how many times we throw a ball into the air,
it will fall to the ground with the same acceleration. Rules of grammar, on
the other hand, are modified by use (i.e. languages change) and it is
therefore not only legitimate, but necessary, to observe language as it is

spoken, and to pay particularly close attention to the various external factors which modify the structure of a linguistic system.

If the nature of these external factors is at times (disappointingly?) transparent, this has absolutely no bearing on the contention that language-learning mechanisms are innate. Whether or not language-learning mechanisms are conscious or unconscious is an entirely different question: personally, I believe that many are unconscious (an opinion of absolutely no scientific value or interest), but I have chosen to concentrate here on some which are conscious, and none the less real for all that. The empirical validity of the isomorphism and motivation hypotheses is attested by established natural languages, and may even be confirmable by experiments similar to Wolfgang Köhler's famous *takete* and *maluma*. Until we know a great deal more about the geography of brain functions than we now do, this may be the best evidence available.

Let me close this book, as I began it, with a plea for the fascination of the evident.

Bibliography

Abercrombie, David. 1967. *Phonetics*. Edinburgh: University of Edinburgh Press.

Aissen, Judith, and David Perlmutter. 1983. Clause reduction in Spanish, pp. 360–404 in Perlmutter, D. (ed.) *Studies in Relational Grammar*. Chicago: University of Chicago Press.

Andersen, Henning. 1972. Diphthongization. *Language* 48:11–50.

– 1973. Abductive and deductive change. *Language* 49:765–91.

– 1980. Morphological change: towards a typology, pp. 1–50 in Fisiak, D. (ed.) *Historical morphology*. The Hague: Mouton.

– 1980a. Summarizing discussion: typology and genetics of language. *Travaux du cercle linguistique de Copenhagen* 20:197–210.

Anderson, Stephen C. 1979. Verb structure, pp. 73–136 in Hyman, L. (ed.)

Andersson, Lars-Gunnar. 1975. *The form and function of subordinate clauses*. Gothenburg Monographs in Linguistics, 1. Department of Linguistics, University of Göteborg.

Anttila, R. 1972. *Introduction to comparative and historical linguistics*. New York: Macmillan.

Ashton, Elizabeth. 1947. *Swahili grammar*. 2nd edition. London: Longmans, Green.

Austin, Peter. 1981. *A grammar of Diyari, South Australia*. Cambridge: Cambridge University Press.

Babby, Leonard. 1975. A transformational analysis of -sja verbs in Russian. *Lingua* 35:297–332.

Baldi, Philip. 1975. Reciprocal verbs and symmetric predicates. *Linguistische Berichte* 36:13–20.

Bamgbose, Ayo. 1966. *A grammar of Yoruba*. Cambridge: Cambridge University Press.

Banfield, Ann. 1973. Narrative style and the grammar of direct and indirect speech. *Foundations of language* 10:1–21.

Barasch, Marc. 1983. *The little black book of atomic war*. New York: Dell.

Bee, Darlene. 1973. Usarufa: a descriptive grammar, pp. 225–232 in McKaughan (ed.).

– 1973a. Comparative and historical problems in Eastern New Guinea Highlands languages, pp. 739–68 in McKaughan (ed.).

Behaghel, Otto. 1909. Beziehungen zwischen Umfang und Reihenfolge von Satzgliedern. *Indogermanischen Forschungen* 25:110–42.

– 1928. *Deutsche Syntax*, Vol. III. Heidelberg: Carl Winter.

– 1932. *Deutsche Syntax*, Vol. IV. Heidelberg: Carl Winter.

Behrens, Leila. 1982. *Zur funktionalen Motivation der Wortstellung: Untersuchungen anhand des Ungarischen.* Veröffentlichungen des Finnisch-Ugrischen Seminars an der U. München, C-13.

Beke, Ödön. 1919. A feltételes mondat eredete. *Nyr* 48:103–6.

Bellugi, Ursula, and Edward Klima. 1976. Two faces of the sign: iconic and abstract, pp. 514–38 in Harnad, S.R. et al. (eds.) *The origins and evolution of language and speech.* New York: New York Academy of Sciences.

Bennett, Tina. 1977. Interrogatives, pp. 171–88 in Byarushengo *et al.* (eds.).

Benveniste, Emile, 1946. Relations de personne dans le verbe. *BSL* 43:1–12.

– 1952. Animal communication and human language. *Diogenes* 1:1–7.

Berent, Gerald. 1973. Absolute constructions as "subordinate clauses". You take the high node and I'll take the low node. *CLS parasession on subordination*: 147–53.

Bhat, D.N.S. 1978. *Pronominalization.* Pune: Deccan College.

Bickerton, Derek. 1981. *The roots of language*, Ann Arbor: Karoma.

Bierwisch, M. and Ferenc Kiefer. 1970. Remarks on definitions in natural language, pp. 55–79 in Kiefer, F. (ed.) *Studies in syntax and semantics.* Dordrecht: Reidel.

Blake, Barry. 1979. Pitta-Pitta, pp. 183–242 in Dixon, R.M.W. and B. Blake (eds.) *Handbook of Autralian languages*, Vol. 1. Amsterdam: John Benjamins.

– 1982. The absolutive: Its scope in English and Kalkatungu, pp. 71–94 in Hopper and Thompson (eds.)

Bloomfield, Leonard. 1946. Algonquian, pp. 85–130 in *Linguistic structures of native America.* New York: The Viking Fund.

Bokamba, E.G. 1971. Specificity and definiteness in Dzamba. *Studies in African linguistics* 2:3.

Bolinger, Dwight. 1956. Contestar vs. contestar a. *Hispania* 39:106.

– 1961. *Generality, gradience, and the all-or-none.* (Janua Linguarum, series minor, 14.) The Hague: Mouton.

– 1975. *Aspects of language*, 2nd edition. New York: Harcourt, Brace, Jovanovich.

– 1977. The form of language. London: Longmans.

Bolinger, Dwight, and Louis Gerstman. 1957. Disjuncture as a clue to constructs. *Word* 13:246–55.

Boyle, Daniel. 1973. Ach and agus as coordinate and subordinate conjunctions in Gaelic. *CLS parasession on subordination*: 220–8.

Brandson, Lee. mss. Essays on aspects of Gende grammar. University of Manitoba.

Bresnan, J. 1972. Theory of complementation in English. Unpublished doctoral dissertation, MIT.

Brewer, W. 1970. Extent of verbal influence and the choice between le and lo in Alphonsine prose. *Hispanic review* 38:133–45.

Bromley, M. 1981. *A grammar of Lower Grand Valley Dani* (Pacific Linguistics C-63). Canberra: Research School of Pacific Studies, Australian National University.

Brown, Roger, and Albert Gilman. 1960. The pronouns of power and solidarity, pp. 253–76 in Sebeok, T. (ed.) *Style in language.* Cambridge, Mass.: MIT Press.

Byarushengo, E. et al. (eds.) 1977. *Haya grammatical structure.* (Southern California Occasional papers in Linguistics, 6.) Los Angeles: University of Southern California.

Bybee, Joan. to appear. Diagrammatic iconicity in stem-inflection relations, in Haiman, J. (ed.).

Caldicott, Helen. 1984. *Missile envy.* New York: Random House.

Capell, Arthur. 1948–9. Distribution of languages in the Central Highlands, New Guinea. *Oceania* 19:104–29; 234–53; 349–77.

Capell, Arthur, and H.E. Hinch. 1970. *Maung grammar.* (Janua Linguarum, series practica, 98.) The Hague: Mouton.

Carden, Guy. 1976. *English quantifiers: logical structure and linguistic variation.* New York: Academic Press.

Chao, Yuen-ren. 1968. *A grammar of spoken Chinese.* Berkeley and Los Angeles: University of California Press.

Chomsky, Noam. 1957. *Syntactic strucures* (Janua Linguarum, series minor, 4). The Hague: Mouton.

– 1959. Review of "Verbal behavior" by B.F. Skinner. *Language* 35:26–58.

– 1965. *Aspects of the theory of syntax.* Cambridge, Mass.: MIT Press.

– 1972. *Language and mind,* 2nd edition. New York: Harcourt, Brace, Jovanovich.

– 1975. *Reflections on language.* New York: Pantheon.

– 1976. On the nature of language, pp. 46–57 in Harnad et al. (eds.) *The origins and evolution of language and speech.* New York: New York Academy of Sciences.

– 1980. *Rules and representations.* New York: Columbia University Press.

– 1981. On the representation of form and function. *The linguistic review* 1:3–40.

– 1981a. *Lectures on government and binding.* Dordrecht: Foris.

Cole, Peter. 1983. Switch-reference in two Quechua languages, pp. 1–16 in Haiman and Munro (eds.).

Comrie, Bernard. 1975. The anti-ergative: Finland's answer to Basque. *CLS* 11:112–21.

– 1980. *Language typology and linguistic universals.* Chicago: University of Chicago Press.

– 1983. Switch-reference in Huichol: a typological study, pp. 17–38 in Haiman and Munro (eds.).

– to appear. Conditionals: a typology, in Traugott, Elizabeth, et al. (eds.) *On conditionals.* Cambridge: Cambridge University Press.

Crazzolara, J. 1938/1955. *A study of the Acooli language.* Oxford: Oxford University Press.

Creider, Chet. 1978. Anaphora in Kalenjin (Nandi Kipsigis), pp. 180–222 in Hinds, John (ed.) *Anaphora in discourse.* Edmonton: Linguistic Research, Inc.

Curme, George. 1931. *A grammar of the English language,* Vol. III: *Syntax.* Boston: Heath.

Darmesteter, Arsène. [1886] 1925. *La vie des mots,* 15th edition. Paris: Librairie Delagrave.

Davies, John. 1981. *Kobon.* Lingua descriptive studies, 3.

Davison, Alice. 1979. Some mysteries of subordination. *Studies in the linguistic sciences* 9(1):105–28.

– 1981. Syntactic and semantic indeterminacy resolved: a mostly pragmatic analysis of the Hindi conjunctive participle, pp. 101–28 in Cole, P. (ed.) *Radical pragmatics*. New York: Academic Press.

Deibler, Ellis. 1976. *Semantic relationships among Gahuku verbs*. Norman, Oklahoma: Summer Institute of Linguistics.

Dešeriev, Ju. 1959. *Grammatika Xinalugskogo jazyka*. Moskva: Akademia Nauk.

Dixon, R.M.W. 1968. Noun classes. *Lingua* 21:104–25.

– 1971. A method of semantic description, pp. 436–71 in Jakobovitz, L. and D. Steinberg (eds.) *Semantics: an interdisciplinary reader*. Cambridge: Cambridge University Press.

– 1977. *A grammar of Yidiɲ*. Cambridge: Cambridge University Press.

Donaldson, Tamsin. 1980. *Ngiyambaa*. Cambridge: Cambridge University Press.

Dougherty, Ray. 1970. A grammar of conjoined coordinate structures, I. *Language* 46:850–99.

Downing, Bruce, and Judith Fuller. 1984. Cultural contact and expansion of the Hmong lexicon. Linguistics club, University of Minnesota 4/25/84.

DuBois, John. to appear. Competing motivations, in Haiman (ed.).

Duran, James. 1979. Nonstandard forms of Swahili in West-Central Kenya, pp. 129–51 in Hancock (ed.).

Duranti, Alessandro. 1977. Relative clauses, pp. 119–32 in Byarushengo et al. (eds.).

Dutton, Tom. 1975. A Koita grammar sketch and vocabulary, pp. 281–412 in Dutton, T. (ed.) *Studies in languages of Central and Southeastern Papua* (Pacific Linguistics C-29). Canberra: Research School of Pacific Studies, Australian National University.

Elbert, Samuel. 1974. *Puluwat grammar* (Pacific Linguistics B-29). Canberra: Research School of Pacific Studies, Australian National University.

Faltz, Leonard. 1977. Reflexivization: A study in universal syntax. Unpublished doctoral dissertation, Berkeley.

Ferguson, C. 1959. Diglossia. *Word* 15:325–40.

– 1971. Absence of copula and the notion of simplicity: a study of normal speech, baby talk, foreign talk, and pidgins, pp. 141–50 in Hymes (ed.).

Ferguson, C. and C. DeBose. 1977. Simplified registers, broken language, and pidginization, pp. 99–125 in Valdman, A. (ed.) *Pidgin and creole studies*. Bloomington: Indiana University Press.

Fidelholtz, James. 1975. Word frequency and vowel reduction in English. *CLS* 11:200–13.

Fischer, John. 1958. Social influences on the choice of a linguistic variant. *Word* 14:47–56.

Flobert, Pierre. 1975. *Les verbes déponents latins*. Paris: Les belles lettres.

Fodor, Jerry. 1970. Three reasons for not deriving "kill" from "cause to die". *Linguistic inquiry* 1:429–38.

Fortune, G. 1955. *An analytical grammar of Shona*. London: Longmans, Green.

Fortune, Reo. 1942. *Arapesh*. (Publications of the American Ethnological Society 19.) New York: Augustin.

Franklin, Karl. 1971. *A grammar of Kewa, New Guinea* (Pacific Linguistics C-16). Canberra: Research School of Pacific Studies, Australian National University.

Franklin, Karl. 1983. Some features of interclausal reference in Kewa, pp. 39–50 in Haiman and Munro (eds.).

Frantz, Chester. 1973. Grammatical categories as indicated by Gadsup noun affixes, pp. 424–38 in McKaughan (ed.).

Frantz, Donald. 1977. A new view of to-contraction. *Workpapers* 21:71–6, Summer Institute of Linguistics (North Dakota Session).

Frei, Henri. 1929. *La grammaire des fautes.* Paris: Geuthner.

Frishberg, Nancy. 1975. Arbitrariness and iconicity: historical change in the American Sign Language. *Language* 51:696–719.

Gamkrelidze, Thomas. 1974. The problem of l'arbitraire du signe. *Language* 50:102–11.

Gardiner, Alan. 1957. *Egyptian grammar.* London: Oxford University Press.

Gazdar, Gerald. 1981. Unbounded dependencies and coordinate structure. *Linguistic inquiry* 12:155–84.

Geertz, Clifford. 1960. *The religion of Java.* Glencoe: The Free Press.

Gibson, J. and Joy McCarthy. 1975. *Kanite grammar sketch.* Ukarumpa: Summer Institute of Linguistics.

Givón, Talmy. 1971. Historical syntax and synchronic morphology: an archaealogist's field trip. *CLS* 7:394–415.

– 1972. Pronoun attraction and subject postposing in Bantu. *Chicago which hunt:* 190–7.

– 1976. Some constraints on Bantu causativization, pp. 325–51 in Shibatani, M. (ed.) *The grammar of causative constructions.* (Syntax and Semantics, Vol. 6.) New York: Academic Press.

– 1979. Prolegomena to any sane creology, pp. 3–35 in Hancock (ed.)

– 1979a. *On understanding grammar.* New York: Academic Press.

– 1980. The binding hierarchy and the typology of complements. *Studies in language* 4:333–77.

– 1980a. *Ute reference grammar.* Ignacio, Colardo: Southern Ute Indian Tribe.

– 1983. Topic continuity: the functional domain of switch-reference, pp. 51–82 in Haiman and Munro (eds.).

– to appear. Iconicity, isomorphism, and non-arbitrary coding, in Haiman (ed.).

Gooch, Anthony. 1970. *Diminutive, augmentative, and pejorative suffixes in Modern Spanish.* Oxford: Pergamon Press.

Goodman, Maurice. 1964. *A comparative study of creole French dialects.* The Hague: Mouton.

Goodwin, Wm., and C. Gulick. 1958. *Greek grammar.* Waltham: Ginn-Blaisdell.

Gordon, Lynn. 1983. Switch-reference in Maricopa, pp. 83–104 in Haiman and Munro (eds.).

Grammont, M. 1965. *Traité de phonétique,* 8th edition. Paris: Klincksieck.

Greenberg, Joseph. 1966. Some universals of language with particular reference to the order of meaningful elements, pp. 73–113 in Greenberg, J. (ed.) *Universals of language.* 2nd edition. Cambridge, Mass.: MIT Press.

– 1966a. *Universals of language with particular reference to feature hierarchies.* The Hague: Mouton.

– 1970. Some generalizations concerning glottalic consonants, especially implosives. *IJAL* 36:123–45.

Gregerson, Kenneth. ms. Sound symbolism in Rengao.

Haas, Mary. 1940. *Tunica*. New York: J.J. Augustin.

Haiman, John. 1976. Agentless sentences. *Foundations of language* 16:19–53.

– 1976a. Presuppositions in Hua. *CLS* 12:258–70.

– 1977. Connective particles in Hua; an essay on the parts of speech. *Oceanic linguistics* 16:53–107.

– 1978. A study in polysemy. *Studies in language* 2:1–34.

– 1980. *Hua: A Papuan language of the Eastern Highlands of New Guinea*. Amsterdam: John Benjamins B.V.

– 1980a. Dictionaries and encyclopaedias. *Lingua* 51:329–57.

– 1982. Dictionaries and encyclopedias again. *Lingua* 56:353–5.

– 1982a. High transitivity in Hua, pp. 177–94 in Hopper and Thompson (eds.).

– 1983a. On some origins of switch-reference marking, pp. 105–28 in Haiman and Munro (eds.)

– 1983b. Iconic and economic motivation. *Language* 59:781–819.

– (ed.) to appear. *Iconicity in syntax* (Typological Studies in Language 6). Amsterdam: John Benjamins.

– ms. The origin of the medial–final distinction in the Gorokan languages.

Haiman, John and Pamela Munro (eds.). 1983. *Switch-reference and universal grammar* (Typological Studies in Language 2). Amsterdam: John Benjamins.

Hale, Kenneth. 1973. Person marking in Walbiri, pp. 308–44 in Anderson, Stephen, and Paul Kiparsky (eds.) *A Festschrift for Morris Halle*. New York: Harper and Row.

– 1973a. Deep-surface canonical disparities and language change: an Australian case, pp. 401–58 in *Current trends in linguistics* 11. The Hague: Mouton.

– 1976. The adjoined relative clause in Australia, pp. 78–105 in Dixon, R.M.W. (ed.) *Grammatical categories in Australian languages*. Canberra: Australian Institute of Aboriginal Studies.

Hale, Wm., and C.D. Buck. 1903. *A Latin grammar* (reprinted 1966). University of Alabama Press.

Hall, Robert. 1966. *Pidgin and creole languages*. Ithaca: Cornell University Press.

Hancock, Ian. (ed.). 1979. *Readings in Creole studies*. Ghent: Storia Scientia.

Hancock, Ian, and DeCamp (eds.). 1974. *Pidgins and creoles: trends and prospects*. Georgetown: Georgetown University Press.

Hankamer, Jorge. 1973. Unacceptable ambiguity. *Linguistic inquiry* 4:17–68.

Hanson, Vicki, and Ursula Bellugi. 1982. On the role of sign order and morphological structure in memory for ASL sentences. *Journal of verbal learning and verbal behavior* 21(5):621–33.

Harrell, Richard. 1965. *A basic course in Moroccan Arabic*. Georgetown: Georgetown University Press.

Harris, Martin. to appear. The historical development of conditional sentences in Romance, in Traugott et al. (eds.) *On conditionals*. Cambridge: Cambridge University Press.

Harrison, Sheldon. 1976. *Mokilese reference grammar*. Honolulu: University of Hawaii Press.

Havers, Wilhelm. 1931. *Handbuch der erklärenden Syntax*. Heidelberg: Carl Winter.

Haviland, John. 1979. Guugu-Yimidhirr, pp. 27–180 in Dixon, R.M.W. and B. Blake, (eds.) *Handbook of Australian languages*, Vol. I. Amsterdam: John Benjamins.

– 1979a. Guugu-Yimidhirr Brother-in-Law language. *Language in society* 8:365–94.

Healey, Phyllis. 1966. *Levels and chaining in Telefol sentences* (Pacific Linguistics B-5). Canberra: Department of Linguistics, Research School of Pacific Studies, Australian National University.

Heine, Bernd. 1979. African based pidgins, pp. 89–98 in Hancock (ed.).

Hermann, E. 1895. Gab es im Indogermanischen Nebensätze? *Kuhns Zeitschrift* 33:481–534.

Hetzron, Robert. 1975. *Surfacing: from dependency relations to linearity*. Padova: Liviana Editrice.

– 1980. On word order and morpheme order, pp. 175–9 in Brettschneider, G. and Ch. Lehmann, (eds.) *Wege zur Universalienforschung*. Tübingen: Günter Narr.

Hill, Kenneth, and Jane Hill. 1978. Honorific usage in Nahuatl. *Language* 54:123–55.

Hinnebusch, T. 1979. Swahili, pp. 189–250 in Shopen, T. (ed.) *Languages and their status*. Cambridge: Winthrop.

Hinnebusch, Thomas, and Robert Kirsner. 1980. On the inference of "inalienable possession" in Swahili. *Journal of African languages and linguistics* 2:1–16.

Hinton, Leanne. 1982. How to cause in Mixtec. *BLS* 8:354–63.

Hoa, Nguyen Dinh. 1974. *Colloquial Vietnamese*. Carbondale: Southern Illinois University Press.

Hoijer, Harry. 1946. Chiricahua Apache, pp. 55–84 in *Linguistic structures of native America*. New York: The Viking Fund.

Hopper, Paul. 1979. Aspect and foregrounding in discourse, pp. 213–42 in Givón, Talmy (ed.) *Discourse in syntax* (Syntax and Semantics, Vol 12). New York: Academic Press.

Hopper, Paul, and Sandra A. Thompson. 1980. Transitivity in grammar and discourse. *Language* 56:250–99.

– to appear. The iconic basis for the categories "noun" and "verb", in Haiman (ed.).

– (eds.). 1982. *Studies in transitivity*. New York: Academic Press.

Hudson, Richard. 1976. Coordination reduction, gapping, and right node raising. *Language* 52:535–62.

Hurst, Dorothy. 1951. Spanish case: influence of subject and connotation of force. *Hispania* 34:74–8.

Hyman, Larry. 1971. Consecutivization in Feʔfeʔ. *Journal of African languages* 10/2:29–43.

– 1979. Phonology and noun structure, pp. 1–72 in Hyman (ed.).

– (ed.) 1979. *Aghen grammatical structure* (Southern California Occasional Papers in Linguistics 7). Los Angeles: University of Southern California.

Hyman, Larry, and Karl Zimmer. 1976. Embedded topic in French, pp. 191–211 in Li, C. (ed.) *Subject and topic*. New York: Academic Press.

Hymes, Dell (ed.). 1971. *Pidginization and creolization of languages*. Cambridge: Cambridge University Press.

Irwin, Barry. 1974. *Salt-Yui grammar* (Pacific Linguistics B-38). Canberra: Research School of Pacific Studies, Australian National University.

Jacob, Judith. 1968. *Introduction to Cambodian*. Oxford: Oxford University Press.

Jakobson, Roman. 1965. Quest for the essence of language. *Diogenes* 51:21–37. (Reprinted in his *Selected writings*, Vol. ɪɪ (1971):345–59. The Hague: Mouton.)

– 1966. Implications of language universals for linguistics, pp. 263–78 in Greenberg (ed.). (Reprinted in his *Selected writings*, Vol. ɪɪ (1971):580–92.)

– 1966a. Grammatical parallelism and its Russian facet. *Language* 42:399–429.

– 1971. The relationship beween Russian stem suffixes and verbal aspects. *Selected writings*, Vol. ɪɪ (1971):198–202.

– 1971a. Da i net v mimike. *Selected writings*, Vol. ɪɪ (1971):360–5.

Jakobson, Roman, G. Fant, and Morris Halle. 1967. *Preliminaries to speech analysis: the distinctive features and their correlates*, 2nd edition. Cambridge, Mass.: MIT Press.

James, Dorothy. ms. Verb serialization in Siane. Ukarumpa: Summer Institute of Linguistics.

Jensen, John. 1977. *Yapese reference grammar*. Honolulu: University of Hawaii Press.

Jespersen, Otto. 1909. *A modern English grammar on historical principles*. Vol. ɪ. Heidelberg: Carl Winter.

– 1933. Symbolic value of the vowel I. Reprinted in *Selected writings of Otto Jespersen* (nd), pp. 557–78. London: George Allen and Unwin.

– 1940. *A modern English grammar on historical principles*, Vol. ᴠ. London: George Allen and Unwin.

– 1949. *A modern English grammar on historical principles*. Vol. ᴠɪɪ. London: George Allen and Unwin.

Johnson, Michael. ms. Coordination and subordination in Parkeri, University of Manitoba.

Johnston, Ray. 1981. Conceptualizing in Nakanai and English, pp. 212–24 in K. Franklin (ed.) *Syntax and semantics in New Guinea languages*. Ukarumpa: Summer Institute of Linguistics.

Kaplan, Fred. 1982. Missile envy. *The new republic,* 17 October 1982.

Karttunen, Lauri. 1971. Implicative verbs. *Language* 47:340–58.

Katz, Jerrold, and Paul Postal. 1964. *An integrated theory of linguistic descriptions*. Cambridge, Mass.: MIT Press.

Kay, Paul, and Gillian Sankoff. 1974. A language-universals approach to pidgins and creoles, pp. 61–72 in Hancock and DeCamp (eds.).

Kayne, Richard. 1975. *French syntax*. Cambridge, Mass.: MIT Press.

Keenan, Edward. 1972. Relative clause formation in Malagasy. *Chicago which hunt*:169–89.

Keenan, Edward, and Bernard Comrie. 1977. Noun phrase accessibility and universal grammar. *Linguistic inquiry* 8:77–100.

Keenan, Edward, and Robert Hull. 1973. The logical syntax of direct and indirect questions. *CLS parasession on subordination*:348–70.

Kellerman, Eric. ms. Now you see it, now you don't. Paper given at the 9th conference on applied linguistics, Ann Arbor.

Kim, K.-O. 1977. Sound symbolism in Korean. *Journal of linguistics* 13:67–75.

Kimenyi, Alexandre. 1980. *A relational grammar of Kinyarwanda* (University of California Papers in Linguistics 91).

Kiparsky, Paul. 1968. Tense and mood in Indo-European syntax. *Foundations of language* 4:30–57.

Klima, Edward, and Ursula Bellugi. 1979. *The signs of language*. Cambridge, Mass.: Harvard University Press.

Koefoed, Gerd. 1979. Baby talk and relexification theory, pp. 36–54 in Hancock (ed.)

Köhler, Wolfgang. 1947. Gestalt psychology. New York: Liveright.

Kühner, Raphael. 1879. *Ausführliche Grammatik der lateinischen Sprache*. Vol. II. Hannover: Hannsche Buchhandlung.

Kuno, Susumu. 1973. *The structure of the Japanese language*. Cambridge, Mass.: MIT Press.

Kuryłowicz, Jerzy. 1964. *The inflectional categories of Indoeuropean*. Heidelberg: Carl Winter.

Labov, W. 1970/1977. On the adequacy of natural languages (Linguistic Agency of the University of Trier B-23).

– 1972. *Sociolinguistic patterns*. Philadelphia: University of Pennsylvania Press.

Lambrecht, Knud. 1984. Frame semantics and German binomial expressions. *Language* 60:753–96.

Langacker, Ronald, and Pamela Munro. 1975. Passives and their meaning. *Language* 51:789–830.

Langdon, Margaret. 1970. *A grammar of Diegueño* (University of California Papers in Linguistics 66).

– 1971. Sound symbolism in Yuman languages (University of California Papers in Linguistics 65:149–73).

Langdon, Margaret, and Pamela Munro. 1979. Subject and (switch-)reference in Yuman languages. *Folia linguistica* 13:321–44.

Lee, Kee-dong. 1975. *Kusaiean reference grammar*. Honolulu: University of Hawaii Press.

Lewis, G.L. 1967. *Turkish grammar*. Oxford: Oxford University Press.

Li, Charles, and Sandra A. Thompson. 1973. Serial verb constructions in Mandarin Chinese. *CLS* 9:96–102.

– 1981. *Mandarin: A functional reference grammar*. Berkeley and Los Angeles: University of California Press.

Longacre, Robert. 1972. *Hierarchy and constituency in New Guinea languages*. Vol. 2 *Discussion*. Georgetown: Georgetown University Press.

Lord, Carol. 1973. Serial verbs in transition. *Studies in African languages* 4(3):269–96.

Loving, Richard, and Aretta Loving. 1973. A preliminary survey of Awa noun suffixes, pp. 19–30 in McKaughan (ed.).

Lukas, Johannes. 1937. *A study of the Kanuri language*. Oxford: Oxford University Press.

Luria, A.S. 1968. *The mind of a mnemonist*. New York: Braziller.

Lynch, John. 1973. Verbal aspects of possession in Melanesian languages. *Oceanic linguistics* 12:69–102.

– 1978. *A grammar of Lenakel* (Pacific Linguistics B-55). Canberra: Research School of Pacific Studies, Australian National University.

– 1983. Switch-reference in Lenakel, pp. 209–22 in Haiman and Munro (eds.).

Lyons, John. 1977. *Semantics*, volume I. Cambridge: Cambridge University Press.

– 1981. *Language, context, and meaning.* Cambridge: Cambridge University Press.

MacDonald, Lorna, to appear. Medial verbs and left-dislocation in Tauya. *Language and linguistics in Melanesia* 14.

– ms. A grammar of Tauya. Unpublished doctoral dissertation, University of Manitoba.

Magomedbekova, Z. 1971. *Karatinskij jazyk.* Tbilisi: Mecniereba.

Magometov, A.A. 1965. *Tabasaranskij jazyk.* Tbilisi: Mecniereba.

Manczak, Witold. 1978. Irregular sound change due to frequency in German, pp. 309–19 in Fisiak, J. (ed.) *Recent developments in historical phonology.* The Hague: Mouton.

Manessy, Gilbert. 1966. Processes of pidginization in African languages, pp. 129–54 in Valdman, A. (ed.) *Pidgin and creole linguistics.* Bloomington: University of Indiana Press.

Mardirussian, Galust. 1975. Noun incorporation in universal grammar. *CLS* 11:383–9.

Marlett, Stephen. 1981. The structure of Seri. Unpublished doctoral dissertation, University of California, San Diego.

Martin, Samuel. 1964. Politeness in Japanese, in Hymes, Dell (ed.) *Language in culture and society.* New York: Harper and Row.

– 1975. *A reference grammar of Japanese.* New Haven: Yale University Press.

Martin, Samuel, and Young-sook C. Lee. 1969. *Beginning Korean.* New Haven: Yale University Press.

Matisoff, James. 1973. *A grammar of Lahu.* Berkeley and Los Angeles: University of California Press.

Matthews, Peter. 1981. *Syntax.* Cambridge: Cambridge University Press.

McBride, Samuel, and Nancy McBride. 1975. *Gimi grammar sketch.* Ukarumpa: Summer Institute of linguistics.

McCarthy, Joy. 1965. Clause chaining in Kanite. *Anthropological linguistics* 7(5):59–70.

McCawley, James. 1968. Lexical insertion in a transformational grammar without deep structures. *CLS* 4:71–80.

– 1968a. The role of semantics in a grammar, in Fillmore, Charles, and D. Terence Langendoen (eds.) *Studies in linguistic semantics.* New York: Holt.

McKaughan, Howard (ed.). 1973. *The languages of the Eastern family of the Eastern New Guinea Highlands Stock.* Seattle: University of Washington Press.

McKaughan, Howard, and Doreen Marks. 1973. Notes on Auyana phonology and morphology, pp. 181–9 in McKaughan (ed.).

McKay, Graham. 1975. A grammar of Rembarrnga. Unpublished doctoral dissertation, Australian National University.

Meeussen, A.E. 1971. Bantu relative clauses. *Studies in African linguistics*, supplement 2.

Meillet, A. 1912/1958. L'évolution des formes grammaticales, pp. 130–49 in his *Linguistique historique et linguistique générale.* Paris: Champion.

Meinhof, Carl. 1936. *Die Entstehung flektierender Sprachen.* Berlin: Reimer.

Merlan, Francesca. 1976. Nahuatl noun incorporation. *International journal of American linguistics* 42:177–92.

Mierow, Charles. 1911. *Latin syntax.* New York: Ginn.

Mikami, Akira. 1963. *Nihongo no koobun.* Tokyo: Kuroshio Shuppan.

Miller, Roy. 1967. *The Japanese language.* Chicago: University of Chicago Press.

Montgomery, Thomas. 1978. Iconicity and lexical retention in Spanish: stative and dynamic verbs. *Language* 54:907–16.

Morani, Moreno. 1973. L'uso del participio assoluto nelle lingue indoeuropee. *Rendiconti del Istituto Lombardo, Classe di lettere* 107:707–59.

Moravcsik, Edith. 1978. The case marking of objects, pp. 249–89 in Greenberg, Joseph (ed.) *Universals of human language.* Vol. IV. Stanford: Stanford University Press.

Morris, Charles. 1955. *Signs, language, and behavior.* New York: Braziller.

Mülhäusler, Peter. 1974. *Pidginization and simplification of languages* (Pacific Linguistics B-26). Canberra: Research School of Pacific Studies, Australian National University.

– 1979. (and S. Wurm and T. Dutton). Language planning and New Guinea Pidgin, pp. 263–76 in Wurm, S. (ed.) *New Guinea and neighbouring areas.* The Hague: Mouton.

Munro, Pamela. 1982. On the transitivity of "say" verbs, pp. 301–18 in Hopper and Thompson (eds.).

– 1983. When "same" is not equal to "not different", pp. 223–44 in Haiman and Munro (eds.).

Murane, Elizabeth. 1974. *Daga grammar.* Norman, Oklahoma: Summer Institute of Linguistics.

Napoli, Donna Jo. 1981. Semantic interpretation versus lexical governance. *Language* 57:841–87.

Naro, Anthony. 1973. The origin of West African Pidgin. *CLS* 9: 442–9.

– 1978. A study on the origins of pidginization. *Language* 54:314–47.

Nichols, Johanna. 1971. Diminutive consonant symbolism in West North America. *Language* 47:826–48.

Nida, Eugene. 1975. The analysis of meaning and dictionary making, pp. 1–23 in his *Language structure and translation,* edited by Anwar S. Dil. Stanford: Stanford University Press.

Nida, Eugene, et al. 1975. Semantic domains and componential analysis of meaning, pp. 139–67 in Cole, Roger (ed.) *Current issues in linguistics.* Bloomington, Indiana: Indiana University Press.

Noss, Philip. 1979. Fula: a language of change, pp. 173–88 in Hancock (ed.).

Ohala, John. 1974. Phonetic explanation in phonology, *CLS parasession on natural phonology*: 251–74.

Olson, Michael. 1981. Barai clause junctures: towards a theory of interclausal relations. Unpublished doctoral dissertation, Australian National University.

Osgood, Charles. 1953. *Method and theory in experimental psychology.* New York: Oxford University Press.

Oswalt, Robert. 1977. The causative as a reference-switching device in Pomo. *Berkeley Linguistic Society* 2:46–53.

Palmer, George, and Dan Bolef. 1984. Laser isotope separation. *Bulletin of the atomic scientists* 40:26–31.

Paul, Hermann. 1880/1968. *Prinzipien der Sprachgeschichte*, 8th edition. Tübingen: Max Niemeyer.

Payne, J. and D. Drew. 1966. *Kamano sketch grammar*. Ukarumpa: Summer Institute of Linguistics.

Peirce, Charles. 1932. *Philosophical writings*, Vol. ii. Cambridge: Harvard University Press.

Perrott, D. 1957. *Teach yourself Swahili*. London: English Universities Press.

Pilhofer, Georg. 1933. Grammatik der Kâte-Sprache. *Zeitschrift für Eingeborenen-Sprachen*, Beiheft 14. Berlin: Reimer.

Postal, Paul. 1970. On the surface verb remind. *Linguistic inquiry* 1:37–120.

– 1970a. Coreferential complement subject deletion. *Linguistic inquiry* 1:439–500.

Postal, Paul, and Geoffrey Pullum. 1982. The contraction debate. *Linguistic inquiry* 13:122–38.

Pul'kina, I.M. and Zaxava-Nakrasova, E.B. 1964. *Učebnik russkogo jazyka*. Moskva: Vyšaja škola.

Pullum, Geoffrey, and Paul Postal. 1979. On an inadequate defence of "trace theory". *Linguistic inquiry* 10:689–706.

Quine, Willard. 1961. Reference and modality, pp. 139–59 in his *From a logical point of view*, 2nd edition. New York: Harper.

Ramsey, F. 1931. General propositions and causality, pp. 237–55 in his *Foundations of mathematics*. London: Kegan Paul.

Rappaport, Gilbert. 1979. Detachment and adverbial participial clauses. Unpublished doctoral dissertation. University of California at Los Angeles.

Reckendorf, H. 1895. *Die syntaktischen Verhältnisse des Arabischen*. Leiden: E.J. Brill.

– 1921. *Arabische Syntax*. Heidelberg: Carl Winter.

Reesink, Ger. ms. Switch-reference and topicality hierarchies. Ukarumpa: Summer Institute of Linguistics.

– to appear. Structures and their functions in Usan. University of Amsterdam.

Renck, Gunther. 1975. *A grammar of Yagaria* (Pacific Linguistics B-40). Canberra: Research School of Pacific Studies, Australian National University.

– 1977. *Yagaria dictionary* (Pacific Linguistics C-37). Canberra: Research School of Pacific Studies, Australian National University.

Riese, Timothy. 1981. Some aspects of the conditional sentence in the Vogul language. *Nyelvtudományi Közlemények 83/2:383–93*.

Rivero, Maria-Luisa. 1972. On conditional sentences in Spanish, pp. 196–214 in Casagrande, Jean, and Bohdan Saciuk (eds.) *Generative studies in Romance languages*. Rowley, Mass.: Newbury House.

Ross, John. 1967. Constraints on variables in syntax. Unpublished doctoral dissertation, MIT.

– 1970. Gapping and the order of constituents, pp. 140–54 in Bierwisch, Manfred, and Karl Heidolph (eds.) *Progress in linguistics*. The Hague: Mouton.

Ross, Malcolm, and John Paol. 1978. *A Waskia grammar sketch and vocabulary*

(Pacific Linguistics B-58). Canberra: Research School of Pacific Studies, Australian National University.

Sadock, Jerry. 1980. Noun incorporation in Greenlandic Eskimo. *Language* 56:300–19.

Saint-Jacques Fauquenoy, Marguerite. 1974. Guyanese: A French creole, pp. 27–37 in Hanock and DeCamp (eds.).

Saitz, Robert. 1955. Functional word order in Old English subject–object patterns. Unpublished doctoral dissertation, University of Wisconsin.

Sankoff, Gillian. 1977. Creolization and syntactic change in Tok Pisin, pp. 131–54 in Blount, Ben, and M. Sanchez (eds.) *Sociocultural dimensions of linguistic change*. New York: Academic Press.

Sankoff, Gillian and S. Laberge. 1974. On the acquisition of native speakers by a language, pp. 73–84 in Hancock and DeCamp (eds.).

Sansom, George. 1928. *An historical grammar of Japanese*. Oxford: The Clarendon Press.

Sapir, Edward. 1929. A study of phonetic symbolism. *Journal of experimental psychology* 12:225–39. (Reprinted in *Selected writings of Edward Sapir*, edited by David Mandelbaum, Berkeley: University of California Press.)

Saussure, Ferdinand de, 1969 (1916) *Cours de linguistique générale*. Paris: Payot.

Saxton, Dean., 1982. Papago, pp. 93–266 in Langacker, Ron (ed.) *Studies in Uto-Aztecan grammar*, Vol. III. Norman, Oklahoma: Summer Institute of Linguistics.

Scaglione, Aldo. 1972. *The classic theory of composition*. Chapel Hill: University of North Carolina Press.

Schachter, Paul. 1973. Focus and relativization. *Language* 4:19–46.

– 1976. The subject in Philippine languages, pp. 491–518 in Li, Charles (ed.) *Subject and topic*. New York: Academic Press.

– 1977. Constraints on coordination. *Language* 53:86–113.

Schachter, Paul, and Susan Mordechay. 1983. A phrase structure account of non-constituent conjunction. *West Coast Conference on Formal Linguistics* 2:260–74.

Schachter, Paul, and Fe Otanes. 1972. *Tagalog reference grammar*. Berkeley and Los Angeles: University of California Press.

Scott, Graham. 1973. *Higher levels of Fore grammar* (Pacific Linguistics B-23). Canberra: Research School of Pacific Studies, Australian National University.

– 1978. *The Fore language of Papua New Guinea* (Pacific Linguistics B-47). Canberra: Research School of Pacific Studies, Australian National University.

Scotton, Carol. 1979. Nairobi and Kampala varieties of Swahili, pp. 111–27 in Hancock (ed.).

Serebrennikov, B.A. 1963. Istoričeskaja morfologia permskix jayzkov. Moskva: Akademia Nauk.

Shapiro, Michael. 1983. *The sense of grammar*. Bloomington: Indiana University Press.

Shibatani, Masayoshi. 1972. *Three reasons for not deriving "kill" from "cause to die" in Japanese* (Syntax and Semantics, Vol. 1:125–37). New York: Academic Press.

– 1976. *Causativization* (Syntax and Semantics, Vol. 5:239–94). New York: Academic Press.

Silverstein, Michael. 1976. Hierarchy of features and ergativity, pp. 112–71 in Dixon, R. (ed.) *Grammatical categories in Australian languages.* Canberra: Australian Institute of Aboriginal Studies.

Slobin, Dan. 1980. The repeated path between transparency and opacity in language, pp. 229–43 in Bellugi, U. and M. Studdert-Kennedy (eds.) *Signed and spoken language: biological constraints on linguistic form.* Deerfield Beach, California: Verlag Chimie.

– to appear. The child as icon maker, in Haiman (ed.).

Sohn, Ho-Min. 1975. *Woleaian reference grammar.* Honolulu: University of Hawaii Press.

Song, Seok Choong. 1978. Causes of confusion in descriptions of causatives in Korean, pp. 207–16 in Kim, Chin-wu (ed.) *Papers in Korean linguistics.* Columbia, South Carolina: Hornbeam Press.

Stahlke, Herbert. 1970. Serial verbs. *Studies in African languages* 1/1:60–99.

Stampe, David. 1979. *A dissertation on natural phonology.* New York: Garland.

Starks, Donna. ms. Coordination and subordination in NWR Montagnais. *University of Manitoba.*

Stern, Gustaf. 1931. *Meaning and change of meaning.* Bloomington: University of Indiana Press.

Stevens, L. 1965. Language levels in Madurese. *Language* 41:294–302.

Strange, David. 1973. Indicative and subjunctive in Asaro. *Linguistics* 110:82–98.

Strange, Gladys. 1975. Nominal elements in Upper Asaro. *Anthropological linguistics* 7/5:71–9.

Sturtevant, Edgar. 1917. *Linguistic change.* Chicago: University of Chicago Press.

Sugita, Hiroshi. 1973. Semi-transitive verbs and object incorporation in Micronesian languages. *Oceanic linguistics* 12:393–406.

Swadesh, Morris. 1971. *The origin and diversification of language.* Chicago: Aldine.

Tai, James. 1969. Coordination reduction. Unpublished doctoral dissertation, University of Illinois.

– to appear. Temporal sequence and Chinese word order, in Haiman (ed.).

Takizala, A. 1972. Focus and relativization in Kihungʔan. *Studies in African Linguistics* 3:2.

Tanz, Christine. 1971. Sound symbolism in words relating to proximity and distance. *Language and speech* 14:266–76.

Taylor, F. W. 1953. *A grammar of the Adamawa dialect of the Fulani language.* Oxford: Oxford University Press.

– 1959. *A practical Hausa grammar.* 2nd edition. Oxford: Clarendon Press.

Thompson, David. 1971. *Chrau grammar.* Honolulu: University of Hawaii Press.

Thurman, Robert. 1978. Interclausal relations in Chuave. Master's essay, University of California at Los Angeles.

Tiersma, Peter. 1982. Local and general markedness. *Language* 58:832–49.

Traugott, Elizabeth. to appear. Conditional markers, in Haiman (ed.).

Ullmann, Stephen. 1962. *Semantics.* New York: Barnes and Noble.

Underhill, Robert. 1976. *Turkish grammar.* Cambridge, Mass.: MIT Press.

Vasmer, Max. 1953. *Russisches etymologisches Wörterburch*, I. Heidelberg: Carl Winter.

Vogt, Hans. 1971. *Grammaire de la langue georgienne*. Oslo: Universitetsforlaget.

Voorhoeve, C.L. 1975. Central and western Trans-New Guinea Phylum languages, pp. 345–460 in Wurm (ed.).

Wacke, O. 1931. Formenlehre der Ono-Sprache. *Zeitschrift für Eingeborenen-Sprachen* 21:161–208.

Wackernagel, Jakob. 1912/13. Fernstellung zusammengehörigen Wörter im Deutschen. *Indogermanische Forschungen* 31:398–431.

Watkins, Calvert. 1962. *Indo-European origins of the Celtic verb. Part one: The sigmatic aorist*. Dublin: Institute of Advanced Studies.

Watters, John. 1979. Focus in Aghem, pp. 137–97 in Hyman (ed.).

Weil, Henri. 1978. *The order of words in the ancient languages compared with that of the modern languages* (edited by Aldo Scaglione). Amsterdam: John Benjamins.

Wells, Rosemary. 1979. *Siroi grammar* (Pacific Linguistics B-51). Canberra: Research School of Pacific Studies, Australian National University.

Welmers, William. 1973. *African language structures*. Berkeley and Los Angeles: University of California Press.

West, Dorothy. 1973. *Wojokeso sentence, paragraph and discourse analysis* (Pacific Linguistics B-28). Canberra: Research School of Pacific Studies, Australian National University.

Whinnom, Keith. 1971. Linguistic hybridization and the "special case" of pidgins and creoles, pp. 91–116 in Hymes (ed.).

Whitehead, Carl. ms. A Menya grammar. Master's essay, University of Manitoba.

Whitney, Dwight. 1875. Phusei or thesei. *Transactions of the American Philological Association for 1874*: 95–116. (Reprinted in *Whitney on Language*, edited by Michael Silverstein. Cambridge, Mass.: MIT Press.)

Wierzbicka, Anna. 1972. The semantics of direct and indirect discourse. *Papers in linguistics* 7:267–307.

– 1980. *Lingua mentalis*. New York: Academic Press.

Williams, Edwin. 1975. *Small clauses in English* (Syntax and Semantics, Vol. 4:249–73). New York: Academic Press.

Williams, Joseph. 1975. *Origins of the English language*. New York: Free Press.

Witkowski, Stanley, and Cecil Brown. 1983. Marking reversals and cultural importance. *Language* 59:569–82.

Wittgenstein, Ludwig. 1958. *Philosophical investigations*. 2nd edition, translated by Elizabeth Anscombe. Oxford: Blackwell.

Wolff, John. 1967. *Beginning Cebuano*. New Haven: Yale University Press.

Woodcock, E.C. 1959. A new Latin syntax. London: Methuen.

Woodward, L. 1973. Maring sentences. *Workpapers in New Guinea languages* 1:1–26.

Wurm, Stephan (ed.). 1975. *Papuan languages and the New Guinea linguistic scene* (Pacific Linguistics C-38). Canberra: Research School of Pacific Studies, Australian National University.

Young, Robert. 1964. The primary verb in BenaBena, pp. 41–88 in Pence, A. (ed.)

Verb studies in five New Guinea Languages. Norman, Oklahoma: Summer Institute of Linguistics.

– 1971. *The verb in BenaBena: its form and function* (Pacific Linguistics B-18). Canberra: Research School of Pacific Studies. Australian National University.

Zipf, George. 1935. *The psychobiology of language.* Boston: Houghton Mifflin.

Zwicky, Arnold, and M. Geis. 1971. On invited inferences. *Linguistic inquiry* 2:561–6.

Index of languages

Index of names

Index of subjects

283